THE
CONSULTANT'S
SCORECARD

THE CONSULTANT'S SCORECARD

Tracking ROI and Bottom-Line Impact of Consulting Projects

Second Edition

JACK J. PHILLIPS
PATRICIA PULLIAM PHILLIPS

New York   San Francisco   Washington, D.C.   Auckland   Bogotá
Caracas   Lisbon   London   Madrid   Mexico City   Milan   Montreal
New Delhi   San Juan   Singapore   Sydney   Tokyo   Toronto

1 2 3 4 5 6 7 8 9 10   DOC/DOC   1 9 8 7 6 5 4 3 2 1 0

ISBN: 978-0-07-174282-5
MHID: 0-07-174282-4

This publication is designed to provide accurate and authoritative information in regard to the subject matter covered. It is sold with the understanding that neither the author nor the publisher is engaged in rendering legal, accounting, securities trading, or other professional services. If legal advice or other expert assistance is required, the services of a competent professional person should be sought.
> —From a Declaration of Principles jointly adopted by a Committee of the American Bar Association and a Committee of Publishers and Associations

Library of Congress Cataloging-in-Publication Data

Phillips, Jack J.
    The consultant's scorecard : tracking ROI and bottom-line impact of consulting projects/ by Jack J. Phillips, Patricia P. Phillips.—2nd ed.
        p. cm.
    Includes index.
    ISBN 978–0–07–174282–5 (alk. paper)
    1. Consultants. 2. Business consultants. I. Phillips, Patricia Pulliam. II. Title.
    HD69.C6P468 2011
    001—dc22   2010036607

Contents

Acknowledgments ix

Introduction xi

PART I

Setting the Stage

Chapter 1: The Need for Consulting Results from the Client Perspective 3

Why Measure Results? 3

Trouble in Paradise 5

When Consultants Are Not Accountable 11

Shifting Paradigms 13

Needing a New Approach to Measure Impact 15

How to Make Sure You Get Your Consultant Focused on Results 17

Final Thoughts 22

Chapter 2: How Consultants Can Prove the Value of Their Work to Clients: What's in It for the Consultant? 23

Why Measure ROI? 24

The Dilemma of ROI Accountability 26

What Is Causing This Concern for Accountability? 27

Finally, a Feasible and Credible Approach 30

The Framework: Evaluation Levels 31

The ROI Process Model 33

The Operating Standards: Guiding Principles 41

Implementation of the Process 41

Applications 42

How Evaluation Data Can Be Used: Benefits of ROI for Consulting 43

Application of the ROI Process: A Case Study 45

Final Thoughts 50

Chapter 3: Initial Analysis and Planning: Key to a Successful ROI Evaluation   **51**

Overall Project Goal   51

Levels of Project Objectives   52

How Is It All Connected? Linking Evaluation with Needs   59

Planning for Measurement and Evaluation   70

Final Thoughts   75

PART II

Data Collection

Chapter 4: Was It Useful and Did You Understand It?: Measuring Reaction and Learning   **79**

Why Measure Reaction?   79

Why Measure Learning?   81

Sources of Data   82

Topics for Reaction and Learning   83

Timing of Data Collection   83

Using Questionnaires and Surveys to Measure Reaction and Learning   85

Using Interviews to Measure Reaction and Learning   91

Using Focus Groups to Measure Reaction and Learning   93

Measuring Learning with Tests   95

Measuring Learning with Simulation   95

Measuring Learning with Less Structured Activities   96

Using Reaction and Learning Data   97

Final Thoughts   99

Chapter 5: Measuring the Progress of Consulting Projects: Tracking Application and Impact   **101**

Why Measure Application?   101

Why Measure Business Impact?   103

Data Collection Key Issues   104

Using Questionnaires to Measure Application and Impact   110

Using Interviews and Focus Groups   117

Using Observation   117

Using Action Plans   120

Using Performance Contracts   124

Monitoring Business Performance Data   125

Selecting the Appropriate Method for Each Level   127

Final Thoughts   130

PART III

Analysis

Chapter 6: Separating the Consulting Impact from Other Factors: How to Isolate the Effects of the Consulting Project   133

    Why Isolate the Effects of Consulting Projects?   133

    Preliminary Issues   134

    Use of Control Groups   136

    Analytical Approaches   138

    Estimates from Credible Sources   142

    Using the Techniques   149

    Final Thoughts   150

Chapter 7: How to Convert Business Measures to Monetary Values   151

    Why Convert Data to Monetary Values?   151

    The Five Key Steps to Convert Data to Money   152

    Standard Monetary Values   154

    When Standard Values Are Not Available   160

    When Conversion Should Not Be Pursued: The Intangible Benefits   171

    Selecting the Techniques and Finalizing the Values   174

    Final Thoughts   177

Chapter 8: Costs and ROI: Monitoring the Costs of Consulting and Calculating ROI   179

    The Importance of Costs and ROI   179

    Developing Costs   180

    Cost-Tracking Issues   183

    Major Cost Categories   186

    Basic ROI Issues   190

    ROI Measures   191

    BCR/ROI Case Application   193

    Other ROI Measures   196

    Benefits of the ROI Process   198

    Final Thoughts   199

PART IV

Reporting and Implementation

Chapter 9: Reporting Results: How to Provide Feedback and
Results to the Client   **203**

Communicating Results: Key Issues   203

Analyzing the Need for Communication   206

Planning the Communication   208

Selecting the Audience for Communications   210

Developing the Information: The Impact Study   213

Selecting the Communication Media   218

Communicating the Information   221

Analyzing Reactions to Communication   226

Final Thoughts   227

Chapter 10: Making It Routine: Overcoming Resistance to Measuring ROI   **229**

The Resistance   229

The Approach to Overcoming Resistance   230

Assessing the Climate   232

Developing Roles and Responsibilities   233

Establishing Goals and Plans   236

Revising/Developing Policies and Guidelines   239

Preparing the Consulting Staff   239

Initiating ROI Projects   241

Preparing the Management Team   242

Removing Obstacles   245

Monitoring Progress   245

Final Thoughts   245

Appendix: Do Your Consulting Projects Focus on Results?   **247**

Notes   **253**

Index   **255**

Acknowledgments

In no way has developing this book been a single-handed effort. Many individuals have helped shape the content and issues contained in each chapter. Much appreciation goes to ROI Institute clients, who have provided us a vast opportunity to experiment with the ROI process. We have had the opportunity to work with hundreds of individuals in organizations around the world. These experiences are the basis for much of the content described in this book.

We owe much appreciation to our international partners. We now operate in 54 countries and are amazed at the capability and quality of our partners as they deliver a variety of consulting services. From them, we have witnessed not only excellent consulting in action but also have picked up accountability tips on making consulting more valuable for the client. We have also learned that the accountability of consulting knows no borders; it cuts across all types of countries and cultures.

Our consulting has grown from private sector applications in the early 1990s to applications in a wide variety of organizations. We provide consulting services to local, state, and federal government agencies, nonprofits, nongovernment organizations (NGOs), foundations, educational institutions, religious organizations, and health-care providers. As we work with these organizations, we learn new ways to approach our consultancy that help us ensure clients get the most value for their money.

Much appreciation goes to our U.S. associates, who have provided ideas, suggestions, and helpful information to fine-tune the ROI process and build a truly successful consulting practice. As a group, they are outstanding consultants.

To write a book that focuses on measuring consulting involves a lot of inspiration from others who are in the same profession. Beyond our own team and partners at the ROI Institute, we have learned from many consultants whose work we admire and in which we are, in some cases, directly involved. We appreciate the work Robert H. Schaffer, whose work on high-impact consulting has been a tremendous addition to this professional field. We respect the contribution of Alan Weiss, who believes in and practices bringing value to the consulting process. Alan is a great consultant with considerable success in inspiring others to tackle this important field by bringing results along the way. We also respect the work of Gordon Perchthold and Jenny Sutton, who know how to extract value from consultants and help clients achieve maximum success from a consulting project. Perhaps one of the most respected consultants is Peter Block, author of *Flawless Consulting*, whose work is one of the most important contributions to this field. Peter is an expert in the consulting field and brings accountability throughout the process. Geoffrey M. Bellman brings practical advice in making sure the consulting process works for the client, consultant, and those involved in the process. We admire, respect, and continue to learn from Elaine Biech, who clearly understands the business of consulting and ensures consultants join the profession for the right reasons, delivering results as defined by the client. Finally, we learned from David H. Maister, who focuses on how to manage a professional services firm, building in accountability throughout the process to ensure the entire team is focused on the desired outcome. To these and many other successful consultants, we owe a debt of gratitude for their pioneering work.

Perhaps more than any other group, we appreciate the support of our team at the ROI Institute. Although certain members of our team are more directly involved with our research and publishing efforts than others, the entire team supports us. For this particular book, we appreciate the work of Crystal Bedwell Langford, who has helped us on many projects over the years. We also appreciate the superb editing skills of Alison Frenzel. This is the fourth book that Alison has taken on as the lead editor, and she never fails to come through with her capability, quality of work, and superb editing and writing skills. We appreciate her contribution to our ambitious publishing program. Thanks, Alison.

Finally, thanks to Knox Huston of McGraw-Hill. McGraw-Hill is one of the outstanding publishers in the world, and Knox is an excellent acquisitions editor. This is our fifth book with McGraw-Hill and our second with Knox. We appreciate the professionalism, patience, understanding, and the ease at which the process has worked with this particular book. Thanks, Knox, for continuing to allow us to be a part of the McGraw-Hill publishing family.

Jack and Patti Phillips

Introduction

Interest in ROI

In the past, the consulting process may have seemed analogous to the potential marital success of a couple introduced on a dating television show. Relying merely on chemistry, interpersonal relationships, and plain old luck, success of the process was evaluated by the quality of the relationship between the consultants and the client. This measure of success, like that of two individuals deemed "made for each other," was often defined in vague and general terms, reflecting qualitative judgments. Only a few attempts were actually made to connect consulting to bottom-line values, which, like many dating show couples, ended up in a lackluster pile of disappointments.

Today, things in the consulting world are different. While relationships are important, executive management requires greater accountability for consulting. With expenditures growing for consulting services and with increasing dissatisfaction with the quality and success of consulting assignments, there is tremendous pressure to show accountability measured in terms that managers, executives, and administrators clearly understand—return on investment (ROI).

Several issues are driving the increased interest in, and application of, the ROI process for consulting assignments. Pressure from clients and executive managers to show the actual return on their consulting investment is probably the most influential driver. Competitive economic pressures are causing intense scrutiny of all expenditures, including consulting costs. A variety of change programs have entered the workplace, including lean engineering, Six Sigma, and continuous process improvement. These initiatives have created renewed interest in measurement and evaluation because of the desire of senior management to show the actual results of these processes.

While these and other change processes have brought great expectations, they have failed to deliver the results promised or expected. In essence, this lack of results has caused many to question the consulting process and call for a more comprehensive approach for showing the actual contribution—ideally prior to the implementation of the process. The growth in consulting budgets, combined with the current scrutiny and economic pressures outlined above, have created an unprecedented need for the ROI process.

The ROI Methodology

The challenging aspect of ROI is the nature and accuracy of its development. The process often seems confusing and is usually surrounded by models, formulas, and statistics that can frighten even the most capable consultants and clients. Coupled with this concern are misunderstandings about the process and the gross misuse of ROI techniques in some consulting projects. These issues leave consultants with distaste for the process and clients wondering if an appropriate ROI process actually exists.

Unfortunately, ROI cannot be ignored. To admit to clients and executive management that the impact of an expensive consulting project cannot be measured is to admit that consulting does not add value or that consulting should not be subjected to this level of accountability. In practice, ROI must be explored, considered, and ultimately implemented as part of the consulting project.

What is needed is a rational, logical approach that can be simplified and implemented even in the midst of budget and resource constraints. This book presents a proven ROI process based on 20 years of development, a process that is rich in tradition and refined to meet the demands facing the consulting field. It meets the requirements of the following three very important groups.

First, the consultants who have used this model and implemented the ROI Methodology™ in their consulting projects continue to report satisfaction with the process and the success it has achieved. The ROI Methodology is user friendly, easy to understand, and has been proven to pay for itself again and again.

A second important group, the clients and executive managers who approve consulting projects and consulting budgets, want measurable results, preferably expressed in terms of financial return on investment. The ROI process described in this book has fared well with these client groups. Senior executives often view the process as credible, logical, practical, and easy to understand. More importantly, they buy into the process, which is critical in gaining their support for future implementation.

The third important group is the professional evaluators, professors, and evaluation researchers who develop, explore, and analyze new processes and techniques for demonstrating accountability. When exposed to the ROI Methodology in a two-day or one-week workshop, the researchers—without exception—give the process very high marks. They often applaud the strategies for isolating the effects of consulting and converting data to monetary values. Unanimously, they characterize the process as an important contribution to the consulting field.

Why This Book at This Time?

Despite the need, there are no other books available that show how ROI is developed in consulting. Also, there are few presentations of comprehensive evaluation processes for consulting. No other approach parallels the comprehensive process presented in this book. Most models and representations of measurement and evaluation processes ignore the essential ingredients for a successful ROI process. They generally provide very little insight into how the processes actually work.

This is not a book about how to provide consulting services; rather, it shows how to structure consulting so that it produces results and how to measure the results. This book provides a mechanism to show the actual contribution of consulting in six data categories. While there are many great books on actual consulting processes, they fail to actually show how to measure the success of consulting from a balanced viewpoint.

The Scorecard Perspective: Six Balanced Measures

This book presents six types of measures collected in a consulting project that offer a balanced viewpoint of the project's success. The measures involve both qualitative and quantitative data collected at different time intervals. The result constitutes a comprehensive profile of success as well as an explanation for those projects that have been less than successful. In essence, the process delivers the following six types of data:

1. Reaction to and satisfaction with the consulting project from a variety of different stakeholders at different time frames.
2. The extent of learning that has taken place as those involved in the consulting project learn new skills, processes, procedures, and tasks necessary to make the project successful.
3. Success with the actual application and implementation of the consulting project as the process is successfully utilized in the client's work and organization.
4. The actual business impact changes in the area where the consulting project has been initiated. These values include hard data as well as soft data and represent typical business measures.
5. The actual return on investment reported as a ratio or as a percentage comparing the monetary benefits to the costs of the project. This measure shows the financial return on the investment in the project.

6. Intangible measures, which are business measures that have improved as a result of the project but that are not converted to monetary values for use in the ROI formula.

These six data items provide a comprehensive, balanced profile of success. In addition, the ROI Methodology provides insight into problems and areas where adjustments can be quickly made to enhance the success of the consulting project. It is a comprehensive approach that can guarantee success for consulting.

A Focus on Results

In addition to actually measuring the contribution with the six measures, the consulting ROI process provides a framework to focus on results throughout the consulting intervention. Beginning with evaluation planning, the process requires concentration on important measures throughout the consulting intervention so that all stakeholders are aware of expectations, measures, and the actual success. In addition, in situations for which a forecast of the ROI process is necessary, the process can be adapted to provide a pre-project ROI forecast or a forecast at different time frames during the actual consulting intervention. In short, the consulting ROI process is an effective tool for bringing needed accountability to the consulting field.

Target Audience

The primary audience for this book can be divided into two categories: client and consultant, with both having equal coverage and direction. For clients who engage consulting services, this book provides an indispensable process for measuring the success of consulting and a framework for measuring success throughout the project. No longer will the client be forced to live with whatever evaluation is provided by the consultant. The client may, at a minimum, impose some parts of the process on future consulting projects, or require the entire ROI process for all major consulting projects, whether internal or external.

For consultants who need a process to show the value of consulting, this book presents such a process that is user friendly and easy to understand and apply. It can provide all the information needed or demanded by the client. Many of the steps can be built into the consulting project in order to minimize costs and resources. More importantly, pursuing this comprehensive evaluation process will build a database of successful ROI projects that clearly shows the impact of consulting, providing one of the best marketing tools for future consulting projects. For small consulting firms, the consultant can use parts or all of the material to focus additional efforts on accountability, stopping short of a complete, comprehensive evaluation. In larger firms, the ROI process may mean a complete change in the way consulting is marketed and implemented from the firm's perspective.

There are three secondary audiences for this book. The first is the individuals involved in support roles for consulting. These could be individuals supporting consulting internally in the consulting firm or in the client organization. This book will be a valuable tool to help them understand the need for accountability and how it is integrated into the processes.

The next secondary audience is management. Managers in a client organization are not necessarily the direct clients of consulting but are influenced or affected by the results of consulting projects. They need to understand the processes for bringing accountability to this important area, and this book should fulfill that need.

The third secondary audience is individuals who are in an external or peripheral role in the consulting process. They include researchers, seminar presenters, professors, and other educators who are involved in the professional development of consultants. The book provides a proven, reliable, and valid way to measure the success of consulting projects and should become a valuable addition to any workshop, seminar, or college course on the consulting process.

Special Issues for the Second Edition

This second edition, produced 11 years after the first edition, brings some important changes in two major categories. First, the book has been updated using more recent examples and also adjustments in the process learned in the past decade from a variety of consultants who currently use this process in their consulting practices. There are also updates from the client perspective as well as recent trends and issues that affect consulting accountability.

Second, the size of the book has been reduced. For some consultants, the first edition was intimidating, with almost 400 pages. This edition has been substantially streamlined based on the feedback of our readers, who wanted less information on data collection. Additionally, a separate chapter was not needed for the ROI calculation, and the chapter on forecasting was expanded into a separate book (*The Consultant's Guide to Results-Driven Business Proposals:*

How to Write Proposals That Forecast Impact and ROI, McGraw-Hill, 2010, Jack J. Phillips and Patricia Pulliam Phillips). This streamlined edition should be a more useful tool, particularly for consultants in smaller organizations.

Structure of the Book

This book has several unique features that make it a useful tool for the target audiences. The material is presented in a practical and useful way, outlining how the ROI process is used in organizations. The first chapter explores the need for an ROI process from the perspective of the client. It shows how the client can hold the consultant accountable for a consulting intervention.

Chapter 2 explains how the ROI process can be used by consultants to show the value of their consulting assignments. It reveals how the process can play a part in every consulting situation, regardless of the budget and resources available.

Chapter 3 focuses on the initial analysis and planning. This has two parts. The first is ensuring that an alignment exists of the consulting project to the business measures and details the issues and questions that must be addressed to elevate and achieve this alignment. The second, the planning for the impact and ROI study are shown as example documents.

Chapters 4 and 5 present the data collection for the first four measures: reaction, learning, application, and business impact. Each chapter presents the rationale for measuring success with the particular measure and describes data collection techniques that are most appropriate for the particular type of measure.

Chapter 6 covers perhaps the most critical issue, isolating the effects of the consulting project. A variety of useful strategies is presented to separate the influence of the consulting intervention from other factors that may affect output data.

Chapter 7 examines the critical issue of converting data to monetary values, explaining the different techniques for developing the overall monetary benefit from a consulting project. This chapter explains how the intangible measures are developed, which represents the sixth type of data. The analysis needed for intangibles is also presented.

Chapter 8 focuses on the cost of consulting, showing all the costs that should be monitored and how those costs should be reported. This is an essential part of the process to develop the cost of a consulting intervention, because it allows the cost of consulting to compare with monetary benefits to develop the ROI. This chapter also examines the actual ROI calculation, which is the fifth measure in the consulting ROI process. It shows how the value is developed and interpreted.

Chapter 9 shows how the various types of data are communicated to targeted audiences. More specifically, it shows how an impact study is developed and communicated to the client group, how to build an appropriate communications tool for the senior management team, and how routine feedback is provided during the consulting intervention.

Finally, Chapter 10 focuses on ways in which the process can become internalized as a routine part of consulting assignments. The chapter explains how to overcome resistance to using the process and presents a variety of ways in which the ROI process has been implemented effectively in consulting firms.

Collectively these chapters provide a comprehensive framework for the ROI use, addressing all of the key issues necessary to make the method an important and essential ingredient in consulting.

Dispelling the ROI Myths

Indeed, measuring the ROI for consulting is a hot topic. ROI appears routinely on conference agendas, in professional journals, and at networking meetings. Internally, from a client's perspective, ROI discussions are popping up in executive planning sessions, senior management staff meetings, and board meetings. Externally, progressive consulting firms all over the globe are developing ROI strategies.

Although most major consulting firms recognize ROI as an important addition to measurement and evaluation, they often struggle with how to address the issue. Many consultants see the ROI process as a ticket to increased funding and prosperity for consulting. They believe that without it, they may be lost in the shuffle, and with it, they may gain the respect they need to continue to achieve funding for consulting. Regardless of their motivation for pursuing ROI, the key question is this: "Is it a feasible process that can be implemented with reasonable resources, and will it provide the benefits necessary to make it a useful, routine tool?"

The ROI Institute is the global leader in the ROI process, conducting its first ROI impact study in 1972. Since that time, the process has been refined and is now used by more than 4,000 organizations in more than 50 countries. ROI Institute consultants are involved in more than 1,000 ROI impact studies each year, and more than 5,000 individuals from 25 countries have completed the ROI certification program. From this evidence, it is clear that

conducting an ROI impact study is feasible and is a way of life in many organizations and consulting firms.

The controversy surrounding ROI stems from misunderstandings about
what the process can and cannot do and how it should be implemented in an
organization. These misunderstandings are summarized in the following
myths about ROI. The myths were identified by the ROI Institute and are
based on years of experience with the ROI process and the perceptions discovered during consulting projects and workshops. Each myth is presented
below, along with an explanation of the truth.

1. **ROI is too complex for most users.** This issue has been a problem
   because of a few highly complex models that have been presented
   publicly. Unfortunately, these models have not helped their users and
   actually cause confusion about ROI. The ROI process is a basic financial formula for accountability that is simple and understandable—
   earnings are divided by investments—where earnings equate to net
   benefits from consulting intervention, and the investment equals the
   cost of the project. Straying from this basic formula can add confusion
   and create misunderstanding. The ROI Methodology, as presented in
   this book, is simplified with a step-by-step, systematic process.

2. **ROI is expensive, consuming too many critical resources.** The
   use of ROI can become expensive if it is not carefully organized, con-
   trolled, and properly implemented. The cost of a consulting ROI
   impact study can be significant, but several options are available to
   keep costs down. For example, the skills for developing ROI studies
   can be developed internally using existing measurement and evaluation staff, if available. Also, the process can be built into projects at the
   design and implementation stages, which should significantly reduce
   the amount of resources needed for a study. The responsibilities for
   different parts of the ROI process can be shared with others, reducing
   the need to use special resources for an ROI study. More importantly,
   the process should be applied only to a sampling of projects—those
   critical and important enough to be subjected to this level of analysis.

3. **If senior management or a client does not require ROI, there is no
   need to pursue it.** This myth captures the most innocent bystanders. It
   is easy to be lulled into providing measurement and evaluation that simply meets the status quo, believing that no requests means no desire for
   the information. If senior executives or clients have only been provided
   reaction data, they may not be asking for higher-level data. We know of

one large consulting firm (in the top five) that uses client reaction as the primary way to evaluate a project. In some cases, consultants have convinced top management that consulting cannot be evaluated at the ROI level or that the specific impact of a project cannot be determined. Given these conditions, it comes as no surprise that client and senior managers may not be asking for ROI data.

4. **ROI is a passing fad.** Unfortunately, this comment does apply to many of the processes being introduced to organizations today. Accountability for expenditures will always be present, and ROI provides the ultimate level of accountability. As a tool, ROI has been used for years. In the initial publication year of the *Harvard Business Review*, in the 1920s, ROI was the noted measurement tool. For years, ROI has been used to measure the investment of equipment and new plants. Now it is being used in many other areas, including consulting solutions. With its rich history, ROI will continue to be used as an important tool in measurement and evaluation.

5. **ROI is only one type of data.** This is a common misunderstanding. The actual consulting ROI process depicted in this book reports several types of data, including the financial ROI.

6. **ROI is not future-oriented. It reflects only past performance.** Unfortunately, many evaluation processes are ex post facto research projects, describing project success retroactively. This approach is the only way to have an accurate assessment of impact. However, the ROI Methodology can easily be adapted to forecast the actual ROI. The challenge is to estimate the actual impact on the measures that will be influenced by a particular project. The rest of the process remains the same. While this is a novel idea and is a routine request, the accuracy of forecasting is limited as with any forecasting model. However, several techniques presented in this book are available for achieving a reasonably accurate assessment of what a project can provide, removing much of the risk of the forecasting concept and reducing the likelihood of resource misuse. In addition, data are collected throughout the consulting project implementation, providing evidence of potential success along the way.

7. **ROI is rarely used by organizations.** This myth is easily dispelled when the evidence is fully examined. More than 4,000 organizations (including consulting firms) use the ROI Methodology, and there are at least 400 case studies published describing its application. Leading organizations throughout the world, in all sizes and sectors, use the ROI process to increase accountability and improve projects.

8. **ROI is not a credible process. It is too subjective.** This myth has evolved because some ROI studies involving estimates have been publicized and promoted in literature and conferences. Many ROI studies can and have been conducted without the use of estimates. The problem with estimates often surfaces when attempting to isolate the effects of other factors. Using estimates from the participants directly involved in the project is only one of several different techniques used to isolate the effects of a project. Sometimes estimating is used in other steps of the process, such as converting data to monetary values or estimating output in the data collection phase. In each of these situations, other options are often available; but for convenience or economic reasons, estimates are often used. While estimations often represent the worst-case scenario in ROI, they can be extremely reliable when they are obtained carefully, adjusted for error, and reported appropriately.

9. **ROI is for manufacturing and service organizations only.** Although initial ROI studies appeared in the manufacturing sector, the service sector quickly picked up the process as a useful tool. Then it migrated to the nonprofit sector as hospitals, educational institutions, foundations, community groups, and nongovernment organizations began endorsing and using the process. Now the ROI process is moving through government sectors around the world.

10. **It is not possible to isolate the influence of consulting.** Isolating the effects of other factors is always achieved when using the ROI process. There are seven ways to isolate the influence of other factors, and at least one method will work in any given situation. The challenge is to select an appropriate isolation method for the resources and accuracy needed in a particular situation.

11. **ROI is appropriate only for large consulting firms.** While it is true that large firms with enormous consulting budgets should have the most interest in ROI, the medium-sized and smaller firms are using ROI in greater numbers, particularly when it is simplified and built into projects. One-person consulting firms have successfully applied the ROI process, using it as a tool to bring increased accountability to consulting and drive future business.

12. **There are no standards for the ROI process.** An important problem facing measurement and evaluation is a lack of standardization or consistency. The ROI Methodology contains standards labeled as guiding principles. These standards bring consistency between studies, credibility for results because of the conservative assumptions, and efficiency in the use of resources.

Conclusion

The ROI Methodology is not for every organization or individual consultant. The use of ROI represents a tremendous paradigm shift as clients attempt to bring more accountability and results to the consulting process from the consultant's perspective. It is client-focused, requiring much contact, communication, dialogue, and agreement with the client.

Admittedly, there are some natural obstacles to this process that may hinder its use. The good news is that the ROI process is being adopted by thousands of organizations in virtually every type of setting. The myths described here are quickly being debunked as consultants recognize ROI as a useful tool that can add tremendous value to the mission and goals of the consulting process.

If you have questions, suggestions, or other feedback, please contact us at:

Jack J. Phillips, Ph.D., Chairman
Patti P. Phillips, Ph.D., President and CEO
ROI Institute
P.O. Box 380637
Birmingham, AL 35238-0637
jack@roiinstitute.net
patti@roiinstitute.net

Setting the Stage

The Need for Consulting Results from the Client Perspective

Why Measure Results?

Consultants know why business is booming and, more importantly, why it's not. Fortunately, their business has experienced considerable boom during the past two decades with the consulting business's growth exceeding that of many professions. The impact of the recent global recession has not stifled their insights about themselves either, as most estimates predict the industry to grow in the range of 15 to 20 percent each year. Whether restructuring, implementing systems, developing staff, changing procedures, buying new companies, or bringing out new products and services, consultants are being asked to assist in a variety of ways. As many companies struggle to overcome the recession's effects, they are fervently seeking consultants for their external perspectives and expert opinions, hoping they can provide solutions that will improve business.

One important insight of a consultant is understanding the viewpoint of the very top executive when it comes to measures of success for all types of projects and programs. The ROI Institute conducted a study in 2009 to understand the executive view of measures of success for typical noncapital expenditures such as consulting, learning and development, human resources, communications, and public relations. This executive view provided an important glimpse into critical mainstays for top executives.

Table 1-1 shows the summary of executive input. For this particular part of the study, executives were provided with eight measurement categories. They were asked if they were now receiving this type of information regarding

Table 1-1 The CEO View of Metrics

Measure	We Currently Measure This	We Should Measure This in the Future	My Ranking of the Importance of This Measure
1. *Inputs*: "This project will consume 3,000 hours' consulting time and about 250 hours' client time."	94%	85%	6
2. *Efficiency*: "The total cost of this project will be $678,000 in consulting fees and expenses."	78%	82%	7
3. *Reaction*: "Employees rated our projects very high, averaging 4.2 out of 5."	53%	22%	8
4. *Learning*: "At least 95 percent of the individuals involved in the project know what they must do to make it successful."	32%	28%	5
5. *Application*: "The project is being implemented properly and on schedule with various groups following through on specific action items."	11%	61%	4
6. *Impact*: "The project is driving two critical business measures ranked among the highest and most important in the organization."	8%	96%	1
7. *ROI*: "The project delivered a 38 percent ROI."	4%	74%	2
8. *Awards*: "This project won an award from the Industry Trade Group."	40%	44%	3

N = 96 respondents
Source: CEO Survey—Fortune 500 and Large Private Companies, © 2010 ROI Institute, www.roiinstitute.net.

projects and programs, and if they should be receiving this information in the future. In addition, the executives were asked to rank the data sets on a scale of 1 to 8, with 1 being the most valuable measurement category, and 8 being the least valuable.

As the table reveals, the executives are not so interested in reaction data or even learning data but are mainly concerned with impact and ROI. Regarding the inputs, executives are interested in the extent of involvement, particularly, as one executive indicated, how much this process is disrupting an organization. Knowing cost is beneficial (and always an interest) for them as an input into the process, although it doesn't measure success. Executive interest begins to increase with application data, demonstrating how things are working; impact data, the business connection; and ROI data, the ultimate level of evaluation.

The concern is the gap with application, impact, and ROI. Eleven percent, 8 percent, and 4 percent of CEOs, respectively, have these categories of data provided to them. Unfortunately, 61 percent, 96 percent, and 74 percent, respectively, want them to be provided, causing a gap in terms of what we provide executives and what they want. The surveys were taken directly from Fortune 500 CEOs and represent one of the most important views of metrics. For consultants, the mandate is clear: we must show executives the business impact for our projects and be credible in the process. Also, we must step up to the ROI challenge and show executives the value for the consulting projects in terms that they all understand—the ROI.

Unfortunately, clients are often disappointed when products and services fail to deliver anticipated results, leaving both the client and the consultant frustrated over the outcome of the project. This chapter explores the current status of consulting, examines the causes behind the accountability crisis, and suggests ways to overcome it.

Trouble in Paradise

While some have regarded the consulting profession as a highly desirable occupation, others have characterized it by the lack of effectiveness of consultants and the consulting industry. The problems facing consultants, although varying with the industry and the type of consulting activities, generally fall into three major categories: lack of accountability, tarnished image, and excessive costs. Each of these brings a cloud over the industry, causing some to question the contributions of consulting projects.

Lack of Accountability

Perhaps one of the most damaging reports about the consulting industry was presented in a book focusing on large consulting companies. *Dangerous Company*, written by insiders to the industry, illustrates how consulting power-houses are inflicting damages on many organizations. The opening paragraph best summarizes the concerns for accountability:

> A secretive and elite army of management consultants is at work deep inside corporations everywhere, from the giants of the Fortune 500 to middle-sized and smaller companies. It is also expanding its influence all over the developing world, wherever economies are coming to life. And it has become partner to government, adviser to heads of state, and confi-dant to countless interests eager to exploit the promise of a growing world economy. It collects top dollar for its work, sometimes delivering all the sparkle and success it promises, and sometimes failing so remarkably that its clients seem more victim than customer. A relative newcomer to the world of business, management consulting has escaped all but the most cursory of levels of scrutiny. It has only good things to say about itself. But there is a growing sense of unease about this exploding and occasionally explosive enterprise, a feeling that it is a palace built on a foundation of shifting sand. From a distance, it glistens like alabaster. Up close, a different image emerges. It centers on a key question: "Whose interest is being served?" All too often, the answer is that it is not the best interest of the client.[1]

We expect consultants to have expertise, to be thorough with analysis, and to be objective in data collection, analysis, and reporting. This is not always the case:

> In 2006, one of the leading consultants, Bain & Company, proclaimed on its website that "Bain's clients have outperformed the stock market 4 to 1." A chart showed that from 1980 to 2004, while the S&P 500 rose by a factor of about 15, the shares of Bain's clients grew by a factor of about 60—four times the rate of the market. The implication? That following Bain's advice leads to higher performance, in fact much higher perfor-mance. But there are two huge flaws in this claim. First, the data in fact show the quarter-by-quarter performance of Bain's then-current clients relative to the S&P index in that quarter. A 400 percent gap over 25 years, or 100 quarters, translates to an average gap of somewhat more than one percent per quarter—1.4 percent, to be exact—which is not insignificant, but you'd have to enjoy that difference every quarter for

25 years in order to outperform your rivals by a 4 to 1 margin. Most consulting engagements last for a few years, not for two and a half decades, which means that the performance gap for a typical client is much less. But the second flaw, and the more important one, is that at best Bain has shown a correlation, not causality. Even if Bain's clients outperformed the market average by a little more than 1 percent each quarter, does that mean working with Bain leads to better performance? That's the suggestion, and maybe it's true. Or could it be that only profitable companies can afford Bain's services. That could be true, too, in which case working with Bain doesn't lead to higher profits; in fact, it might well be the other way around—only companies with high profits can afford Bain. Again, a simple correlation tells us very little.[2]

It would be unfair to label all consultants and consulting firms as incapable of producing results or supplying a useful product or service. There are many success stories where consulting firms have enhanced organizations and even turned them around. However, in far too many cases, the results are just not there. And sometimes, the process itself causes a breakdown in accountability.

Many consultants agree with this assessment and have developed a new approach. According to Robert Schaffer in his book *High-Impact Consulting*:

Most management consultants subscribe to a model of consulting that is inherently loaded against success. This consulting paradigm, followed throughout the world by external and staff consultants alike, is unnecessarily labor-intensive, long in cycle time, and low in return on investment. It locks both clients and consultants into a fundamentally ineffective mode of operation. In this, the conventional consulting model, there is a clear divide between the parties: The experts are accountable for creating the best possible solutions and tools, and the clients are accountable for exploiting those solutions and tools to improve organization results. In too many cases, however, clients do not or cannot implement the consultant-developed solutions in ways that yield significant improvement.[3]

Beyond the flawed issues surrounding implementation and support are the problems of a lack of clear definition up front, focus on specific objectives, and emphasis on obtaining results throughout the process. While many consulting projects do yield results, they often fall short of the significant results they could achieve, and in far too many cases they produce no results at all.

This book presents the tools and processes needed to measure the success of consulting projects, ensure that consulting projects are properly initiated (with the end in mind), and place the necessary emphasis on results, including various feedback mechanisms to keep the project clearly on track. When implemented, this process will ensure that a consulting project not only produces results but also produces significant results that should be expected from major interventions.

Tarnished Image

Closely related to a lack of accountability in the consulting industry is a problem with the tarnished image. Top management has had a love-hate relationship with consultants. Jack Welch, former CEO of General Electric and the all-time most admired CEO, weighs in on the consultant issue. He cautions executives to spend very little on consulting. Be careful is his advice, adding, "Before you know it, they could be doing the ongoing work of your business. After all, that's what they want, even if you don't."[4]

Elaine Biech, in her book *The Business of Consulting*, lists as one of her myths that "consulting is a respected profession." Elaine explains that she thought she had chosen a respected profession but was shocked the first time she was called a "beltway bandit"—a term assigned to consulting firms in and around the Washington, D.C., beltway. Since her initial encounter, she has been called a "pest" and a "con-person."[5] Indeed, the consulting profession has come under fire, particularly from the employees who have to work with consultants and deal with the outcomes of a consulting assignment. Perhaps this is underscored best, or at least in a more humorous way, in the role of consultants depicted in the *Dilbert* comic strip. In Scott Adams's bestselling book *The Dilbert Principle*, which was a number one *New York Times* bestseller, nearly 10 percent of the book's coverage is devoted to consultants and consulting. The *Dilbert* cartoon depicts the petty and stupid requests and activities of consultants and consulting projects that litter cubicles throughout the corporate world.[6] Some of Adams's observations of consultants are:

- A consultant is a person who takes your money and annoys your employees while tirelessly searching for the best way to extend the consulting contract.
- Consultants will hold a seemingly endless series of meetings to test various hypotheses and assumptions. These exercises are a vital step toward tricking managers into revealing the recommendation that is most likely to generate repeat consulting business.
- After the correct recommendation is discovered, it must be justified by a lengthy analysis. Analysis is designed to be as confusing as possible,

thus discouraging any second-guessing by staff members who are afraid of appearing dunce.

- Consultants use a standard set of decision tools that involves creating alternative scenarios based on different assumptions. Any pesky assumption that does not fit the predetermined recommendation is quickly discounted as being uneconomical by the consultants.
- Consultants will often recommend that you do whatever you are not doing now.
- Consultants do not need much experience in industry in order to be experts; they learn quickly.

Adams continues with his list of advantages that consultants bring to a company:

- Consultants have credibility with customers because consultants are not dumb enough to be regular employees with your company.
- Consultants eventually leave, which makes them excellent scapegoats for major management blunders.
- Consultants can schedule time on your boss's calendar because they do not have your reputation as a troublemaker who constantly brings up unsolvable issues.
- Consultants often are more trusted than your regular employees.
- Consultants will return phone calls because it is all billable time to them.
- Consultants work preposterously long hours, thus making the regular staff feel worthless for only working 60 hours a week.

While this is a humorous attack on the consulting field, it unfortunately rings true for many consultants, bringing confirmation at least on some of the points.

The attack on consultants appears in all types of communications, even on the Internet. The following top ten list comes from Dusty Miller, who took it off of the Internet. Here is the Top Ten List of Things You Will Never Hear a Consultant Say:

10. You're right; we're billing you way too much for this.
9. Bet you I can go a week without saying "synergy" or "value-added."
8. How about paying us based on the success of the project?
7. This whole strategy is based on a Harvard business case I read.
6. Actually, the only difference is that we charge more than they do.
5. I don't know enough to speak intelligently about that.

4. Implementation?
3. I can't take the credit. It was Linda in your marketing department.
2. The problem is, you have too much work for too few people.
And number 1. Everything looks OK to me.[7]

Certainly some of the criticism toward consulting is unjustified. Employees who are often the subject of job loss, job redesign, transfer, or relocation as a result of a consulting initiative will undoubtedly view that process as unfair and distasteful. However, the hostility and negative attacks go beyond the outcome of the consulting process. They underscore the fact that many consulting interventions are not value-added processes—they do not provide a payoff for the organization for its time and resources allocated to the process. A well-designed and properly focused project that brings value to the organization will not be subjected to the type of ridicule and negative comments consultants often draw.

Excessive Costs

The cost of consulting is increasing significantly. The story of the employee who was fired and rehired as a consultant at twice the salary is becoming commonplace, except these days it may be three or four times the salary. While most employees understand that an hourly rate for a consultant must be more than a corresponding hourly rate for an employee, the differential is staggering. An MBA fresh out of school may command $200 an hour for a big consulting firm working hand in hand with employees who know far more about the process than the consultant. In essence, the consultant is learning on the job. The middle level or senior consultants in a large consulting firm may command $250 to $350 an hour, while a senior partner will charge more than $500 an hour. These are not short-term assignments but often are long-term projects that continue for as much as a year. The notion of a higher hourly rate was built on the idea that there are only a certain number of billable days, usually 60 percent of the day's work. Today that number has increased, and in some firms, junior consultants bill between 80 and 90 percent of their time— sometimes on a requirement or expectations. These costs, when spread over a large organization, add up quickly. Some top consulting firms will not bid on a project unless it hits a $10 million threshold.

The underlying theme of the three issues is the lack of a focus on results— the absence of a process that defines results, emphasizes results, and delivers results throughout the project. While this book is not about how to consult, it does show you how the value of consulting is determined. It provides a process to measure any type of consulting, quickly and routinely, to keep it on track to reach its ultimate objectives, including the actual return on investment.

When Consultants Are Not Accountable

With that glimpse of the problems in the consulting industry, let's review the damages. Although the issues sometimes overlap, five consequences can come from a flawed consulting assignment when it goes astray.

Squandered Funds

Perhaps the most important consequence is that precious funds are wasted on consulting—funds that could be used in other places. Consulting projects are usually very expensive, and in larger organizations, the funding for a consulting project can be significant and often grows without accountability. With the fierce competition for funds, worthwhile processes, functions, or projects may need the money—and may go unfunded.

Most likely you have also experienced this disappointment. How could this be possible? After all, you pay consultants considerable sums of money with the expectation that they will achieve specific, agreed-upon business objectives in return. Failure occurs for a number of reasons, some in combination, including the following:

- **The consultants are working on the wrong problem either because you have not defined the problem clearly or they have persuaded you to allow them to work on something other than what you hired them for—usually something easier or that generates more fees.**
- **You have selected the wrong type of consultants for the problem at hand and therefore they do not have the domain knowledge, local presence, or industry expertise to determine the appropriate solution to the problem.**
- **The consultants do not have the skills or experiences that were proposed because of substitutions: the individual consultants with the credentials on which you based your selection decision have been replaced with less qualified people.**
- **You are not controlling or managing the consultants effectively so the consultants are running amok in your organization and/or the project is significantly delayed or over budget without realizing it.**

- **The consultants have lost their effectiveness in your organization either because they are too familiar with you and have become part of your organization's groupthink, or they have been marginalized by your managers, thus blocking their meaningful participation.**[8]

Wasted Time

Consultants eat up precious staff time, as dozens and sometimes hundreds of employees perform tasks for, and provide information to, consultants. This is often done with the assumption that the current staff can provide this information at less cost. Also, they often know where to find the information and how to interpret it. If the consulting project has gone astray and not produced results, this experience represents a tremendous waste of internal time—time that could be devoted to important, profit-generating activities.

Demoralized Staff

The waste of time negatively affects morale of the staff. Too many employees see consultants as individuals who collect information from them and pass their recommendations on to the executives. They see little contribution from consultants.

Consider, for example, the following consulting project for a regional financial institution. A well-known and respected consulting firm was engaged to analyze areas where efficiency could be developed to add immediate bottom-line value to the organization. The consultants pored through financial records, analyzed operating reports, and interviewed dozens of managers and specialists. In the end, the consulting firm seized the ideas and suggestions of the operating managers—taking projects that were already under way or in the planning stages—and presented them as recommendations to improve operating efficiencies. When the senior staff of the firm objected to the consultants' report, the CEO, who had hired the consultants previously, praised the work of the consultants and suggested their recommendations be adopted. The staff resisted in every way and ultimately did nothing with what was originally planned. The senior staff never implemented the recommendations. In a reference check by another organization seeking consulting advice, the CEO praised the report and gave the consulting firm very high marks for their efforts. Privately, he said, "Although we did not implement all the recommendations and some were already in planning, it was a good exercise for the organization."

Harmful Advice

If improper advice is given, the consequences can be devastating. If a system is implemented improperly or a product line is introduced incorrectly, business is unnecessarily harmed. If an acquisition is pursued improperly, the business may suffer irreversible damage. When a feasibility study is off target, a decision is incorrect. Although these consequences are not the routine, they occur with enough frequency to be alarming. In rare cases, bad advice can be so devastating that it brings the company to bankruptcy. In other cases, it causes reduced revenues or diminished profits. Unfortunately, many articles appear routinely in business publications explaining how organizations are now taking consultants to court and holding them legally liable for their bad advice.

Devastated Careers

Consulting assignments have been known to tarnish the careers of those individuals who advocated or supported faulty assignments. Having realized the company misspent money or received very little advice for the money spent, the executive or executives involved in the process often lose their luster (and sometimes their jobs). Also, in a political environment, those who resist consulting interventions often suffer career anxieties and disappointments as well. The use of consultants is often a political activity within organizations.

Many of the above consequences of ineffective consulting interventions can be prevented if proper steps are taken to hold consultants accountable from the beginning of the process and throughout, to the end of the assignment. The tools presented in this book will show how to avoid these disasters, which can wreak havoc within an organization.

Shifting Paradigms

Consulting paradigms are shifting for both consultants and clients. Processes are being developed to focus directly on accountability. For years, consulting activity, consulting processes, and consulting progress have been activity- or input-focused, with success being derived by the inputs into the process rather than the outcomes. The situation is changing, though, as consulting interventions and processes are now results-based. Table 1-2 shows the shift from activity-based consulting to results-based consulting, an important paradigm shift for the consulting profession.

Table 1-2 Paradigm Shift in Consulting Accountability

Activity-Based Consulting Characterized by:	Results-Based Consulting Characterized by:
No business need for the consulting project	Project linked to specific business needs
No assessment of performance issues related to project	Assessment of performance issues related to project
No specific, measurable objectives for application and business impact	Specific objectives for application and business impact
No effort to prepare stakeholders/ participants to achieve results	Results/expectations communicated to stakeholders/participants
No effort to prepare the work environment to support implementation	Environment prepared to support implementation
No efforts to build partnerships with key managers	Partnerships established with key managers and clients
No measurement of results or cost-benefit analysis	Measurement of results including cost-benefit analysis
Planning and reporting on consulting projects are input-focused	Planning and reporting on consulting projects are output-focused

As shown, results-based consulting includes the following characteristics:

- Consulting projects developed with the end in mind, linked to specific business needs represented by business impact measures that matter.
- A detailed assessment of performance issues and performance effectiveness to determine the specific causes or inhibitors to the improvement of business needs.
- Specific objectives developed at multiple levels, including application and business impact objectives.
- Expectations of results communicated through a variety of individuals, particularly for those stakeholders and participants directly involved in the consulting project. This helps keep the end in mind in very specific, measurable terms.
- Full exploration and preparation of the work environment to support the implementation of the consulting solution.
- Partnerships with key managers and clients to build their support for the process and solution, helping to ensure that they will provide the resources and commitment to make the project a success.

- Measurement of results, including a cost-benefit analysis showing the payoff for major consulting projects.
- Output-focused planning and reporting on consulting projects, indicating the successes obtained through the project rather than listing the resources deployed.

This represents a dramatic shift in reporting as organizations report data along the six measures outlined in this book. This paradigm shift is long overdue. Fortunately, a few consulting firms have adopted the results-based philosophy and are delivering results, meeting the expectations of the client. Unfortunately, not enough are basing their approach on results. Clearly, there is more talk than action on this issue.

Needing a New Approach to Measure Impact

Clients—who must approve consulting budgets, request consulting projects, and live with the results of consulting—have a strong interest in consulting accountability in four major areas. First, clients want to see what actually changed as a result of the consulting assignment. They want to know if it was implemented properly, on time, on schedule, as planned, and if the appropriate support was delivered. This is critical to its success. Second, clients want to know if the process had an impact on the business units. Did it improve the measures that matter? Third, clients want to know if this assignment was a good investment for the organization. Was the payoff appropriate? Did money benefits exceed the actual cost of the project? Finally, did the project drive key intangible measures, which are often difficult to value yet critical to the success of an organization? These four concerns of the client group represent the most important four of the six outcome measures advocated in this book.

Clients have been skeptical of attempts to quantify the success of consulting projects. Sometimes, other influences or factors were not considered; the costs were not fully loaded, or the benefits were actually overstated. Attempts to require an ROI process have been met with much skepticism and sometimes even criticism—from the consultants. While the evaluation process described in this book is explained in more detail in the following chapter, it is important to consider the requirements for this type of process from the viewpoint of the client.

To satisfy the needs of clients, an ROI process must meet several requirements. Ten essential criteria for an effective ROI process are:

1. The ROI process must be **simple**, void of complex formulas, lengthy equations, and complicated methodologies. Most ROI attempts have failed on this requirement. In an attempt to obtain statistical perfection and use too many theories, several ROI models and processes have become too complex to understand and use. Consequently, they have not been implemented.

2. The ROI process must be **economical,** with the ability to be implemented easily. The process should be capable of becoming a routine part of consulting without requiring significant additional resources. Sampling for ROI calculations and early planning for ROI are often necessary to make progress without adding staff.

3. The assumptions, methodology, and techniques must be **credible**. Logical, methodical steps are needed to earn the respect of practitioners, senior managers, and researchers. This requires a very practical approach to the process.

4. From a research perspective, the ROI process must be **theoretically sound** and based on generally accepted practices. Unfortunately, this requirement can lead to an extensive, complicated process. Ideally, the process must strike a balance between maintaining a practical and sensible approach and a sound and theoretical foundation. This is perhaps one of the greatest challenges to those who have developed models for an ROI process.

5. The ROI process must **account for other factors** that have influenced business measures. One of the most often overlooked issues, isolating the influence of consulting is necessary to build credibility and accuracy within the process. The ROI process should pinpoint the contribution of the project when considering the other influences.

6. The ROI process must be appropriate for a **variety of consulting projects**. Some models apply to only a small number of projects, such as marketing, technology, or productivity consulting. Ideally, the process should be applicable to all types of consulting in all types of settings.

7. The ROI process must have the **flexibility** to be applied on a pre-project (as a forecast) basis as well as a post-analysis basis. In some situations, an estimate of the ROI is required before the project is approved. Ideally, the process should be able to adjust to a range of potential time frames.

8. The ROI process must be **applicable with all types of data**, including hard data, which is typically represented as output, quality, costs, and time; and soft data, which include image, employee engagement, customer satisfaction, brand awareness, teamwork, and corporate social responsibility.
9. The ROI process must **include all the costs of consulting**. The ultimate level of evaluation is comparing the benefits with costs. Although the term ROI has been loosely used to express any benefit of consulting, an acceptable ROI formula must include costs. Omitting or underestimating costs will only destroy the credibility of the ROI values.
10. Finally, the ROI process must have a successful **track record** in a variety of applications. In far too many situations, models are created but never successfully applied. An effective ROI process should withstand the wear and tear of implementation and be improved because if it.

Because these criteria are considered essential, an ROI process should meet the vast majority, if not all, of them. The bad news is that most ROI processes do not. The good news is that the ROI process presented in this book meets all of the criteria.

How to Make Sure You Get Your Consultant Focused on Results

Now comes the critical question: what can the client do to make sure the consultant focuses on results? Actually, the client is in the driver's seat. The client can demand, require, specify, as well as expect results. How is this done? From a practical basis, this can be achieved by focusing on the following issues. All of these issues may not be appropriate for a particular consulting project, but they represent important areas to consider in ensuring that the project is developed properly, structured adequately, and delivers the results needed and promised. The checklist in Table 1-3 will help the client determine the degree to which the consultant focuses on results.

Ask for Impact and ROI Results from Other Projects

As a first step in a new consulting possibility, clients should ask for results from other projects. The results needed should be specific and include the impact and return on investment from the consulting project. Although results achieved in previous projects do not guarantee success in another

Table 1-3 Does Your Consultant Focus on Results?

	YES	NO
1. Does your consultant have impact and ROI results from other projects?	____	____
2. Will your consultant agree to guarantee results?	____	____
3. Is there a clear focus on business results early in the process?	____	____
4. Will the consultant forecast the ROI?	____	____
5. Have multiple levels of objectives (including application and impact) been established for the project?	____	____
6. Will expectations be communicated to all stakeholders?	____	____
7. Can the consultant develop an impact and ROI study?	____	____
8. Will the consultant examine a variety of data on different sources at different times?	____	____
9. Are the data collection, analysis, and reporting independent?	____	____
10. Is there a plan to monitor the long-term effects of the project?	____	____

project, they do show the extent to which the consulting firm focuses on results, reviewing the methodology, process, and, more importantly, the effectiveness of the consulting project. If there is no success, then there should be cause for concern. If the consultant or consulting firm cannot produce results or prefers not to disclose the confidential information from previous assignments, then the client should be concerned. Reports can be desensitized and names changed to protect the confidentiality of the client. In today's environment, there is little justification for not having previous successes to provide a glimpse of what might happen in the proposed project.

Seek a Guarantee for Results

A few consulting firms are willing to guarantee results. Unfortunately, not enough are taking this approach. Perhaps it is time to ask for a guarantee. Consultants will quickly comment that there are so many factors out of their control that it is impossible to guarantee results. While this is true, guarantees can be conditional on issues out of their control. For example, one consulting firm will guarantee the results of the project with the condition that management supports the project and endorses the recommended solutions. They go on to detail specifically what is meant by "management support," including time frames and specific activities. This provides the consultant leverage but also addresses the concern about other influences.

Other consulting firms will have a contingency for results. They will share the savings or profits from the consulting assignment, placing everything at risk with much to gain if it is successful. Still others will have lower-than-normal consulting fees, barely capturing the direct cost for the consulting project and adding a contingency for splitting cost savings after a 25 percent return on investment is achieved. The important issue is the message that it sends to the client. SAP, the world's largest business software and services company, reports that success guarantees are now required for their projects. Some clients are asking for an ROI forecast. Now it is time to ask for a guarantee of results or inject some type of risk from the consultant's perspective.

Focus on Results Early, with the End in Mind

As with so many issues or situations, the project should begin with the end in mind in terms of clear expectations of implementation and business impact. Ideally, the business impact measures should form the beginning point, specifying exactly what should change or improve as a result of the consulting project. Then it builds on these results. When business measures are the beginning point, measurement of business impact at the conclusion of the project becomes much easier. Also, all of the activities in between focus on those end results. Therefore, the client should insist on a results-focused project at the outset.

Consider an ROI Forecast—with an Update

In some projects it is helpful, and sometimes essential, to forecast the ROI prior to implementing the consulting project. This is particularly useful if there is a large-scale project or tremendous cost or risk associated with the consulting project. In today's climate, clients may need to know the anticipated impact and payoff prior to engaging consulting services. Pre-project forecasts can be developed for many situations, although they may suffer from accuracy and credibility because they are estimates. Ideally, if an estimate is needed for a pre-project ROI, it should be obtained using the best data available, often from previous studies or experts who can provide input on the expected results. This topic is covered in more detail in a later chapter.

Specify Multiple-Level Objectives, Including Application and Impact

When consulting is initiated, multiple levels of objectives should be required or specified. Ideally, objectives should be developed at five levels: reaction, learning, application, impact, and ROI. The most important level is impact objectives, which define the specific business needs or measures that must change or improve as a result of consulting. These multiple levels of objectives ensure that there is a focus on results throughout the project.

Addressing these items, which will sometimes require half a day to a full day, will allow you to make all the major decisions about how data are collected, analyzed, and reported to various target audiences.

Communicate Expectations to Stakeholders

The stakeholders directly involved in the process should understand what is expected from consulting, particularly from the application and impact objectives. Continuous communication of expectations maintains the focus on the desired results and helps make adjustments when things are off track or out of line. Many issues can cause a consulting project to go astray. Free-flowing data from different points and different sources can help keep the process on track and the focus on the outcome.

Require an Impact Study with ROI

For major consulting projects, an impact study may be desired. This shows a variety of data up to and including the business impact and actual return on investment where benefits are compared to costs. Intangible benefits are also identified. For the study to be credible, the effects of consulting should be isolated from other influences. All of this represents an extra expense, but it may be worth it for the client to see the impact of the consulting project. Otherwise, the impact may never be known. If it becomes too costly for the client, perhaps some agreement to share the costs may be appropriate between the consulting firm and the client. The important point is to discuss the impact study up front and include it in the deliverables.

Require a Variety of Data

Both qualitative and quantitative data need to be collected at different time frames from different sources to provide a complete profile of the success of the project. This book suggests that six types of outcome data be collected on every consulting project, as shown in Table 1-4.

Table 1-4 The Six Outcome Measures

Type of Data	Description
Reaction	Measures the satisfaction/reaction from those directly involved in the consulting project
Learning	Measures the learning necessary for project implementation
Application/ implementation	Measures the success of implementation and utilization of the consulting project
Business impact	Measures the change in business impact measures directly related to the consulting project
ROI	Measures the cost versus benefits of the consulting project
Intangible benefits	Important impact measures not converted to money

Ensure That Data Collection and Analysis Are Independent

To be objective, the measurement process should be independent. A consulting firm reporting the success of its own consulting project is much like the fox guarding the hen house. If feasible, steps should be taken to ensure that data are collected, analyzed, and reported independently of the consulting firm. One option is for the client to review the data and make the analysis. A more viable option may be to employ a firm that specializes in impact analysis, including ROI. If both options are unacceptable, perhaps some initial understanding of how the data is analyzed, collected, or reported is necessary. Perhaps all of the raw data are presented along with the consulting firm's analysis. The most important point is that this issue must be addressed early in the evaluation process.

Monitor Long-Term Effects of Projects

The final item is a provision to monitor the long-term effects for consulting projects that will not fully pay off for several years. Although no one wants to wait for an extended time period to measure success, some mechanism should be considered to monitor the long-term impact. Perhaps a predetermined follow-up, conducted externally by a third party or conducted jointly by the client and the consulting firm, would be appropriate. Many projects are revisited each year to update the success, although the accuracy may deteriorate as other influences enter the process.

Final Thoughts

This first chapter explores major changes on the consulting landscape as consultants are being held more accountable. The global economic turmoil, competitive pressures, and competition for funds are causing organizations to demand more results from consulting. The situation is changing with more focus on business results. Processes are available to ensure that there is a focus on results, but the focus must be driven by the client in terms of expectations, demands, and requirements. The client is in the driver's seat and can make the difference in the value delivered from consulting.

The next chapter will outline a specific process developed for overall accountability, including how it was developed. The remaining chapters will address the six measures and discuss various issues surrounding implementing this process.

How Consultants Can Prove the Value of Their Work to Clients

What's in It for the Consultant?

CHAPTER 1 FOCUSED on the rationale for comprehensive measurement and evaluation from the client's perspective. This chapter approaches the same issue but from the consultant's perspective. Consultants must address several important accountability issues. Questions must be answered, such as: What is involved in the process? What is my role in measuring the impact and ROI? How should I approach evaluation? Is a credible process available? Can it be implemented within my resources? What are the consequences of a negative ROI? What would happen if I do nothing? These and other critical issues need attention. This chapter explores each issue and others as the case is presented for consultants to adopt a more comprehensive measurement and evaluation process, including measuring the ROI.

In this chapter, a rational, credible approach to measurement and evaluation is presented, showing how the process can be applied within the resources of the consulting firm. It shows the various elements and issues needed to build credibility with a proven process.

Why Measure ROI?

Developing a balanced set of measures, including measuring ROI, has earned a place among the critical issues in the consulting field. The topic appears on conference agendas and comes up at professional meetings. Journals and newsletters embrace the concept with increasing print space. Several consulting experts are recommending ROI calculations. Even top executives have increased their appetite for ROI information, particularly since the global recession.

Although the interest in the topic has heightened and progress has been made, it is still an issue that challenges consulting firms. Some consultants argue that it is not possible to calculate the ROI in consulting, while others quietly and deliberately proceed to develop measures and ROI calculations. Regardless of the position taken on the issue, the reasons for measuring the ROI are still there. Most consultants share a concern that they must eventually show a return on investment for their consulting projects. Otherwise, they won't have the projects, and their image may be tarnished.

Although the rationale for focusing on ROI may be obvious, it is helpful to explore the various reasons why now is the time to pursue ROI. The consulting industry has been in existence for many years and has earned an important place in the mainstream activities of most medium and large organizations. Why is now the time to begin measuring the success in more detail than ever imagined? Several issues create a logical answer to this question.

Client Demands, "Show Me the Money."

Today, more clients are requesting additional evaluation data, up to and including measuring the ROI. It is common for clients to ask for value at the beginning of most consulting projects with "Show me the money," "What is the ROI?" and "Will this be a good return on my investment?" Although this issue has always been there, it has never been at the level that exists today.

Figure 2-1 shows how the "Show me" request has evolved. Two decades ago, clients wanted to see data, resulting in a "Show me data!" request. They wanted to see how well a consulting project was connected to the business. This request evolved into "Show me the money," perhaps even a decade ago. Here, executives recognize that a project is costing money, so they demand, "Show me the money I'm getting out of the project." This request evolved into "Show me the real money (but only that part that's connected to the project)." This particular request recognizes that many factors can influence a

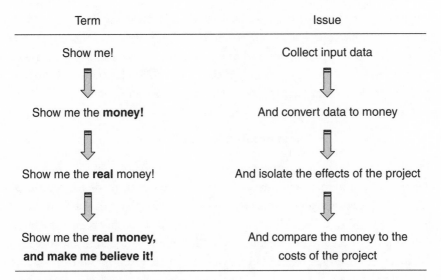

Figure 2-1   The "Show me" evolution.

business measure. This issue hasn't been addressed very often, as it is needed to satisfy an executive's request for a credible connection to the business. Finally, particularly the since the recent recession, executives are asking, "Show me the money and make me believe it's a good investment." Here, the cost of the project must be compared to the monetary benefits derived from it, to present the ultimate evaluation, the financial ROI. Also, it means that it must be a credible process, following conservative standards. The latest request is the best way to meet the executive's demands. For consultants, this means they must focus on the monetary value and return on investment for the project.

When the client demands a process, it must be explored and implemented, and the process must be credible enough for the client to believe the results. Client questions must be addressed in a simple, rational way. Avoiding the issue will erode the relationship between the client and consultant and ultimately may cause the loss of the project.

Competitive Advantage

Perhaps one of the most important reasons to pursue a more comprehensive measurement and evaluation, including ROI, is to meet or beat the competition. Many progressive consulting firms are beginning to develop the ROI for consulting projects to stay competitive or perhaps stay ahead of others who are developing similar processes. These firms address the issue in a proactive manner with a comprehensive approach to ROI. It just may be the best way to position the consulting firm ahead of much of the competition. A database of ROI studies for consulting projects using a credible, undisputed evaluation process can be a crucial advantage and a persuasive selling point.[1]

Increased Revenues and Profits

When a consulting firm can show the actual contribution of the consulting engagement in monetary terms, an excellent case can be made for additional fees—or at least additional projects. Some firms are taking the process to the level of using it to drive additional bonuses (e.g., discounting regular fees in a consulting project and placing the rest of the compensation at risk with a pay-off linked to a target ROI). The payment can be a set amount or savings beyond the target. This approach provides an excellent way to increase revenues and build profits while generating client satisfaction and loyalty.[2]

Satisfaction and Engagement

Individuals engaged in professional work want to know that their efforts make a difference. Consultants need to see that they are making a contribution in terms that clients and managers respect and appreciate. Showing the ROI on a project may be one of the most satisfying parts of a consulting project. Not only do things go well in terms of schedule, budget, and client feedback, but the value added in monetary terms with an impressive ROI adds the final touch to a major project. This provides additional evidence that what we do does make a difference.

The Dilemma of ROI Accountability

The dilemma surrounding ROI for consulting is a source of frustration with many clients and consultants and even within the consulting field itself. Most clients realize that consulting is a necessity when organizations are experiencing problems, significant growth, or increased competition. In these cases, consultants can prepare employees and the organization to meet competitive challenges. Consultants are also important during business restructuring and rapid change.

While many clients see the need for consulting, they intuitively feel that there is value in a consulting project. They can logically conclude that consulting pays off in important bottom-line measures such as productivity improvements, quality enhancements, cost reductions, and time savings. Also, they believe that a consulting project can enhance customer satisfaction, improve engagement, and build teamwork. Yet the frustration comes from the lack of evidence showing that the process is really working. While the payoffs are assumed to be there, and consulting appears to be needed, more evidence is needed for consulting funds to be allocated in the future. The ROI Methodology represents the most promising way to show this accountability through a logical, rational approach.

What Is Causing This Concern for Accountability?

Another important issue to face is examining the rationale for the use of ROI in consulting. Just what is causing so much focus on accountability, including ROI? Several key forces are coming together at this time to create a tremendous pressure to pursue ROI.

Failure of Consulting Projects

Let's face it—many consulting projects have not lived up to their promises or expectations. Experienced consultants can identify an uncomfortable number of projects that have not delivered the results that the client and the consulting firm expected—at least not in the terms that management understands, primarily bottom-line contributions. As more and more consulting projects are undertaken, consuming precious resources in an organization, the results have simply not materialized for many projects.[3] And when the results are reported, there is often skepticism and concern about the credibility of the data, objectivity of data, and the thoroughness of the analysis. This has caused many clients to rethink the role of consulting as well as the accountability of consulting and to place more restraints and demands on consultants.

Economic Pressures of Clients

As firms strive to be successful in a global economy, there are tremendous pressures on costs and efficiency. Companies must squeeze all the savings possible out of every process, activity, and resource. They must account for every expenditure and every project. For some, survival is an issue. This competition for resources has caused organizations to examine the payoff of consulting to make sure they are getting the most out of their consulting expenditures.

The pressures to show the value of projects are not just present in an economic slump but instead evolve and grow over time. Prior to the recession, pressures already existed to show the value of all types of projects and programs because of the global, competitive environment and fierce pricing competition in most industries. Organizations have to be efficient and effective in almost everything they do, including consulting projects.

The global recession has had a major impact on consulting, and many firms have cut their consulting budget significantly, leaving some consulting firms struggling. A few went bankrupt, including a large one, BearingPoint, based in Washington, D.C. It's not surprising to find that consulting budgets were cut in larger proportions than other functional budgets. This flies in the face of what should be happening. Many individuals would agree that during a recession, you need consultants to help you through difficulties and sometimes replace the work that was previously performed by terminated employees.

After the recession, there is more pressure to show the value than ever before, up to and including the forecast of ROI. Some firms are already experiencing this request to show the value before projects are initiated. It's not unusual to see the ROI requirement working its way into the RFP (request for proposal) process.

Budget Growth

With the increased use of consultants comes increased spending for consulting activities. In 2008, when the most recent recession began, consulting was a big business with $305 billion spent annually, according to Kennedy Consulting Research and Advisory. The recession caused a dip of 5.5 percent. By 2012, consulting is expected to reach $315 billion. Because of this, consulting fees and charges have become a target for critics inside the clients' organizations. It is one thing to spend $50,000 on a consulting project, but it is another to spend $1 million and still have nothing to show for it. Consulting has secured a greater percentage of many firms' operating budgets. They see the percentage of expenditures dedicated to consulting growing significantly, not only in magnitude but also as a percentage of operating costs. This growth makes consulting a likely target for increased accountability—if nothing else—to satisfy critics of the process.

Even firms that do not have economic pressures to reduce consulting expenditures are also finding themselves heading in the same direction. For example, consider a large petroleum company based in the Middle East. Every morning, clients and consultants enter their headquarters, ready to tackle a variety of issues. This firm engages all types of consultants. Consultants are used on feasibility studies and implementation projects, bringing in new procedures, processes, technology, and even products. Although the organization is profitable, top executives are scrutinizing the consulting process.

During our most recent visit to this company, we were told that consulting budgets are now being more clearly identified. Previously, they were often scattered throughout a variety of accounting entries, making it difficult to see the full cost of consulting. With an understanding of what's being spent on consulting, there were more efforts to control it. According to our personal resource, this is needed because the consultants often provide conflicting views on the same issue, even delaying and sometimes preventing proper decisions from being made.

Accountability Trends

Today, the trend of increased accountability is sweeping across organizations not only in consulting activities but with almost every type of process. Quality initiatives, technology implementation, human resources projects, marketing projects, and major change initiatives are all being subjected to increased accountability. In today's environment, any new process implemented must address accountability. The focus on accountability is not a new issue. It has been increasing for years, and recently it has been growing in intensity across organizations. Global competition, scarce resources, and demand for funds for new projects and growth initiatives will continue to drive the need for more accountability for projects in the future.

Balanced Measures

For years, there has been debate over what should or should not be measured and how. Some prefer soft data directly from the client or customers. Others prefer hard data focused on key issues of output, quality, cost, and time. Still others have argued for a balance of measures, including financial results. The latter camp seems to be winning. Data from a variety of groups at different time frames and for different purposes are collected representing qualitative and quantitative, tangible and intangible, and financial and nonfinancial categories. This mixture of data, often referred to as a balanced approach, is driving the need for the process described in this book and is an important part of consulting accountability.

Executive Interest

ROI is now enjoying increased interest from the executive suite. Top executives who have watched their consulting budgets grow without the appropriate accountability measures have become frustrated and, in an attempt to respond to the situation, have demanded a return on investment for consulting. The payoff of consulting is becoming a conversation topic in executive publications. The *Wall Street Journal*, the *Financial Times*, the *Economist*, *Fortune*, *Bloomberg Businessweek*, and *Forbes* regularly feature articles about consulting and the need for increased accountability. They describe the frustration of senior executives as they search for results from major consulting projects. They describe failures in detail, examining complaints, consults, and government regulation.

Measuring ROI is becoming a global issue, as executives from all over the world are concerned about the accountability of consulting. Whether the economy is mature or developing, the economic pressures of running a global enterprise are making the accountability of consulting an issue.

Passing Fads

Finally, ROI applications have increased because of the growing interest in a variety of organizational improvement and change interventions offered by consulting firms, particularly in North America. Organizations have embraced almost any trend that appears on the horizon. Unfortunately, many of these change efforts have not worked and have turned out to be nothing more than passing fads, however well intentioned. Unfortunately, the ROI Methodology was not used to measure the accountability of these projects.

The consulting firm is often caught in the middle of this activity, either by supporting the potential fad with a project or actually coordinating the new fad in these organizations. A process is needed to prevent the implementation of an unnecessary program. The implementation of the ROI Methodology requires a thorough assessment of business needs and significant planning before the ROI is attempted. If these two elements are in place, unnecessary passing fads doomed for failure will be avoided. With the ROI process in place, a new change program that does not connect to business needs will be exposed. Management will be fully aware of it early so that adjustments can quickly be made.

Finally, a Feasible and Credible Approach

To develop a credible approach for calculating the ROI on consulting, elements must be in place as shown in Figure 2-2. First, there should be an

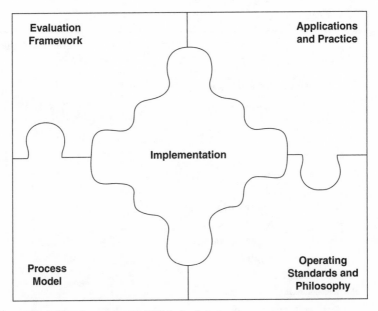

Figure 2-2　The elements of ROI Methodology.

evaluation framework that defines the various levels of evaluation, objectives, and needs assessment and shows the connection between them. Next, an ROI process model is developed that shows a step-by-step procedure for developing the actual ROI calculation. Inherent in this process is the isolation of the effects of consulting from other factors. Next, there should be a set of operating guidelines or operating standards, designed to keep processes on track and build credibility by taking a very conservative approach. Next, appropriate resources should be devoted to implementation issues, addressing responsibilities, policies, procedures, guidelines, goals, and internal skill building. Finally, there should be ample applications that build experience with a process to show how it actually works in real-world settings. Together, these five elements are necessary to develop an evaluation system that contains a balanced set of measures, has credibility with the various stakeholders involved, and can be replicated from one group to another. The following sections offer more detail on these five elements.

The Framework: Evaluation Levels

The ROI Methodology collects or generates five levels of data. The concept of different levels of evaluation is both helpful and instructive in understanding how the return on investment is calculated. Table 2-1 shows the five-level framework used in this book.

Table 2-1 Measurement in Consulting

Level	Measurement Category	Current Status*	Goal in 5 Years*	Comments about Status
1	**Reaction and Perceived Value** Measures reaction to, and satisfaction with, the consulting project	100%	100%	Need more focus on content and perceived value 92%[†]
2	**Learning** Measures what consulting participants learned in the project—information, knowledge, skills, and contacts	30 – 40%	80 – 90%	Must use simple learning measures 83%[†]
3	**Application and Implementation** Measures progress with the project—the use of information, knowledge, skills, and contacts	20%	40%	Need more follow-up 39%[†]
4	**Impact and Consequences** Measures changes in business impact variables such as output, quality, time, and cost linked to the consulting project	9%	20%	The connection to business impact 26%[†]
5	**ROI** Compares the monetary benefits of the business impact measures to the costs of the consulting project	2%	10%	The ultimate level of evaluation 14%[†]

* Percent of programs evaluated at this level
[†] Best practice benchmarking (user for 5 plus years)

At Level 1, **Reaction** from consulting stakeholders is measured. Almost all consulting firms evaluate at Level 1, usually with generic questionnaires and surveys. While this level of evaluation is important as a customer satisfaction measure, a favorable reaction does not ensure that participants will implement the improvements from the project.

At Level 2, **Learning** measurements focus on what consulting participants and other stakeholders learned during the project. A learning check is helpful to ensure that consulting participants have absorbed new skills and knowledge and know how to use it to make the consulting project successful. However, a positive measure at this level is no guarantee that the project will be successfully implemented.

At Level 3, **Application and Implementation**, a variety of follow-up methods are used to determine if participants applied what is necessary to make the project successful. The frequency and use of knowledge, information, technology, and skills are important measures. In addition, measures at this level include all the steps, actions, tasks, and processes involved in the implementation of the project. While Level 3 evaluation is important to gauge the success of the implementation, it still does not guarantee that there will be a positive impact for the project.

At Level 4, **Business Impact**, the measurement focuses on the business results achieved by the consulting project. Typical Level 4 measures include revenue, productivity, quality, waste, transaction, cost, cycle time, and customer satisfaction. Although the consulting intervention may produce a measurable business impact, there is still a concern that the intervention may cost too much.

At Level 5, the ultimate level of evaluation, **Return on Investment**, compares the project's monetary benefits with the fully loaded consulting costs. Although the ROI can be expressed in several ways, it is usually presented as a percentage or benefit-cost ratio.

While almost all consulting firms conduct evaluations to measure reaction, very few conduct evaluations at the ROI level. Perhaps the best explanation for this is that ROI evaluation is often characterized as a difficult and expensive process. Although business results and ROI are desired, it is very important to evaluate the other levels. A chain of impact should occur through the levels as the skills and knowledge learned (Level 2) in the consulting project are applied as the project is implemented (Level 3) to produce business impact (Level 4). If measurements are not taken at each level, it is difficult to conclude that the results achieved were actually produced by the consulting project. Because of this, it is recommended that evaluation be conducted at all levels when a Level 5 evaluation is planned.

The ROI Process Model

The ROI process, presented briefly in this chapter and explored throughout this book, had its beginnings several years ago as the process was applied to a variety of types of projects. Since then, the process has been refined and modified to represent what is presented in Figure 2-3. As the figure illustrates, the process is comprehensive, as data are developed at different times and gathered from different sources to develop the six types of outcome measures (five levels plus intangibles) that are the focal point of this book. To date, more than 300 case studies describing the use of the ROI process model have been published, and the number is growing rapidly. It is estimated that 4,000 users have conducted 5,000 studies. The process meets all of the criteria outlined in

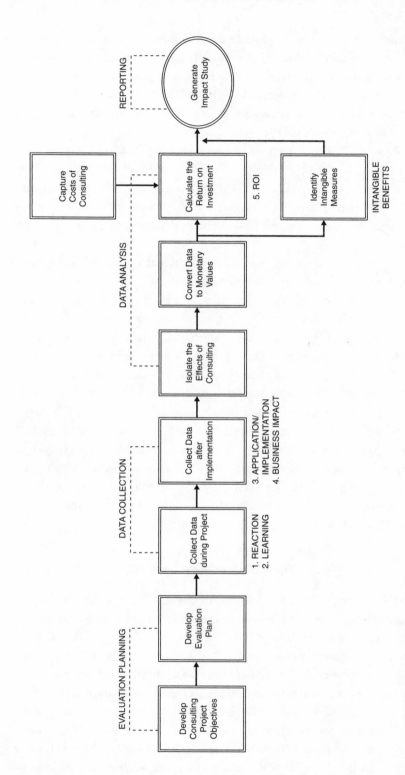

Figure 2-3 The ROI process model.

the previous chapter. Each part of the process is briefly described here. More detail is provided in later chapters.

Planning the Evaluation

The first two parts of the ROI process model focus on two critical planning issues. The first step is to develop appropriate objectives for the consulting project. These are often referred to as the objectives of the solution when a consulting project involves the implementation of a solution. Project objectives range from developing objectives for reaction to developing an objective for the ROI and are defined in more detail in the next chapter.

With the objectives in hand, the next step is to develop a detailed evaluation plan. This involves two important documents. A data collection plan indicates the type of data collected, the method for data collection, data sources, the timing of collection, and the various responsibilities. The next document, the ROI analysis plan, details how the effects of the consulting project are isolated from other influences, how data are converted to monetary values, the appropriate cost categories, the expected intangible measures, and the anticipated target audience for communication. These planning documents are necessary for the process to be implemented appropriately.

Collecting Data

Data are collected during the early stages of the project measure reaction (Level 1) and learning (Level 2). Collecting data during the project ensures that adjustments are made and the process is altered as necessary to make sure the project is on track. Reaction and learning data are critical for immediate feedback and necessary to make the project successful.

Data collection is central to the calculation of the ROI. Post-project data are collected and compared to pre-project situations, control group differences, and expectations. Both hard data (representing output, quality, cost, and time) and soft data (including work habits, work climate, and attitudes) are collected. Data are collected using a variety of methods, such as:

- Follow-up surveys measure satisfaction from stakeholders.
- Follow-up questionnaires measure reaction and uncover specific application issues with consulting interventions.
- On-the-job observation captures actual application and use.
- Tests and assessments are used to measure the extent of learning (knowledge gained or skills enhanced).

- Interviews measure reaction and determine the extent to which the consulting project has been implemented.
- Focus groups determine the degree of application of the consulting project.
- Action plans show progress with implementation on the job and the impact achieved.
- Performance contracts detail specific outcomes expected or obtained from the consulting project.
- Business performance monitoring shows improvement in various performance records and operational data.

The important challenge in data collection is selecting the method or methods appropriate for the setting and the specific intervention, within the time and budget constraints. Data collection methods are covered in more detail in Chapters 4 and 5.

Isolating the Effects of Consulting

An often-overlooked issue in most evaluations is the process of isolating the effects of a consulting project. In this step of the process, specific strategies are explored, which determine the amount of performance improvement directly related to the intervention. This step is essential because there are many factors that will influence performance data after a consulting intervention. The specific strategies in this step will pinpoint the amount of improvement directly related to the intervention. The result is increased accuracy and credibility of the ROI calculation. These strategies have been utilized by organizations to tackle this important issue:

- A pilot group with the consulting initiative is compared to a control group without consulting to isolate the consulting impact.
- Trend lines are used to project business impact measures, and the trend is compared to the actual data after a consulting project is implemented.
- A forecasting model is used to isolate the effects of a consulting project when mathematical relationships between input and output variables are known.
- Participants/stakeholders estimate the amount of improvement related to a consulting project.
- Supervisors and managers estimate the impact of a consulting project on the output measures.

- External studies provide input on the impact of a consulting project.
- Independent experts provide estimates of the impact of a consulting project on the performance variable.
- When feasible, other influencing factors are identified, and the impact is estimated or calculated, leaving the remaining unexplained improvement attributable to the consulting project.
- Customers provide input on the extent to which the consulting project has influenced their decision to use a product or service.

Collectively, these strategies provide a comprehensive set of tools to tackle the important and critical issue of isolating the effects of consulting. Chapter 6 provides more information on this important process.

Converting Data to Monetary Values

To calculate the return on investment, business impact data are converted to monetary values and are compared to intervention costs. This requires a value to be placed on each unit of data connected to the consulting project. Here are the key techniques that are available to convert data to monetary values:

- Output data are converted to profit contribution or cost savings using a standards value.
- The cost of a quality measure, such as a reject, is reported as a standard value.
- Employee time saved is converted to wages and benefits for the time saved.
- Historical costs of a measure, such as a customer complaint, are calculated.
- Internal and/or external experts estimate the value of a data item.
- External databases are searched for an approximate value or cost of a data item.
- A hard-to-value measure is linked to other measures where the value is easily developed.
- Participants estimate the cost or value of the data item.
- Supervisors or managers provide estimates of costs or value of the data item.
- The consultant estimates the value of a data item.

The specific strategy selected usually depends on the type of data and the situation.

This step in the ROI model is very important and is absolutely necessary for determining the monetary benefits for the ROI calculation. The process is challenging, particularly with soft data, but can be methodically accomplished using one or more of these strategies. Because of the importance of converting data to monetary values, most of Chapter 7 is devoted to this issue.

Capturing the Cost of the Consulting

The other part of the equation in a benefit-cost analysis is the consulting cost. Capturing the cost involves monitoring or developing all the costs related to the consulting project. A fully loaded approach is recommended where all direct and indirect costs are captured. Here are the cost components that should be included:

- The cost of initial analysis and assessment connected to the consulting project
- The cost to develop consulting solutions
- The cost to acquire technology, equipment, and external services
- The cost of materials and supplies used in the project
- The cost for the use of facilities and support expenses
- The cost for the time of all stakeholders involved in the project
- The cost of application and implementation of the project
- The cost of maintenance and monitoring
- The costs of administration and overhead for the consulting project allocated in some convenient way
- The cost of evaluation and reporting

For internal consulting projects, all these costs are included. For external consulting projects, many of the costs items are included in the consulting fee. Still, the client absorbs other costs. Both groups should be included to develop the ROI from the client perspective. The conservative approach is to include all of these costs so that the total is fully loaded. Chapter 8 provides more detail on this issue.

Calculating the Return on Investment

The return on investment is calculated using benefits and costs of the consulting project. This comparison is made using the benefit/cost ratio (BCR) or the return on investment percentage (ROI). The BCR is the monetary benefit of the consulting project divided by the cost of the consulting project. In formula form it is:

$$BCR = \frac{\text{Consulting monetary benefits}}{\text{Consulting costs}}$$

The ROI uses the net monetary benefits divided by consulting costs. The net benefits are the monetary benefits minus the costs, multiplied by 100 to convert the quotient to a percentage. In formula form, the ROI becomes:

$$ROI \% = \frac{\text{Net consulting monetary benefits}}{\text{Consulting costs}} \times 100$$

This is the same basic formula used in evaluating capital investments where the ROI is traditionally reported as earnings divided by investment. Chapter 8 is devoted to ROI calculations.

The BCR and the ROI present the same general information, but with a slightly different perspective. An example will illustrate the use of these formulas. A wellness and fitness project yielded monetary benefits of $752,000 based on reduced medical expenses, absenteeism, and accidents. The fully loaded costs are $549,000. The BCR is:

$$BCR = \frac{\$752,000}{\$549,000} = \$1.37$$

As this calculation shows, for every $1 invested, $1.37 in benefits is returned. In this example, net benefits are $752,000 - $549,000 = $203,000. Thus, the ROI is:

$$ROI \% = \frac{\$203,000}{\$549,000} \times 100 = 37\%$$

This means that for each $1 invested in the consulting project, there is a return of $0.37 in *net* benefits, after costs are covered. The benefits are usually expressed as annual benefits for short-term consulting projects, representing the amount saved or gained for a complete year after the consulting project has been implemented and the business impact has occurred. While the benefits may continue after the first year, the impact usually diminishes and is omitted from calculations in short-term situations. For long-term projects, the benefits are spread over several years. The number of years is determined at the beginning of the project, with a view of being conservative. This conservative approach is used throughout the application of the ROI process described in this book.

Identifying Intangible Benefits

In addition to tangible, monetary benefits, most consulting projects will drive intangible, nonmonetary benefits. During data analysis, every attempt is made to convert all data to monetary values. All hard data—such as output, quality, and time—are converted to monetary values. The conversion of soft data is attempted for each data item. However, if the process used for conversion is too subjective or inaccurate, and the resulting values lose credibility in the process, then the data are listed as intangible benefits with the appropriate explanation. Intangible benefits include items such as:

- Corporate social responsibility
- Brand awareness
- Job satisfaction
- Reputation
- Organizational commitment
- Employee engagement
- Technology leadership
- Stress
- Teamwork
- Culture
- Image

For some consulting projects, intangible, nonmonetary benefits are extremely valuable, often commanding as much influence as the hard data items. Chapter 7 provides more detail on intangible benefits.

Reporting Results

A final operational step of the ROI process model is to generate an impact study to document the results achieved by the consulting project and communicate results to various target audiences. The impact study presents the process used to generate the six measures of outcome data. The process, assumptions, key concepts, and guiding principles are all outlined before the results are presented. Next, the six categories of data, beginning with reaction and moving through to ROI and intangible measures, are presented in a rational, logical process, showing the building blocks to measure the success of the study. This becomes the official document of the complete assessment of success of the consulting project. Its length ranges from 20 to 30 pages for a small project to 200 to 300 pages for a substantial, long-term consulting impact study. A variety of methods are used to communicate results to several target audiences. Chapter 9 is devoted to communicating results.

The Operating Standards: Guiding Principles

To ensure that each study takes the same conservative philosophy and to increase the likelihood of replication, a set of guiding principles has been developed for the consulting ROI process. The list below presents the guiding principles used throughout this book. While the principles may be obvious, each will be explored and revisited throughout the book. Collectively, these principles will ensure that the proper conservative approach is taken and that the impact ROI study can be replicated and compared to others.

1. When a higher-level evaluation is conducted, data must be collected at lower levels.
2. When an evaluation is planned for a higher level, the previous level of evaluation does not have to be comprehensive.
3. When collecting and analyzing data, use only the most credible sources.
4. When analyzing data, select the most conservative alternative for calculations.
5. At least one method must be used to isolate the effects of the project.
6. If no improvement data are available for a population or from a specific source, it is assumed that no improvement has occurred.
7. Estimates of improvements should be adjusted for the potential error of the estimate.
8. Extreme data items and unsupported claims should not be used in ROI calculations.
9. Only the first year of benefits (annual) should be used in the ROI analysis of short-term solutions.
10. Costs of a solution, project, or program should be fully loaded for ROI analysis.
11. Intangible measures are defined as measures that are purposely not converted to monetary values.
12. The results from the ROI Methodology must be communicated to all key stakeholders.

Implementation of the Process

The best tool, technique, or model will be unsuccessful unless it is properly utilized and becomes a routine part of the consulting process. As a new process, both the consultants and clients may resist it, just as with any other significant change. Consultants may fear it; clients may not trust it. Some of the resistance is based on realistic barriers, while some will be based on misunderstandings and perceived problems that may be mythical. In either case, specific steps must be taken to overcome the resistance by carefully and methodically implementing the ROI process. Implementation involves many issues, including assigning responsibilities, building the necessary skills, and developing the plans and goals around the process. It will also involve preparing the environment, individuals, and support teams for this type of comprehensive analysis. The consulting firms with the most success with this process are those that have devoted adequate resources to implementation and deliberately planned for the transition from the current state to where they desire the organization to be in terms of accountability. Chapter 10 covers the implementation issues.

Applications

It is recommended that the material and content in this book be put to practice quickly. A quick application ensures there is successful learning from the book to actual consulting projects. This quick application comes to life in the ROI Institute's certification process. The business model of the ROI Institute is to transfer the capability to conduct ROI studies to organizations through the ROI Certification process, which began in 1995. Since then, more than 5,000 people have participated in the process, resulting in almost 4,000 people achieving the status of Certified ROI Professional. To achieve this designation, the individual must complete a study meeting the standards of the ROI Institute. Based on our experience at the ROI Institute, once people have conducted one study, they are apt to do more. The value of the ROI Methodology is, in its use, systematically and routinely changing practices and approaches, and it is showing the value of projects along the way.

Although a significant number of case applications have been developed, the status of ROI among consultants in the field is difficult, if not impossible, to pinpoint. Top consulting firms and senior consultants are reluctant to disclose internal practices, and even in the most progressive consulting firms, they confess that too little progress has been made. Progress has been made as the literature shows more examples of how a consulting firm has attempted to measure the return on investment in a consulting project.

While examples of the progress of ROI in consulting are growing, it has become a critical topic that is constantly yielding new discoveries in the consulting field. The need is clear. The interest in ROI will be persistent as long as consulting budgets continue to increase and consulting holds the promise of helping organizations improve. Much progress must be made to meet this important need.

How Evaluation Data Can Be Used: Benefits of ROI for Consulting

Although the benefits of adopting a comprehensive measurement and evaluation process for consulting may be obvious, several important benefits can be derived from the routine use of this process.

Show the Contribution of Selected Consulting Projects

With the ROI process, the consultant and the client will know the specific contribution of the consulting project in terms that were not previously developed and in a language understood by the client group. The ROI will show the benefits versus the cost, elevating the evaluation data to the ultimate level of accountability. This process presents indisputable evidence that the project was successful (or how to improve it if it was unsuccessful).

Gain the Confidence of Clients

The client who requests and authorizes a consulting project will now have a complete set of data to show the overall success of the process. Not hampered by a lack of qualitative or quantitative data, this provides a complete profile from different sources, within different time frames, and with different types of data. The ROI study documents the process that has occurred step by step and validates the client's initial decision to move forward with the consulting project. Even if the project is negative, the client has detailed information about how to improve it.

Earn the Respect of Senior Management

Measuring the ROI of a consulting project is one of the best ways to earn the respect and support of the senior management team—not only for a particular consulting project, but for other consulting projects as well. For internal projects, executives will respect processes that add bottom-line value presented in terms they understand. For client organizations, top executives will see the added value of consulting. The result of this analysis is comprehensive, and when it is applied consistently and comprehensively in several projects, it can convince the management group that consulting is an important investment and not just an expense. This is a critical step toward building an appropriate partnership with senior management.

Improve Consulting Processes

Because there is a variety of feedback data collected during the consulting project, a comprehensive analysis (including ROI) provides data to drive changes in consulting processes and make adjustments during a project. It also provides data that will help improve consulting projects in the future when it is realized that certain processes are nonproductive while others add value. Thus, the ROI Methodology is an important process-improvement tool. In rare occasions, the project may have to be halted if it is not adding the appropriate value and can never add value. While that will take courage, it will reap important benefits with the client if it is clearly evident that the project will not produce results.

Develop a Results-Focused Approach

The communication of expectations at different time frames and with the detailed planning that is involved with the ROI Methodology focuses the entire team, including stakeholders, on bottom-line results. This focus often enhances the results that can be achieved because the ultimate goals are clearly in mind. In essence, the process begins with the end in mind. All of the processes, activities, and steps are clearly focused on the ultimate outcomes. As the project shows success, confidence is built in using the process, which enhances the results of future projects.

Justify Other Consulting Projects

If the consulting project is successful, perhaps the same type of project can be applied to other areas. A positive ROI story makes a convincing argument that if one division (or company) has a successful project and another division (or company) has the same needs, the project may add the same value and enhance the overall success and replication of all consulting projects.

Some client organizations will try a project on a pilot basis and then use the results to make a decision to implement it on a broader scale. For example, Walmart will often try a project in about 25 stores, collect a balanced set of data, including ROI, and use the data to make a decision for system-wide implementation.

Application of the ROI Process: A Case Study

To illustrate how the data collected in the consulting ROI is reported, an example is presented. The problem addressed by the consulting firm focuses directly on alternative work solutions with a work-at-home project for employees. A health and insurance company is seeking ways to increase efficiency, productivity, and retention of claims processors and examiners. In addition, executives are interested in the company doing its share to help with the environment. For top executives, this may be the most important issue.

At Family Mutual Insurance Company (FMI), work-at-home opportunities appeared to be a very effective solution from several perspectives. First, productivity was not at the level executives thought it should be in two job categories, claims processors and claims examiners. Claims processors process the claims as they are filed, ensuring that all paperwork is proper, procedures are followed, and the process is consistent with specifications. Claims examiners review claims only when there is a challenge or complaint. They essentially examine what has been done and then work directly with the customers to ensure that they are satisfied. Both of these groups have high turnover, and a work-at-home option seemed to be a great way to minimize this, as many individuals see this option as an attractive offer. At the same time, the company is growing, and it is has reached maximum working capacity with the current office space. Consequently, more real estate space is needed. This project would free up office space that may be used by others to accommodate the growth without additional construction or leasing other buildings. Finally and foremost, the firm wanted to take an important stand in helping the environment. Executives realize that one of the best ways to help the environment is reduce carbon emissions by reducing or eliminating the amount of travel of employees who come to work, thus reducing pollution and congestion.

The consultants were asked to analyze the causes of the problem, develop the best solution, and implement the solution to improve costs, productivity, and retention. A summary of the project is presented in Table 2-2.

As the case summary illustrates, the project involved the employees in claims processing and claims examiners' job categories. The approach was comprehensive and was based on an analysis to develop a solution and implement those solutions. Detailed objectives were developed at Levels 1 through 5. Table 2-2 presents the methods selected for data collection during

Table 2-2 A Case Study: Family Mutual Health and Life Insurance Co.

Project Profile

Title:	Alternative Work Solutions: Work at Home
Target Audience:	Claim processors and claims examiners (950)
Duration:	Six months—from initial analysis and assessment, solution development, and implementation
Overall Objective:	Explore the feasibility of working at home for this group, recommend a specific solution, and implement the solution
Origination:	Management directive with needs analysis and assessment
Coordination:	HR managers

Detailed Objectives

After implementing this project:

Reaction

• Employees should react favorably to the work-at-home project in terms of satisfaction and motivation.
• Managers must see this project as important and necessary.

Learning

• Employees must understand the roles and responsibilities for success.
• Managers must be able to discuss performance issues related to working at home.
• Managers must be able to explain the company's policy for working at home.

Application

• Managers should conduct a meeting with all direct reports to discuss policy and expected behavior and actions.
• At least 30 percent of eligible employees volunteer for at-home assignments.
• Work-at-home employees should work effectively at home.
• The workplace at home should be free from distractions and conflicting demands.
• Managers will administer the company's policy properly.
• Managers should manage the remote employees effectively.

Impact

• The office expense per person should be reduced by 20 percent in six months.
• The productivity of participants should increase by 5 percent in six months.
• Employee turnover for this target group should reduce 12 percent in six months.
• The company's image as a green company should improve.
• Employee engagement should improve.

ROI

Achieve a 25 percent return on investment

Data Collection during Project

- Interview
- Questionnaires
- Business performance monitoring

Data Collection after Implementation

- Questionnaires
- Interviews
- Business performance monitoring

Isolating the Effects of the Consulting Project

- Productivity—control group comparisons
  —participant estimates as a backup
- Turnover—control group comparisons
  —participant estimates as a backup
- Office expenses—control group comparisons
  —expert estimates
  —participant estimates as a backup

Converting Data to Monetary Values—Techniques

- Office expenses—standard values based on historical costs and expert input
- Turnover—external studies, same industry
- Productivity—standard values

Monetary Benefits from Productivity Improvement

- Value of one claim = $10.00
- Value of one disputed claim = $12.00
- Daily improvement = 2.2 claims per day
- Daily improvement = 1.9 disputed claims per day
- Annual value = 234 × 220 work days × 2.2 × 10.00 = $1,132,560
- Annual value = 77 × 220 days × 1.9 × 12.00 = $386,232

Monetary Benefits from Office Expense Reduction

- Office expenses in company office: per person $17,000 annually
- Office expenses at home office: per person $12,500 first year; $3,600 second year
- Net improvement: $4,500, first year
- Total annual value = 311 × $4,500 = $1,399,500

Monetary Benefits from Turnover Reduction

- Value of one turnover statistic = $25,400
- Annual improvement related to program = 45 turnovers (prevented), first year
- Annual value = $25,400 × $45 = $1,143,400

(Continues)

Table 2-2   A Case Study: Family Mutual Health and Life Insurance Co. *(Continued)*

Consulting Project Costs

• Initial analysis and assessment	$21,000
• Solution development	35,800
• IT support and maintenance	238,000
• Administration and coordination	213,000
• Materials (400 @ $50)	20,000
• Facilities and refreshments—21 meetings	12,600
• Salaries plus benefits for employee and manager meetings	418,280
• Evaluation and reporting	33,000
Total First-Year Costs	**$991,680**

Level 1 Results—From Managers

- Rating of 4.2 out of 5 on importance of the work alternative
- Rating of 4.3 out of 5 on the need for the work alternative

Level 1 Results—From Participating Employees

- Rating of 4.6 out of 5 on satisfaction with new work arrangement
- Rating of 4.1 out of 5 on motivational effect of new work arrangement

Level 2 Results—From Managers

- Rating of 4.2 out of 5 on understanding the policy for working at home
- Rating of 3.9 out of 5 on ability to explain policy
- Successful skill practice demonstration on performance discussions

Level 2 Results—From Employees

- Rating of 4.3 out of 5 on roles and responsibilities

Level 3 Results—Key Issues

- 93 percent of managers conducted meetings with employees to discuss working at home.
- 36 percent of eligible employees volunteered for at-home work assignments (342 participants).
- Work-at-home employees rate 4.3 out of 5 on working effectively at home.
- 95 percent of employees report that workplace is free of distractions and conflict.
- Managers rate 4.1 out of 5 on administering policy properly.
- Managers rate 3.8 out of 5 on managing remote employees effectively.

Level 4 Results

Business Performance	Work-at-Home Group	Comparison Group	Change	Number of Participants
Daily claims processed	35.4	33.2	2.2	234
Daily claims examined	22.6	20.7	1.9	77
Office expense per person	$12,500	$17,000	$4,500	311
Turnover*	9.1%	22.3%	13.2%	311

* Processors and examiners

Level 5 Results

Monetary Benefits

Productivity	=	$1,132,560 + 386,232 = $1,518,792
Office expense	=	$4,500 × 311 = $1,399,500
Turnover	=	$1,143,000
Total	=	$4,061,292

ROI Calculating

$$BCR = \frac{\text{Consulting Monetary Benefits}}{\text{Consulting Costs}} = \frac{\$4,061,292}{\$991,680} = 4.10$$

$$ROI = \frac{\text{Net Consulting Benefits}}{\text{Consulting Costs}} = \frac{\$4,061,292 - \$991,680}{\$991,680} \times 310\%$$

Intangible Benefits

- Reduced commuting time
- Reduced carbon emissions
- Reduced fuel consumption
- Reduced sick leave
- Reduced absenteeism
- Stronger job engagement
- Improved image as environmentally friendly company
- Increased corporate social responsibility
- Improved job satisfaction
- Reduced stress
- Improved recruiting image

the project as well as after the implementation of the solution. In addition, the methods used to isolate the effects of consulting and the methods to convert data to monetary values are shown.

The results are then presented, beginning with Level 1, and working through Level 5, and the intangibles. The monetary benefits are based on a one-year time frame achieved from improving office expenses, turnover, and productivity. The cost of the project is presented in the table and shows a fully loaded cost profile. A high ROI was achieved.

This brief example shows the richness of this approach in terms of presenting a comprehensive profile of success, ranging from reaction to ROI and intangible benefits. Additional detail on this case study is found in other parts of the book.

Final Thoughts

This chapter provides a brief overview of the process presented in the remainder of the book. The chapter underscores the urgency of the challenge from the consultant's perspective, and now is the time to use a comprehensive measurement and evaluation process, including the ROI for consulting. Several forces are creating this important need for more accountability. The ROI Methodology presented in the book was defined with five important elements: evaluation framework, ROI process model, application, implementation, and guiding principles. When combined with determination, a reliable, credible process is developed that can be replicated from one project to another. Some detail on the ROI process was provided along with the benefits of using it. A sample case study highlights all of the issues in the chapter. The remainder of the chapters detail many of the issues developed in this chapter.

Initial Analysis and Planning

Key to a Successful ROI Evaluation

THE SCENARIO IS FAMILIAR. A project concludes and you find yourself a few days or months later, huddled with your team around a conference table, agreeing to the same admittance: there should have been more planning. Few things are more important in a consulting process than the initial analysis and planning, particularly the planning for evaluation processes. When attempting to measure the success of consulting after the project is complete—as an add-on, follow-up assignment—this obvious conclusion of the need for more planning is often reached. The initial analysis and planning involve several key issues explored in this chapter. The first issue is specifying in detail the objectives of the project arranged by levels. Next, and perhaps more importantly, the chapter shows how to link objectives to initial needs for the project, focusing on different levels of needs analysis. Finally, the chapter introduces a variety of planning tools that can be helpful in setting up the consulting project evaluation.

Overall Project Goal

The goal for the consulting project indicates specifically what will be accomplished and delivered. This is sometimes referred to as the purpose, overall objectives, or aim of the project.

Table 3-1 Examples of Project Goals

- Evaluate the feasibility of three alternative approaches to new product development and rollout. For each approach, provide data on projected success, resources required, and timing.
- Implement a new accounts payable system that will maximize cash flow and discounts and minimize late-payment penalties.
- Identify the causes of excessive, unplanned absenteeism, and recommend solutions with costs and timetable.
- Design, develop, and implement automated sales-tracking system that will provide real-time information on deliveries, customer satisfaction, and sales forecasts.
- Enhance the productivity of the call center staff as measured in calls completed, without sacrificing service quality.
- Build a customer feedback and corrective action system that will meet customer needs and build customer relationships.
- Explore the feasibility of a work-at-home program to improve productivity, efficiency, and retention, while helping to protect the environment.
- Reorganize the sales and marketing division from a product-based unit to a regional-based, fully integrated structure.
- Provide review, advice, and oversight input during the relocation of the headquarters staff. Input is provided by memo each week. The project will address concerns, issues, problems, and delays.
- Recommend and implement a social media marketing approach, given our current marketing strategy and customer base.

Every consulting project should have a goal, and in some cases, there are multiple goals. These goals should be as specific as possible and focused directly on the assignment. Examples of project goals are presented in Table 3-1. As this table illustrates, the goal is broad in scope, outlining from an overall perspective what is to be accomplished within basic parameters. The details of timing, specifications, and specific deliverables come later. Project goals are critical because they bring focus to the project quickly, often serving as the beginning point in the discussion of the consulting project.

Levels of Project Objectives

Most consulting projects lead to solutions. In some situations, the consulting project is aimed at solving a particular problem, preventing a problem, or taking advantage of an opportunity. In other situations, the initial consulting project is designed to develop a range of feasible solutions, or one desired solution prior to implementation. Whatever the case, these solutions or opportunities should have multiple levels of objectives as described in Table 3-2. These

Table 3-2 Multiple Levels of Objectives

Levels of Objectives	Focus of Objectives
Level 1 Reaction	Defines a specific level of reaction to the consulting project as it is revealed and communicated to the stakeholders
Level 2 Learning	Defines specific levels of knowledge, information, and skills as the stakeholders learn how to make the consulting project successful
Level 3 Application and implementation	Defines specific measures and levels of success with application and implementation of project
Level 4 Impact	Defines the specific levels business measures will change or improve as a result of the project's implementation
Level 5 ROI	Defines the specific return on investment from the project, comparing costs against monetary benefits from the project

levels of objectives, ranging from qualitative to quantitative, define precisely what will occur as a particular project is implemented in the organization. These objectives reflect the levels of evaluation and types of data described in Chapters 1 and 2. They are so critical that they need special attention in their development and use.

Reaction Objectives

For any project to be successful, various stakeholders must react to the project favorably, or at least not negatively. Ideally, the stakeholders should be satisfied with the project since the best project solutions offer win-win outcomes for the client and consultant. The stakeholders are those who are directly involved in implementing the project. This diverse group can comprise employees who are involved in implementing the work, team leaders who are responsible for a change process, customers who must use a redesigned product, suppliers who must follow a new system, citizens who must use a new procedure, or volunteers who must adjust to a new process. Stakeholders could also be managers who must support or assist the project in some way. Table 3-3 shows a few of the typical areas for specific reaction objectives with examples. This type of information should be collected routinely through a consulting project so that feedback can be used to make adjustments, keep the project on track, and perhaps even redesign certain parts of it. These are necessary to maintain proper focus. Unfortunately, many consulting projects do not have specific objectives at this level, and data collection mechanisms are not put in place to ensure appropriate feedback for making needed adjustments.

Table 3-3 Reaction Objectives

Typical Areas

• Usefulness	• Overall satisfaction
• Relevance	• Challenging
• Feasibility	• Rewarding
• Difficulty	• Motivational
• Necessity	• Fair
• Importance	• A good investment
• Perceived value	• A good use of time
• Appropriateness	

Typical Reaction Objectives

1. Citizens should perceive the new procedure as important to them with a rating of 4 on a 5-point scale.
2. Sales team should rate the new tracking as relevant to their needs, scoring 4.5 on a 5-point scale.
3. Suppliers should view the new sustainability requirement as appropriate with a 5 rating on a 7-point scale.

Learning Objectives

Almost every consulting project will involve a learning objective. In some cases involving major change projects and new technology implementations, the learning component is quite significant. To ensure that the various stakeholders have learned what they need to learn to make the project successful, learning objectives are developed. Learning objectives are critical because they communicate expected outcomes from the learning component of the project and information needed, and they define the desired competence or the required performance to make the consulting project successful. These objectives provide a basis for evaluating the learning since they often reflect the type of measurement process. Learning objectives should clearly indicate what participants must learn—sometimes with precision. Table 3-4 shows typical action verbs and examples typical of learning objectives.

The three types of learning objectives are often defined. These include:

- **Awareness.** Familiarity with terms, concepts, and processes.
- **Knowledge.** General understanding of concepts, processes, or procedures.
- **Performance.** Ability to demonstrate skills at least on a basic level.

Table 3-4 Learning Objectives and Typical Action Verbs

Action Verbs

• Name	• Explain	• Complete
• Write	• Search	• State
• Prepare	• Sort	• Build
• Describe	• Locate	• Start up
• Recite	• Stop	• List
• Reboot	• Solve	• Compare
• Differentiate	• Calculate	• Recall
• Identify	• Eliminate	• Contrast
• Load	• Construct	• Use
• Score	• Determine	• Document

Typical Learning Objectives

After completing the program, participants will be able to:
- Identify the six features of the new ethics policy
- Complete each software routine in the standard time for the routine
- Use problem-solving skills, given a specific problem statement
- Determine whether they are eligible for the early retirement program
- Score 75 or better in 10 minutes on the new-product quiz
- List all five customer-interaction skills
- Explain the five categories for the value of diversity in a work group
- Document suggestions for award consideration
- Score at least 9 out of 10 on a sexual harassment policy quiz
- Identify five new technology trends explained at the conference
- Name the six pillars of the division's new strategy
- Complete the leadership simulation in 15 minutes

The best learning objectives describe observable, measurable behavior or performance that is necessary for the success of the consulting project. They are often outcome-based, clearly worded, and specific. They specify what the particular stakeholder must know and do to implement the project successfully. Learning objectives can have three components:

- Performance—what the participant or stakeholder will be able to do as a result of the consulting project
- Conditions under which the participant or stakeholder will perform the various tasks and processes
- Criteria—the degree or level of proficiency necessary to perform a new task, process, or procedure that is part of the solution

Application Objectives

As a consulting project is implemented, it should be guided by application objectives that define clearly what is expected and often to what level of performance. Application objectives reflect the action desired from the project. They also involve particular milestones, indicating specifically when steps or phases of the process are completed. Application objectives are critical because they describe the expected outcomes in the intermediate area, that is, between learning what's necessary to make the project successful and the actual impact that will be improved because of it. Application objectives describe how people should perform, processes should evolve, or technology should be used as the project is implemented. The emphasis is on action.

The best application objectives identify behaviors that are observable and measurable or action steps in a process that can easily be observed or measured. They specify what the various stakeholders will change or have changed as a result of the consulting project. As with learning objectives, application or implementation objectives may have three components— performance, condition, and criteria.

Table 3-5 shows typical key questions asked at this level and typical application objectives. Application objectives have almost always been included to some degree in consulting projects but have not been as specific as they could be or need to be. To be effective, they must clearly define the environment where the project is successfully implemented.

Table 3-5 Application Objectives

Typical Questions for Application Objectives

1. What new or improved knowledge will be applied on the job?
2. What is the frequency of skill application?
3. What specific new task will be performed?
4. What new steps will be implemented?
5. What action items will be implemented?
6. What new procedures will be implemented or changed?
7. What new guidelines will be implemented?
8. What new processes will be implemented?
9. Which meetings need to be held?
10. Which tasks, steps, or procedures will be discontinued?

Typical Application Objectives

When this project is implemented:

- At least 99.1 percent of software users will be following the correct sequences after three weeks of use.
- Within one year, 10 percent of employees will submit documented suggestions for saving costs.
- The average 360-degree leadership assessment score will improve from 3.4 to 4.1 on a 5-point scale in 90 days.
- 95 percent of high-potential employees will complete individual development plans within two years.
- Employees will routinely use problem-solving skills when faced with a quality problem.
- Sexual harassment activity will cease within three months after the zero-tolerance policy is implemented.
- 80 percent of employees will use one or more of the three cost-containment features of the health-care plan in the next six months.
- 50 percent of conference attendees will follow up with at least one contact from the conference within 60 days.
- By November, pharmaceutical sales reps will communicate adverse effects of a specific prescription drug to all physicians in their territories.
- Managers will initiate three workout projects within 15 days.
- Sales and customer service representatives will use all five interaction skills with at least half the customers within the next month.

Impact Objectives

Almost every consulting project should have an impact, even in the public sector and among nonprofits and nongovernment organizations. Business impact is expressed in the key business measures that should be improved as the application objectives are achieved. The impact objectives are critical to measuring business performance because they define business-unit performance that should be connected to the consulting project. Above all, they place emphasis on achieving bottom-line results that key client groups expect and demand.

The best impact objectives contain data that are easily collected and are well known to the client group. They are results-based, clearly worded, and specify what the stakeholders have ultimately accomplished in the business unit as a result of the consulting project.

The four major categories of hard data impact objectives are output, quality, cost, and time. Major categories of soft data impact objectives are customer service, work climate, and image. Typical measures that frame the objectives are presented in Chapter 5. Table 3-6 shows examples of impact objectives.

Table 3-6   Typical Impact Objectives

After project completion, the following conditions should be met:

- After nine months, grievances should be reduced from three per month to no more than two per month at the Golden Eagle tire plant.
- The average number of new accounts should increase from 300 to 350 per month in six months.
- Tardiness at the Newbury Foundry should decrease by 20 percent within the next calendar year.
- An across-the-board reduction in overtime should be realized for front-of-house managers at Tasty Time restaurants in the third quarter of this year.
- Employee complaints should be reduced from an average of three per month to an average of one per month at Guarantee Insurance headquarters.
- By the end of the year, the average number of product defects should decrease from 214 per month to 153 per month at all Amalgamated Rubber extruding plants in the Midwest region.
- The company-wide employee engagement index should rise by one point during the next calendar year.
- Sales expenses for all titles at Proof Publishing Company should decrease by 10 percent in the fourth quarter.
- There should be a 10 percent increase in Pharmaceuticals, Inc., brand awareness among physicians during the next two years.
- Customer returns per month should decline by 15 percent in six months.

Return on Investment Objectives

A fifth level of objectives for consulting projects is the expected return on investment. These objectives define the expected payoff from the consulting project and compare the cost of consulting with the monetary benefits from the consulting project. This is typically expressed as an acceptable return on investment percentage that compares the annual monetary benefits minus the cost, divided by the actual cost, and multiplied by 100. A 0 percent ROI indicates a break-even consulting project. A 50 percent ROI indicates that the cost of the consulting is recaptured and an additional 50 percent "earnings" are achieved.

For many consulting projects, the ROI objective is larger than what might be expected from the ROI of other expenditures, such as the purchase of a new company, a new building, or major equipment, but the two are related. In many organizations the ROI objective for a consulting project is set slightly higher than the ROI expected from capital investments because of the relative newness of applying the ROI concept to consulting. For example, if the expected ROI from the purchase of a new company is 20 percent, the ROI from a consulting project might be set in the 25 percent range. The important point is that the ROI objective should be established up front and in discussions with the client.

Importance of Specific Objectives

Developing specific objectives at the application and impact levels for consulting projects provides important benefits. First, they provide direction to the consultants directly involved in the process to help keep them on track. Objectives define exactly what is expected at different time frames from different individuals. These objectives provide guidance to the support staff as they offer assistance to the consultants. Impact objectives help the client to fully understand the ultimate goal and impact of consulting. These objectives provide the focus and motivation for the consultants who must achieve success with the project. In most consulting projects, the participants are actively involved and will influence the results of the project. They will clearly see the gains that should be achieved. Objectives provide important information for all stakeholder groups to clearly understand what the landscape will look like when the consulting is complete. Finally, from an evaluation perspective, the objectives provide a basis for measuring success.

How Is It All Connected? Linking Evaluation with Needs

Where do objectives come from? There is a distinct linkage between objectives and original needs driving a consulting project. The previous chapter focused on the five levels of evaluation and showed how they are critical to providing an overall assessment of the impact of a consulting project—particularly when a solution is implemented as part of the consulting project. This chapter shows the importance of setting objectives for the consulting project at different levels. Now we will make a further connection to the original needs assessment. Figure 3-1 shows the connection between evaluation and needs assessment for consulting projects. This figure shows the important linkage from the initial problem or opportunity that created the needs for consulting to the evaluation of the project. Level 5 defines the potential payoff and examines the possibility for a return on investment before the project is even pursued. Level 4 analysis focuses directly on the business needs that precipitated the need for consulting. At Level 3, the specific performance or action is defined that must change to meet the business needs. At Level 2, the specific information, knowledge, or skills that are needed to address the performance needs are identified. Finally, the preferences for the project implementation define the Level 1 needs. This connection is very important to understanding all of the elements that must go into an effective consulting project.

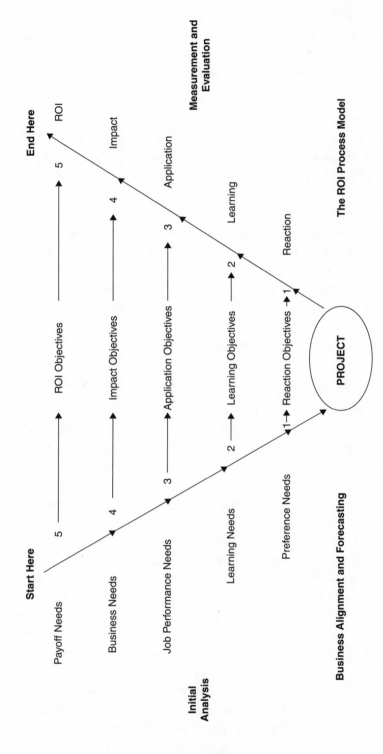

Figure 3-1 Consulting alignment: the V model.

An example will help illustrate this linkage. Figure 3-2 shows an example of linking needs assessment with the evaluation of a consulting project involving a work-at-home initiative, presented in Chapter 2. As the figure shows, the first step is to see if this is a problem worth solving or an opportunity worth pursuing. This sometimes causes a validation of the problem using Level 4 data.

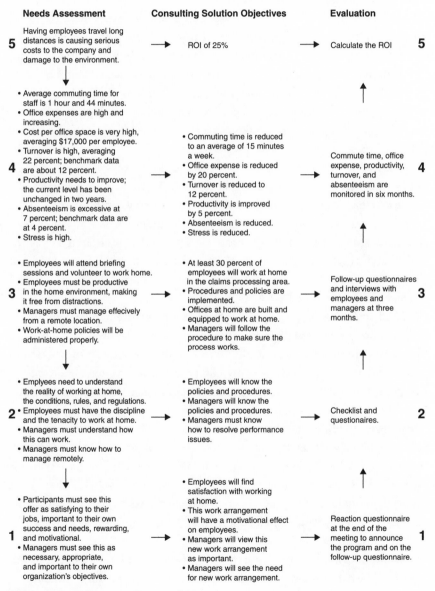

Figure 3-2 Alignment for consulting.

In this example, the payoff need is based on the problem of employees having to travel long distances that generate costs to them and damage to the environment. At Level 4, the problem unfolds with more detail, and it's obvious that it's worth solving. The average commuting time for the team is almost two hours; office expenses are very high and increasing as staff additions are made. Turnover, which is expensive, is extremely high, averaging 22 percent, while benchmark data suggest that it should be about 12 percent or lower. Productivity needs to improve; it has not increased in the last two years. Absenteeism is excessive, and stress is high. When all these measures are all considered, this is a serious problem, and to a certain extent, a great opportunity for improvement.

With the confirmation in Level 4 that there is a problem, a potential payoff can be estimated. This involves estimating the cost of the measures of office expenses, turnover, and lost productivity and estimating the reduction that can come from the consulting project. This develops a profile of potential payoff to see if the problem is worth solving.

At Level 3, the causes of the problem are explored using a variety of techniques. Ideally, each measure should be analyzed to see what's causing it to be where it is (e.g., why is productivity not improving, or what is the cause of the excessive turnover?). For this project, the consultants conducted interviews and focus groups, examined exit interview data, and administered surveys to understand why business measures were at the current level. Some causes of the problem were obvious, such as office expenses incurred due to growth and the increasing cost of real estate and leasing.

The key issue is to identify the solution to the problem. The commuting time will not get better unless the office space is either moved to the people, the people are moved closer to the office, or they're allowed to work from home. The turnover issue has many components, but having an alternative work schedule, such as working at home, would reduce turnover significantly according to an analysis of exit interviews. Some employees have left to work either closer to home or at home. The productivity issue is a little more confusing. It could be better, but it is not clear as to how this should be addressed. Interviews and focus groups hint that working at home might raise the productivity. Absenteeism is traced to problems that could be solved if there were some flexibility in work arrangements. Flexibility in their work arrangements may help avoid this stress, and it appears that it could be resolved with a work-at-home situation as well.

At the next level, Level 2, the learning issue is explored. Do employees understand what's necessary to make this work? Are employees confident that they can work at home? Are they fully aware of all the issues and the ramifications of working at home? Do the managers understand what's involved in this arrangement, and can they adapt to a work-at-home arrangement? These issues involve the content of the project, detailing what people must understand to work successfully at home.

At Level 1, the desired reaction must be detailed. At first, a realistic picture of the work-at-home environment must be presented so that individuals may understand this choice may not be for everyone. Also, when the ground rules are fully understood, employees must see this as helpful, necessary, and, for some, even motivational. Managers must see this as a tool to help them and the organization, not as a process that's going to cause them to lose control. These perceptions are very important and must be approached very deliberately.

These five levels provide an overall profile for determining if the problem is worth solving, and they align the project solution with key measures and identify the issue necessary to develop the objectives. The consulting objectives for each level are shown in the figure as well, along with the evaluation method to verify that the objectives were met. This process is important to the development and implementation of a consulting project. Many consulting projects are involved in developing a solution and implementing the solution, as in this particular example. When this occurs, the above linkage connects the needs to objectives and then to evaluation.

The solution to the problem or opportunity to pursue is an important part of this linkage. Some consulting projects may be involved in uncovering needs with the initial analysis to determine the causes of the problem and then recommend solutions. In those situations, it is up to the client to then implement the solution, or implementation becomes part of another consulting project. In either case, the solutions are ultimately developed for a complete consulting project. If this has not been accomplished, multiple levels of analysis may be necessary for the project. While there are other references that focus more specifically on the performance analysis to uncover different levels of needs, a brief summary is presented here.

Payoff Needs

The first part of the process is to determine if the problem is worth solving or the opportunity warrants serious consideration. In some cases, this is obvious when there are serious problems that are affecting the organization's operations and strategy. Still others may not be so obvious.

Table 3-7 shows some requests for consulting that represent obvious payoff opportunities and thus have business value written all over them. These payoff opportunities make it clear that this is a problem that needs to be solved or an opportunity that should be pursued with a clearly identified business

Table 3-7 Obvious Payoff Opportunities

- System downtime is at its highest level, up to 36 percent from last year.
- Carbon footprint is excessive for this type of organization, and increasing rapidly.
- Excessive turnover of critical talent: 35 percent above benchmark data.
- Very low market share in a market with few players.
- Inadequate customer service: 3.89 on a 10-point customer satisfaction scale.
- Safety record is among the worst in the industry.
- This year's out-of-compliance fines total $1.2 million, up 82 percent from last year.
- Excessive product returns: 30 percent higher than previous year.
- Excessive absenteeism in call centers is 12.3 percent, compared to the 5.4 percent industry average.
- Revenue is declining for the top two projects, although the overall market is growing.
- Sexual harassment complaints per 1,000 employees are the highest in the industry.
- Grievances are up 38 percent from last year.
- The health-care, legal, administrative, and incarceration costs for each homeless person are averaging $78,000 per year.

---

need. Some requests represent not-so-obvious payoff opportunities, such as those presented in Table 3-8. In either case, it is not clear as to what business measures will actually change as a result of this project. The focus at the next level is to clearly define the business measure or variety of measures. In the previous project of converting employees from a work to work-at-home arrangement, the initial request was not so obvious: to reduce employee travel time to lower costs and have a positive impact on the environment. A work-at-home solution was anticipated. Additional detail was needed, and this need led to the connection of several measures. These requests may be difficult for the not-so-obvious opportunities and may raise concerns. The project may not be connected to business needs, and if so, the client should be made aware of this.

At this level, it is important not only to identify the business measures that need to improve but also to convert them into monetary values so the antici-pated improvement can be converted to money. The "Show me the money" requirement is occurring more often. The second part of the process is to develop an approximate cost for the entire consulting project. This could come from a detailed proposal or may be a rough estimate. At this stage only an esti-mate is needed. The projected cost of the project is then compared to the potential monetary benefits to show the ROI forecast. A forecast of ROI is important in very expensive, strategic, or critical projects. This step may be omitted in situations when the problem must be solved regardless of the cost, or if it becomes obvious that it is a high-payoff activity. Still, other projects may be

Table 3-8 Not-So-Obvious Payoff Opportunities

- Become a technology leader.
- Organize a business development conference.
- Establish a project management office.
- Launch a new product.
- Provide job training for unemployed workers.
- Create a green company.
- Develop highly effective employees.
- Provide shelter for the homeless.
- Implement a sexual harassment project for all associates.
- Develop an "open-book" company.
- Implement the same workout process that GE has used.
- Improve leadership competencies for all managers.
- Create a great place to work.
- Implement a transformation program involving all employees.
- Implement a career advancement program.
- Create a wellness and fitness center.
- Build capability for future growth.
- Create an empowered workforce.

---

initiated and the potential payoff is not desired. For example, as an organization strives to be a technology leader, it may be difficult to place a value on that goal.

Business Needs

At Level 4, business data are examined to determine which measures need to improve. This involves a review of organizational records and reports, examining all types of hard and soft data. It is usually the performance of one of the data items that triggers the consulting project. For example, when market share is not as much as it should be, operating costs are excessive, product quality is deteriorating, or productivity is low, the business measure is easily pinpointed. These are the key issues that come directly from the data in the organization and are often found in the operating reports or records.

Table 3-9 shows examples of business needs arranged in categories of hard data to include output, quality, cost, and time. These measures exist in any type of organization, even in the public sector and among nonprofits and nongovernment organizations (NGOs). These measures often attract the attention of executives, as they represent business impact. An important goal is to connect the consulting project to one or more of these issues.

Table 3-9 Examples of Hard Data

Output	Quality	Costs	Time
• Completion rate	• Failure rates	• Shelter costs	• Cycle time
• Units produced	• Dropout rates	• Treatment costs	• Equipment downtime
• Tons manufactured	• Scrap	• Budget variances	• Overtime
• Items assembled	• Waste	• Unit costs	• On-time shipping
• Money collected	• Rejects	• Costs by account	• Time to project completion
• Items sold	• Error rates	• Variable costs	• Processing time
• New accounts generated	• Rework	• Fixed costs	• Supervisory time
• Forms processed	• Shortages	• Overhead costs	• Time to proficiency
• Loans approved	• Deviations from standard	• Operating costs	• Learning time
• Inventory turnover	• Product defects	• Project cost savings	• Meeting schedules
• Patients visited	• Product failures	• Accident costs	• Repair time
• Applications processed	• Inventory adjustments	• Program costs	• Efficiency
• Students graduated	• Time card corrections	• Sales expenses	• Work stoppages
• Tasks completed	• Incidents	• Participant costs	• Order response
• Output per hour	• Compliance discrepancies		• Late reporting
• Productivity	• Agency fines		• Lost time days
• Work backlog			
• Incentive bonus			
• Shipment			

Table 3-10 shows impact measures that are more on the softer side, which includes some of the more common measures, such as those involving customer service, image, and work climate. Although these may be perceived as not as important as hard data, they are important, and in some cases, a consulting project will be connected to one of these soft data items. This book defines a soft measure that can be converted to money as a tangible. If it cannot be converted to money credibly with a minimum amount of resources, it is left as an intangible. This definition means that most of the hard data categories are usually converted to money and are thus tangible.

Table 3-10   Examples of Soft Data

Work Habits

Tardiness
Excessive texting
Violations of safety rules
Communication breakdowns
Excessive breaks
Conflicts

Work Climate/Satisfaction

Grievances
Discrimination charges
Employee complaints
Job satisfaction
Organization commitment
Employee engagement
Employee loyalty
Intent to leave
Stress

Customer Service

Customer complaints
Customer satisfaction
Customer dissatisfaction
Customer impressions
Customer loyalty
Customer retention
Customer value
Lost customers

(Continues)

Table 3-10 Examples of Soft Data *(Continued)*

Employee Development/Advancement

Promotions
Capability
Intellectual capital
Programs completed
Requests for transfer
Performance appraisal ratings
Readiness
Networking

Creativity/Innovation

Creativity
Innovation
New ideas
Suggestions
New products and suggestions
Trademarks
Copyrights and patents
Process improvements
Partnerships
Alliances

Image

Brand awareness
Reputation
Leadership
Social responsibility
Environmental friendliness
Social consciousness
Diversity
External awards

The supporting data may come not only from the operating reports but from annual reports, marketing data, industry data, major planning documents, or other important information sources that clearly indicate operating performance.

Performance Needs

The Level 3 analysis involves determining performance needs. The task is to determine what's causing the problem (or created the opportunity) identified at

Level 4 (i.e., what is causing the business measure not to be at the desired level). Something in the system is not performing as it should and may include, among others, the following:

1. Inappropriate behavior
2. Dysfunctional behavior
3. Ineffective systems
4. Improper process flow
5. Ineffective procedures
6. Unsupported processes
7. Inappropriate technology
8. Inaction of stakeholders

The analysis usually reveals that a group of people are not performing as they should. The reason for this inadequate performance is the basis for the solution, the consulting project. For example, if employee health-care costs are increasing more than they should and sick leave usage is increasing, this may be caused by the unhealthy habits of employees. A wellness and fitness program may be needed.

Performance needs will have to be uncovered using a variety of problem-solving or analysis techniques, such as those listed in Table 3-11. This may involve the use of data collection techniques discussed in this book such as surveys, questionnaires, focus groups, or interviews. It may involve a variety of problem-solving or analysis techniques such as root-cause analysis, fish-bone diagrams, and other analysis techniques. Whatever is used, the key is to determine all of the causes of the problem so that solutions can be developed. Often, multiple solutions are appropriate.

Table 3-11   Diagnostic Tools

• Statistical process control	• Diagnostic instruments
• Brainstorming	• Focus groups
• Problem analysis	• Probing interviews
• Cause-and-effect diagram	• Job satisfaction surveys
• Force-field analysis	• Engagement surveys
• Mind mapping	• Exit interviews
• Affinity diagrams	• Exit surveys
• Simulations	• Nominal group technique

Learning Needs

The analysis at Level 3 usually uncovers specific learning needs of the people who would be involved in the project. It may be that learning deficiencies, in terms of knowledge and skills, may contribute to the problem if they are not the major cause of it. In other situations, the solution will need a learning component as participants learn how to implement a new process, procedure, or technology. The learning would typically involve acquisition of knowledge or the development of skills necessary to improve performance. In some cases, perceptions or attitudes may need to be altered to make the process successful in the future. The extent of learning required will determine whether formalized training is needed or if more informal, on-the-job methods can be utilized to build the necessary skills and knowledge.

Preference Needs

The final level is to consider the preference for the project solution. This involves determining the preferred way in which those involved in the process will need or want it to be implemented. A fundamental issue at this level is the perceived value of the project. Typical questions that surface are, "Is this important?" "Is this necessary?" and "Is it relevant to me?" Preference needs may involve implementation and/or learning issues. Learning issues may involve decisions such as when learning is expected and in what amounts, how it is presented, and the overall time frame. Implementation issues may involve timing, support, expectations, and other key factors. The important issue is to try to determine the specific preferences to the extent possible so that the complete profile of the solution can be developed based on all of the needs.

Planning for Measurement and Evaluation

An important ingredient in the success of the use of the ROI Methodology is to properly plan for the ROI study early in the consulting cycle. Appropriate up-front attention will save much time later when data are collected and analyzed, thus improving accuracy and reducing the cost of the ROI study. Planning also avoids any confusion surrounding what will be accomplished, by whom, and at what time. Two planning documents are necessary and should be completed before the consulting project is initiated.

Data Collection Plan

Table 3-12 shows a completed data collection plan for the work-at-home consulting project described previously. The project was initiated to reduce

Table 3-12 Data Collection Plan

Evaluation Purpose: Measure Success of Program **Date:** March 30
Program: FMI Work-at-Home Project **Responsibility:** HR/Consultants

Level	Broad Program Objective(s)	Measures	Data Collection Method/Instruments	Data Sources	Timing
1	*Reaction and Planned Action* • Employees should react favorably to the work-at-home project in terms of satisfaction and motivation. • Managers must see this project as important and necessary.	• Rating scale (4 out of 5)	• Questionnaires • Interviews	• Participants • Managers	• 30 days • 30 days
2	*Learning and Confidence* • Employees must understand the roles and responsibilities for success. • Managers must be able to discuss performance issues related to working at home. • Managers must be able to explain company's policy for working at home.	• Rating scale (4 out of 5)	• Questionnaires • Interviews	• Participants • Managers	• 30 days • 30 days
3	*Application and Implementation* • Managers should conduct a meeting with all employees to discuss policy and expected behavior and actions. • At least 30 percent of eligible employees volunteer for at-home assignments. • Work-at-home employees should work effectively at home. • The workplace at home should be free from distractions and conflicting demands. • Managers will administer the company's policy properly. • Managers should manage the remote employees effectively.	• Checklist • Sign up • Rating scale (4 out of 5)	• Data monitoring • Data monitoring • Questionnaires	• Company records • Company records • Participants • Managers	• 30 days • 30 days • 90 days • 90 days
4	*Business Impact* • The office expense per person should be reduced by 20 percent. • The productivity of participants should increase by 5 percent. • Employee turnover for this target group should decline 4 percent. • The company's image as a green company should improve. • Employee engagement should improve.	• Direct costs • Claims per day • Voluntary turnover • Rating scale (4 out of 5) • Rating scale (4 out of 5)	• Business performance monitoring • Survey	• Company records • Participants • Managers	• 6 months • 6 months • 6 months • 90 days • 90 days
5	*ROI 25%*	Baseline Data:			

turnover, reduce office expenses, and improve productivity. An ROI calculation, shown in Table 3-13, was planned to show the value of this project.

This document provides a place for the major elements and issues regarding collecting data for the five evaluation levels. In the first column, specific project objectives are stated. In the second column, the specific measures or data descriptors are indicated when they are necessary to explain the linkage of objectives to the data collection. In the next column, the specific data collection method is briefly described using standard terminology. Next, the source of the data is entered. Data sources will vary considerably but usually include participants, team leaders, company records, and/or the client. In the next column, the time frame for data collection is listed, usually referenced from the beginning of the project. Finally, the responsibility for data collection is noted.

The objectives for reaction usually include the desired reactions to the consulting project and suggested improvements. Planned actions may be included here. Reaction data may be collected at different intervals. In this example, feedback is taken only at one time, when the work-at-home project is implemented.

Because Level 2 evaluation focuses on the measures of learning, specific objectives include those areas where participants are expected to learn new tasks, procedures, technology knowledge, skills, or processes. The data collection method is the specific way in which learning is assessed, in this case using a self-assessment questionnaire. The timing for Level 2 evaluation is during the implementation of the project.

For application evaluation, the objectives represent key areas of application, including significant on-the-job activities and implementation steps. In this example, the methods include questionnaires, surveys, and monitoring company records. This information is usually collected a matter of months after the implementation. Because responsibilities are often shared among several groups, including the consulting staff, it is important to clarify this issue early in the process. The timing depends on the scope and nature of the project, and it is usually in the range of three weeks to three months after the launch of the project.

For impact evaluation, objectives focus on business impact measures influenced by the consulting project. The measures/data column includes the specifics and may provide a hint about the location of the measure. For example, if one of the objectives is to improve productivity, a specific measure would indicate how productivity is actually measured. In the example, productivity is measured for each group, processors and examiners. The preferred evaluation method is performance monitoring, though other methods may be appropriate. The sources of data utilized at this level are the company records. The timing depends on how quickly the intervention can generate a sustained impact on the three measures—usually a matter of months after the consulting project is completed. In this example, data are collected at six-month intervals. A project evaluator is responsible for data collection at this level. If appropriate, an ROI objective (Level 5) is included.

The data collection plan is an important part of the evaluation strategy, and it should be completed prior to moving forward with the consulting project; the plan is completed before pursuing an ROI evaluation. The plan provides a clear direction of what types of data will be collected, how they will be collected, where they will be collected, when they will be collected, and who will collect them.

ROI Analysis Plan

Table 3-13 shows a completed ROI analysis plan for the same project. This planning document is the continuation of the data collection plan presented in Table 3-12 and captures information on several key items that are necessary to develop the actual ROI calculation. In the first column, significant business impact data items are listed. These items will be used in the ROI analysis. The method for isolating the effects of consulting is listed next to each data item in the second column. For most projects, the method will be the same for each data item, but there could be variations. For example, if no historical data are available for one data item, then trend-line analysis is not possible for that item, although it may be appropriate for other items. In this example, a control group arrangement was feasible, and a trend-line analysis was also considered. Participant estimates were used as a backup.

The method for converting data to monetary values is included in the third column. In this example, office expenses are converted to monetary values with two approaches: using costs in the company records and collecting expert input from the staff directly involved in the process. The cost categories planned for capture are outlined in the fourth column. Instructions about how certain costs should be prorated are noted here. Normally the cost categories will be consistent from one consulting project to another. However, a specific cost that is unique to this consulting project is also noted. The anticipated intangible benefits expected from this project are outlined in the fifth column. This list is generated from discussions about the project with sponsors, subject matter experts, and other stakeholders.

Table 3-13 ROI Analysis Plan

Program: FMI Work-at-Home Project　　　**Responsibility:** HR/Consultants　　　**Date:**

Data Items (Usually Level 4)	Methods for Isolating the Effects of the Program/Process	Methods of Converting Data to Monetary Values	Cost Categories	Intangible Benefits	Communication Targets for Final Report	Other Influential Issues during Application
Office expenses	• Control group • Expert estimates	• Standard value based on costs	• Initial analysis and assessment • Solution development • IT support and maintenance • Administration and coordination • Materials • Facilities and refreshments • Salaries plus benefits for employee and manager meetings • Evaluation and reporting	• Reduced commuting time • Reduced carbon emissions • Reduced fuel consumption • Reduced sick leave • Absenteeism reduction • Job engagement • Environmental friendly company • Corporate social responsibility • Job satisfaction improvement • Stress reduction • Recruiting image	• Participants • Managers • HR team • Executive group • Consultants • External groups	• Must observe marketing and economic forces • Search for barriers/obstacles for progress
Productivity	• Control group • Participant estimates	• Standard values				
Turnover	• Control group • Participant estimates	• External studies				

Communication targets are outlined in the sixth column. Although there could be many groups that should receive the information, four target groups are always recommended: senior management, consulting participants, managers of participants, and the consulting staff. Each of these four groups needs to know about the results of the ROI analysis. Finally, other issues or events that might influence the success of the consulting project are highlighted in the last column. Typical items include the capability of participants, external issues, the degree of access to data sources, political influence, and unique data analysis issues.

The ROI analysis plan, when combined with the data collection plan, provides detailed information on calculating the ROI, illustrating how the process will develop from beginning to end. When completed, these two plans should provide the direction necessary for the ROI evaluation and should integrate with the overall project plan.

Final Thoughts

This chapter presented the analysis and planning for the evaluation of a consulting project. Because of the need for alignment with business measures, initial analysis and objectives was explored. The first phase of business alignment occurs when the project is connected to specific business measures in the beginning. Impact objectives keep the alignment during the project. The linkage of levels of evaluation, objectives, and initial needs was presented. This connection greatly simplifies the success of consulting projects. Next, evaluation-planning tools were introduced. When the ROI process is thoroughly planned, taking into consideration all potential strategies and techniques, it becomes manageable and achievable. The remaining chapters focus on the major elements of this process.

PART II

Data Collection

CHAPTER

4

Was It Useful and Did You Understand It?

Measuring Reaction and Learning

BECAUSE OF THE VARIETY of approaches to collecting data at the first four levels (reaction, learning, application, and impact), two chapters are devoted to presenting the techniques and issues surrounding this major phase of evaluation. This chapter focuses on measuring reaction (Level 1) and learning (Level 2). Chapter 5 covers measuring application (Level 3) and impact (Level 4).

Collecting data at all four levels is necessary because of the chain of impact that must exist for a project to be successful. Participants in the consulting project should experience a positive reaction to the project and its potential application (Level 1). They should acquire new skills or knowledge to implement the project successfully (Level 2). Changes in on-the-job behavior, actions, or completion of tasks and procedures should prompt a positive and successful implementation (Level 3). A successful implementation should drive changes in business impact. The only way to know if the chain of impact has occurred is to collect data at all four levels. This is guiding principle #1.

Why Measure Reaction?

Collecting reaction data during the first operational phase of the ROI process is critical. Client feedback data are powerful for making adjustments and measuring success. It would be difficult to imagine a consulting project being conducted without collecting feedback from those involved in the project, or at least from the client. Client feedback is important to understanding how well the process is working or to gauge its success after it has been completed. It is always included in every consulting project because of its importance. Here are a few reasons why measuring learning is important.

Customer Satisfaction Is Essential

Without sustained, favorable reactions to projects, it would be difficult for a consulting firm to continue in business. Three important categories of customers exist for almost every consulting project. First, there are those directly involved in the project. These individuals have a direct role in the project and are often referred to as the consulting participants. They are key stakeholders who are directly affected by the consulting project and often have to change processes and procedures and make other job adjustments related to the project. In addition, they often have to learn new skills, tasks, and behaviors to make the project successful. Their feedback is critical to make adjustments and changes in the project as it unfolds and is implemented.

The second category of customers is the supporters, who are on the sidelines, not directly involved, but have some interest in the project. Their perception of the success of the project or potential success is important feedback, as this group will be in a position to influence the project in the future. The third set of stakeholders is the client, the individual or group of individuals who request consulting projects, approve project budgets, allocate resources, and ultimately live with the success or failure of the project. This important group must be completely satisfied, or it will not have to pay for the project.

Making Adjustments Early

Projects can go astray quickly, and sometimes a specific project is the wrong solution for the specified problem. A project may be mismatched from the beginning, so it is essential to get feedback early in the process so that adjustments can be made. This helps avoid misunderstandings, miscommunications, and, more importantly, misappropriations, as an improperly designed project is altered or changed quickly before more serious problems are created. Obtaining feedback, making changes, and reporting changes back to the groups who provide the information should be routine.

Benchmarking Data from Other Projects

Some consultants collect reaction data from several sources using standard questions, and the data are then compared with data from other projects so that norms and standards can be developed. This is particularly helpful at the completion of a project as client satisfaction is gauged, and correlation between reaction data is compared to the success of other projects. Sometimes an overall project success is developed. Some firms even base part of the consulting fee on the level of client satisfaction, making reaction data very critical to the success of every project. Data collection must be deliberately pursued in a systematic, logical, rational way.

Why Measure Learning?

It may seem unnecessary to measure learning in a consulting projects. However, projects can fail because those involved did not know what to do to make the project successful. This is particularly important in projects where there is a significant number of job changes, procedure changes, new tools, new processes, and new technology. The extent to which the participants involved in a project actually learn their new jobs and new processes is an important success factor for the project.

Knowledge Management Is Important

Many organizations are increasing their focus more on knowledge, expertise, and competencies. Consulting projects may involve developing expertise with employees using tools and techniques not previously used. Some projects focus directly on core competencies and building important skills, knowledge, and behaviors into the organization. With a continuous focus on knowledge management, participants understand and acquire a vast array of information, assimilate it, and use it in a productive way.

Learning Is Critical for Complex Projects

Although some consulting projects may involve new equipment, processes, procedures, and new technology, the human factor is still critical to the process. The participants must learn new systems, complex procedures, comprehensive processes, and innovative technology. Whether there is significant restructuring or the addition of new systems, employees must learn how to work in the new environment and develop new knowledge and skills. Learning is becoming a larger part of consulting. Automation has its limitations. Instead, there are complex environments with confusing processes and complicated tools that must be used in an intelligent way to reap the benefits of consulting.

Employees must learn in a variety of ways, not just in a formal classroom environment but also through technology-based learning and on-the-job assistance. Also, the project team leaders and managers of participants often serve as reinforcers, coaches, or mentors in some projects. In a few cases, learning coaches or on-the-job trainers are used as a part of the consulting project to ensure that learning is acquired so that it can be transferred to the job, and the project is implemented as planned.

Sources of Data

When considering the possible data sources for collecting data in a consulting project, the categories are easily defined. Here are the major categories of stakeholders.

Client/Senior Managers

One of the most useful data sources for ROI analysis is the client group, usually a senior management team. Whether an individual or a group, the client's perception and understanding is critical to project success. Clients can provide input on all types of issues and are usually available and willing to offer feedback. Collecting data from this source is preferred, because the data usually reflect what is necessary to make adjustments and measure success.

Consulting Participants

The most widely used data source for an ROI analysis is the consulting participants, who are directly involved in the consulting project from the client. They must use the skills and knowledge acquired via the project and apply them on the job. Sometimes they are asked to explain the potential impact of those actions. Participants are a rich source of data for almost every issue or part of the project. They are credible, since they are the individuals who make the project work. Also, they often possess the most knowledge of the processes and other influencing factors. The challenge is to find an effective and efficient way to capture data in a consistent manner.

Consulting Team

In situations where teams of consultants are involved in the consulting project, all team members can provide information about reaction and learning by the consulting project. Input is appropriate for issues directly involved in their work on the project. In many situations, they observe the participants as they attempt to use the knowledge and skills acquired in the project. Consequently, they can report on the successes linked to the project as well as the difficulties and problems associated with it.

Internal Customers

The individuals who serve as internal customers of the consulting participants are another source of data for a few types of projects. In these situations, internal customers provide input on perceived changes linked to the consulting project. This source of data is more appropriate when consulting projects directly affect the internal customers. They report on how the project has (or will) influence their work or the service they receive. For example, consider a project involving the implementation of a new ERP (enterprise resource planning) system. The participants are the users of the system. The internal customers are the individuals who receive the information and reports from the system.

Topics for Reaction and Learning

Many topics are critical targets for reaction and learning because there are so many issues and processes involved in a typical consulting project. Feedback is needed for almost every major issue, step, or process to make sure things are moving forward properly. Table 4-1 shows the typical major areas of feedback for most projects. The list shows the key success factors in a consulting project, beginning with the objectives of the project and concluding with the likelihood of success. Different stakeholders react to the project and the progress made. The relevance and importance of the project are critical. Knowledge, skills, capability, and capacity are important learning measures. For a particular project, there can be other issues, and each can have specific parts. Each step, element, task, or part of the project represents an opportunity for feedback. The challenge is to sort out those things that are most important so the participants and others can provide valuable input.

Timing of Data Collection

The timing of data collection revolves around particular events connected with the consulting project. Any particular activity, implementation issue, or milestone is an appropriate time to collect reaction and learning data. Figure 4-1

Table 4-1 Areas for Reaction

Intent to implement the project successfully
Feasibility of schedule
Progress made
Relevance of project
Importance of project
Support for project
Resources for project
Integration of project
Project leadership
Project staffing
Project coordination
Project communication
Motivation of project participants
Cooperation of project participants
Knowledge about the project
Capability of project participants
New skills acquired
Capacity achieved
Likelihood of project success

---

shows the timing of feedback on a six-month project. This particular project has pre-project data collection. This is important to make sure that the environment is proper and supportive of the project. A pre-project assessment can be an eye-opening exercise, as particular inhibitors and barriers can be identified that will need adjusting or altering in the project to achieve success. In this particular example, assessment is taken at the beginning of the project as the announcement is made and the project is fully described. Next, a one-month follow-up is taken, followed by a four-month follow-up that is actually three months later. Finally, at the end of the project, the sixth month, an assessment

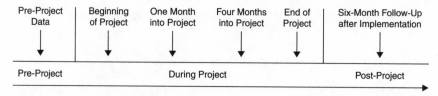

Figure 4-1 Project timetable.

is taken. Using five time frames for data collection may be too comprehensive for some projects but is appropriate for major projects. In addition to these data collection opportunities, a six-month follow-up is planned after implementation. Project timing will depend on the resources available, the need to obtain feedback directly from participants, and the magnitude of events or activities scheduled throughout the project. In addition, they need to make quick adjustments and changes that will also affect the timing. Finally, the need to gain commitment and support and measure the pulse all the way through the process is an important factor in determining the actual timing.

Using Questionnaires and Surveys to Measure Reaction and Learning

The questionnaire is probably the most common data collection method. Questionnaires come in all sizes, ranging from short surveys to detailed instruments. They can be used to obtain subjective data about participants' perceptions as well as to document data for use in a projected ROI analysis. With this versatility and popularity, it is important that questionnaires and surveys be designed properly to satisfy both purposes.

Types of Questions and Statements

Five basic types of questions or statements are available. Depending on the purpose of the evaluation, the questionnaire may contain any or all of the following types of questions:

- **Open-ended question.** Has an unlimited answer. The question is followed by ample blank space for the response.
- **Checklist.** A list of items. A participant is asked to check those that apply to the situation.
- **Range of responses.** Has alternate responses, such as yes/no or other possibilities. This type of question can also include a range of responses from disagree to agree.
- **Multiple-choice question.** Has several choices, and the participant is asked to select the most appropriate.
- **Ranking scales.** Requires the participant to rank a list of items.

Figure 4-2 shows examples of each of these types of questions.

1. Open-ended question:

   What problems will you encounter when attempting to use the system implemented in this project?

2. Checklist:

   For the following list, check all of the business measures that may be influenced by the application of the system in this project in this program.

   ❑ Responsibility   ❑ Cost control
   ❑ Productivity   ❑ Response time
   ❑ Quality   ❑ Customer satisfaction
   ❑ Efficiency   ❑ Job satisfaction

3. Range of responses:

   As a result of this project, I have a better understanding of my job as a customer service representative.

   ❑ Definitely yes   ❑ Maybe   ❑ Definitely no

4. Multiple-choice question:

   Since the project has been initiated, the customer response time has:

   a. Increased
   b. Decreased
   c. Remained the same
   d. Don't know

5. Ranking scales:

   The following list contains six important factors that will influence the success of this project. Please write a one (1) by the item that is most influential, a two (2) by the item that is second most influential, and so on. The item ranked six (6) will be the least influential item on the list.

Rewards systems	_____	Training	_____
Job responsibility	_____	Management support	_____
Communications	_____	Resources	_____

Figure 4-2 Types of questions.

Design Issues

Questionnaire design is a simple and logical process. An improperly designed or worded questionnaire will not collect the desired data and is confusing, frustrating, and potentially embarrassing. The following steps will help ensure that a valid, reliable, and effective instrument is developed. Attitude surveys represent a specific type of questionnaire with several applications for measuring reaction and satisfaction in consulting projects designed to improve work, policies, procedures, the organization, or even the team. Before-and-after project measurements are important to show changes. Sometimes an organization will conduct a survey to assess the correct solution with one of the areas previously listed. Then, based on these results, consulting projects are undertaken to change areas in which improvements are needed.

- **Determine the information needed.** The first step of any instrument design is to itemize the topics, issues, and success factors for the project. Questions are developed later. It might be helpful to develop this information in outline form so that related questions can be grouped together.
- **Select the type(s) of questions.** Determine whether open-ended questions, checklists, ranges, multiple-choice questions, or ranking scales are the most appropriate for the purpose of the questions. Take into consideration the planned data analysis and variety of data to be collected.
- **Develop the questions—keep it simple.** The next step is to develop the questions based on the types of questions planned and the information needed. The questions should be simple and straightforward enough to avoid confusion or leading the participant to a desired response. Unfamiliar terms or expressions should be avoided.
- **Test the questions.** After the questions are developed, they should be tested for understanding. Ideally, the questions should be tested on a small sample of participants in the project. If this is not feasible, the questions should be tested on employees at approximately the same job level as the participants. Collect as much input and criticism as possible, and revise the questions as necessary.
- **Prepare a data summary.** A data summary sheet should be developed so data can be tabulated quickly for summary and interpretation. This step will help ensure that the data can be analyzed quickly and presented in a meaningful way.
- **Develop the completed questionnaire/survey.** The questions should be finalized in a professional questionnaire with proper instructions. After completing these steps, the questionnaire is ready to be administered. Because questionnaire administration is a critical element in evaluation, several ideas will be presented later in this chapter.
- **Design for easy tabulation.** Uniform responses make it easier for tabulation and comparisons. Open-ended questions should be minimized. Forced choice responses are better.
- **Communicate the purpose of the survey.** Participants tend to cooperate in an activity when they understand its purpose. When a survey is administered, participants should be given an explanation of its purpose and told what will be done with the information. Also, they should be encouraged to give correct and proper statements or answers.

Improving the Response Rate for Questionnaires and Surveys

Given the wide range of potential issues to explore in a follow-up questionnaire or survey, asking all of the questions can cause the response rate to be reduced considerably. The challenge, therefore, is to approach questionnaire and survey design and administration for maximum response rate. This is a critical issue when the questionnaire is a key data collection activity and much of the evaluation hinges on the questionnaire results. The following actions can be taken to increase response rate. Although the term questionnaire is used, the same rules apply to surveys:

- **Provide advance communication.** If appropriate and feasible, consulting participants and other stakeholders should receive advance communications about the plans for the questionnaire or survey. This minimizes some of the resistance to the process, provides an opportunity to explain in more detail the circumstances surrounding the evaluation, and positions the evaluation as an integral part of the consulting project rather than as an add-on activity that someone initiated three months after the project was completed.

- **Communicate the purpose.** Stakeholders should understand the reason for the questionnaire, including who or what initiated this specific evaluation. They should know if the evaluation is part of a systematic process or a special request for this consulting project only.

- **Explain who will see the data.** It is important for respondents to know who will see the data and the results of the questionnaire. If the questionnaire is anonymous, it should clearly be communicated to participants what steps will be taken to ensure anonymity. If senior executives will see the combined results of the study, the respondents should know it.

- **Describe the data integration process.** The respondents should understand how the questionnaire results will be combined with other data, if available. Often the questionnaire is only one of the data collection methods utilized. Participants should know how the data are weighted and integrated into the entire impact study, as well as interim results.

- **Keep the questionnaire/survey as simple as possible.** A simple questionnaire does not always provide the full scope of data necessary for a comprehensive analysis. However, the simplified approach should always be kept in mind when questions are developed and the total scope of the questionnaire is finalized. Every effort should be made to keep it as simple and brief as possible.

- **Simplify the response process.** To the extent possible, it should be easy to respond to the questionnaire. If appropriate, a self-addressed stamped envelope should be included. Perhaps e-mail could be used for responses, if it is easier. In still other situations, a response box is provided near the project work area.
- **Utilize local management support.** Management involvement at the local level is critical to response-rate success. Managers can distribute the questionnaires themselves, make reference to the questionnaire in staff meetings, follow up to see if questionnaires have been completed, and generally show support for completing the questionnaire. This direct managerial support will prompt many participants to respond with usable data.
- **Let the participants know they are part of the sample.** For large consulting projects, a sampling process may be utilized. When that is the case, participants should know they are part of a carefully selected sample and that their input will be used to make decisions regarding a much larger target audience. This action often appeals to a sense of responsibility for participants to provide usable, accurate data for the questionnaire.
- **Consider incentives.** A variety of incentives can be offered, and they usually fall into three categories. First, an incentive is provided in exchange for the completed questionnaire. For example, if participants return the questionnaire personally or through the mail, they will receive a small gift, such as a T-shirt or mug. If identity is an issue, a neutral third party can provide the incentive. In the second category, the incentive is provided to make participants feel guilty about not responding. Examples are money clipped to the questionnaire or a pen enclosed in the envelope. Participants are asked to "take the money, buy a cup of coffee, and fill out the questionnaire." A third group of incentives is designed to obtain a quick response. This approach is based on the assumption that a quick response will ensure a greater response rate. If an individual delays completing the questionnaire, the odds of his or her completing it diminish considerably. The initial group of participants may receive a more expensive gift, or they may be part of a drawing for an incentive. For example, in one project, the first 25 returned questionnaires were placed in a drawing for a $400 gift certificate. The next 25 were added to the first 25 in the next drawing. The longer a participant waits, the lower the odds of winning.
- **Have an executive sign the introductory letter.** Participants are always interested in who sent the letter with the questionnaire. For maximum effectiveness, a senior executive who is responsible for a major area where

the participants work should sign the letter. Employees may be more willing to respond to a senior executive than to a member of the consulting team.

- **Use follow-up reminders.** A follow-up reminder should be sent a week after the questionnaire is distributed and another sent two weeks later. Depending on the questionnaire and the situation, these times can be adjusted. In some situations, a third follow-up is recommended. Sometimes the follow-up is sent in a different media. For example, a questionnaire may be sent through regular mail, whereas the first follow-up reminder is from the immediate supervisor and a second follow-up is sent via e-mail.

- **Send a copy of the results to the participants.** Even if it is an abbreviated report, participants should see the results of the questionnaire. More importantly, participants should understand that they will receive a copy of the impact study when they are asked to provide the data. This promise will often increase the response rate, as some individuals want to see the results of the entire group along with their particular input.

- **Estimate the length of time to complete the questionnaire.** Respondents often have a concern about the time it may take to complete the questionnaire. A very lengthy questionnaire may quickly turn off the participants and cause it to be discarded. Sometimes, lengthy questionnaires can be completed quickly because many of them have forced-choice questions or statements that make it easy to respond. However, the number of pages may discourage the respondent. Therefore, it is helpful to indicate the estimated length of time needed to complete the questionnaire—perhaps in the letter itself or at least noted in the communications. This provides extra information so that respondents can decide if they are willing to invest the required amount of time into the process. A word of caution is necessary, though: the amount of time must be realistic. Purposely underestimating it can do more harm than good.

- **Explain the timing of the planned steps.** Sometimes the respondents want to know more detail regarding when they can see the results or when the results will be presented to particular groups. It is recommended that a timetable be presented, showing when different phases of the process will be completed, such as responding to the questionnaire, indicating when the data will be analyzed, when the data will be presented to different groups, and when the results will be returned to the participants in a summary report. This timetable provides some assurance that the process is well organized and professional and that the length of time to receive a data summary will not be too long. Another word of caution: the timetable must be followed to maintain the confidence and trust of the individuals.

- **Make it appear professional.** While it should not be an issue in most organizations, unfortunately, there are too many cases when a questionnaire is not developed properly, does not appear professional, or is not easy to follow and understand. The participants must gain respect for the process and for the organization. To do this, a sense of professionalism must be integrated throughout data collection, particularly in the appearance and accuracy of the materials. Sloppy questionnaires will usually command sloppy responses, or no response at all.

- **Explain the questionnaire during the project meetings.** Sometimes it is helpful to explain to the participants and other key stakeholders that they will be required or asked to provide certain types of data. When this is feasible, questionnaires should be reviewed question by question so that the participants understand the purpose, the issues, and how to respond. This will take only 10 to 15 minutes but can increase the response rate, enhance the quality and quantity of data, and clarify any confusion that may exist on key issues.

- **Collect data anonymously, if necessary.** Participants are more likely to provide frank and candid feedback if their names are not on the questionnaire, particularly when the project is going astray or is off target. When this is the case, every effort should be made to protect the anonymous input, and explanations should be provided as to how the data are analyzed, minimizing the demographic makeup of respondents so that the individuals cannot be identified in the analysis.

Collectively, these items help boost response rates of follow-up questionnaires. Using all of these strategies can result in a 70 to 90 percent response rate, even with lengthy questionnaires that might take 30 minutes to complete.

Using Interviews to Measure Reaction and Learning

Another helpful data collection method is the interview, although it is not used as frequently as the questionnaire. The consultants, the client's staff, or a third party can conduct interviews. Interviews can secure data not available in performance records, or data difficult to obtain through written responses or observations. Also, interviews can uncover success stories that can be useful in communicating evaluation results. Consulting participants may be reluctant to describe their results in a questionnaire but will volunteer the information to a skillful interviewer using probing techniques. The interview is versatile and appropriate for reaction, learning, and application data. A major disadvantage of the interview is that it is time consuming. It also requires time and the preparation of interviewers to ensure that the process is consistent.

Types of Interviews

Interviews usually fall into two basis types: structured and unstructured. A structured interview is much like a questionnaire. Specific questions are asked with little room to deviate from the desired responses. The primary advantages of the structured interview over the questionnaire are that the interview process can ensure the questionnaire is completed and that the interviewer understands the responses supplied by the participant.

The unstructured interview permits probing for additional information. This type of interview uses a few general questions, which can lead to more detailed information as important data are uncovered. The interviewer must be skilled in the probing process. Typical probing questions are:

- Can you explain that in more detail?
- Can you give me an example of what you are saying?
- Can you explain the difficulty that you say you encountered?

Interview Guidelines

The design steps for interviews are similar to those of the questionnaire. A brief summary of key issues with interviews is outlined here:

- **Develop questions to be asked.** After the decision has been made about the type of interview, specific questions need to be developed. Questions should be brief, precise, and designed for easy response.
- **Test the interview.** The interview should be tested on a small number of participants. If possible, the interviews should be conducted as part of the early stages of the project. The responses should be analyzed and the interview revised, if necessary.
- **Prepare the interviewers.** The interviewer should have appropriate skills, including active listening, the ability to form probing questions, and the ability to collect and summarize information into a meaningful form.
- **Provide clear instructions.** The consulting participant should understand the purpose of the interview and know what will be done with the information. Expectations, conditions, and rules of the interview should be thoroughly discussed. For example, the participant should know if

statements will be kept confidential. If the participant is nervous during an interview and develops signs of anxiety, he or she should be made to feel at ease.

- **Administer interviews with a plan in mind.** As with other evaluation instruments, interviews need to be conducted according to a predetermined plan. The timing of the interview, the person who conducts the interview, and the location of the interview are all issues that become relevant when developing an interview plan. For a large number of stakeholders, a sampling plan may be necessary to save time and reduce the evaluation cost.

Using Focus Groups to Measure Reaction and Learning

An extension of the interview, a focus group is particularly helpful when in-depth feedback is needed. The focus group involves a small group discussion conducted by an experienced facilitator. It is designed to solicit qualitative judgments on a planned topic or issue. Group members are all required to provide their input, as individual input builds on group input.

When compared to questionnaires, surveys, or interviews, the focus group strategy has several advantages. The basic premise of using focus groups is that when quality judgments are subjective, several individual judgments are better than one. The group process, where participants often motivate one another, is an effective method for generating new ideas and hypotheses. It is less expensive than the interview and can be quickly planned and conducted. Its flexibility makes it possible to explore a consulting project's unexpected outcomes or applications.

Applications for Evaluation

The focus group is particularly helpful when qualitative information is needed about the success of a consulting project. For example, the focus group can be used in the following situations:

- Evaluating the reaction to the consulting project and the various components of it
- Assessing learning of specific procedures, tasks, schedules, or other components of the project
- Assessing the overall effectiveness of the consulting project as perceived by the participants immediately following the project's completion
- Assessing the potential impact of the project

Essentially, focus groups are helpful when evaluation information is needed but cannot be collected adequately with a simple questionnaire or survey.

Guidelines

While there are no set rules on how to use focus groups for evaluation, the following guidelines should be helpful:

- **Ensure that management and the client embrace focus groups.** Because this is a relatively new process for evaluation, it might be unknown to some management groups. Managers need to understand focus groups and their advantages. This should raise their level of confidence in the information obtained from group sessions.
- **Plan topics, questions, and strategy carefully.** As with any evaluation instrument, planning is the key. The specific topics, questions, and issues to be discussed must be carefully planned and sequenced. This enhances the comparison of results from one group to another and ensures that the group process is effective and stays on track.
- **Keep the group size small.** While there is no magical group size, a range of 8 to 12 seems appropriate for most focus group applications. A group has to be large enough to ensure different points of view but small enough to give every participant a chance to talk freely and exchange comments.
- **Ensure a representative sample of the target population.** It is important for groups to be stratified appropriately so that participants represent the target population. The group should be homogeneous in experience, rank, and influence in the organization.
- **Insist on facilitators with appropriate expertise.** The success of a focus group rests with the facilitator, who must be skilled in the focus group process. Facilitators must know how to control aggressive members of the group and diffuse the input from those who want to dominate the group. Also, facilitators must be able to create an environment in which participants feel comfortable to offer comments freely and openly. Consequently, some organizations use external facilitators.

In summary, the focus group is an inexpensive and quick way to determine the strengths and weaknesses of projects. However, for a complete evaluation, focus group information should be combined with data from other instruments.

Measuring Learning with Tests

Testing is important for measuring learning in project evaluations. Pre- and post-project comparisons using tests are very common. An improvement in test scores shows the change in skill, knowledge, or capability of the participant attributed to the consulting project. The questionnaires and surveys described earlier can be used in testing for learning.

Performance testing allows the participant to exhibit a skill (and occasionally knowledge or attitudes) that has been learned in a consulting project. The skill can be manual, verbal, analytical, or a combination of the three. Here are two examples. Computer systems engineers are participating in a system-reengineering project. As part of the project, participants are given the assignment to design and test a basic system. The consultant observes participants as they check out the system, then carefully builds the same design and compares his results with those of the participants. These comparisons and the performance of the design provide an evaluation of the project and represent an adequate reflection of the skills learned in the project.

As part of a reorganization project, team members learn new products and sales strategies. Part of the evaluation requires team members to practice skills in an actual situation involving a sales presentation. Then participants are asked to conduct the skill practice on another member of the group using a real situation and applying the principles and steps learned in the consulting project. The consultant observes the skill practice and provides a written critique at the end of the practice. These critiques provide part of the evaluation of the consulting project.

Measuring Learning with Simulation

Another technique for measuring learning is job simulation. This method involves the construction and application of a procedure or task that simulates or models the work involved in the consulting project. The simulation is designed to represent, as closely as possible, the actual job situation. Participants try out their performance in the simulated activity and have it evaluated based on how well the task is accomplished. Simulations may be used during the project or as part of a follow-up evaluation.

Task Simulation

One approach involves a participant's performance in a simulated task as part of an evaluation. For example, in a new system implementation, users are provided a series of situations, and they must perform the proper sequence of tasks in a minimum amount of time. To become certified to use this system, users are observed in a simulation where they perform all the necessary steps on a checklist. After they have demonstrated that they possess the skills necessary for the safe performance of this assignment, they are certified by the consultant. This task simulation serves as the evaluation.

Business Games

Business games have grown in popularity in recent years. They represent simulations of a part or all of a business enterprise. Participants change the variables of the business and observe the effects of those changes. The game not only reflects the real-world situation but may also represent a consulting project. The participants are provided certain objectives, play the game, and have their output monitored. Their performance can usually be documented and measured. Typical objectives are to maximize profit, sales, market share, or operating efficiency. Participants who maximize the objectives are those who usually have the highest performance.

Role-Playing

When skill building is part of the consulting project, role-playing may be helpful. Sometimes referred to as *skill practice*, role-playing involves the participant practicing a newly learned skill while being observed by other individuals. Participants are given their assigned roles with specific instructions, which sometimes include an ultimate course of action. The participants then practice the skill with other individuals to accomplish the desired objectives. This is intended to simulate the real-world setting to the greatest extent possible. Difficulty sometimes arises when other participants involved in the skill practice make the practice unrealistic by not reacting the way individuals would in an actual situation. To help overcome this obstacle, trained role players (nonparticipants trained for the role) may be used in all roles except that of the participant. This can possibly provide a more objective evaluation.

Measuring Learning with Less Structured Activities

In many situations, it is sufficient to have an informal check of learning to provide some assurance that participants have acquired the needed skills and knowledge or perhaps that there have been some changes in attitudes. This approach is appropriate when other levels of evaluation are pursued. For example, if a

Level 3 application and implementation evaluation is planned, it might not be so critical to conduct a comprehensive Level 2 evaluation. An informal assessment of learning is usually sufficient. After all, the resources are scarce, and a comprehensive evaluation at all levels becomes quite expensive. The following are some alternative approaches to measuring learning when inexpensive, low-key, informal assessments are needed.

Exercises/Activities

Many consulting projects involve activities, exercises, or problems that must be explored, developed, or solved during the project implementation. Some of these are constructed in terms of involvement exercises, while others require individual problem-solving skills. When these tools are integrated into the learning activity, the results of the exercise can be submitted for review and for possible scoring by the consultant. This becomes a measure of learning.

Self-Assessment

In many consulting situations, self-assessment may be appropriate. Participants are provided an opportunity to assess their acquisition of skills and knowledge. This is particularly applicable in cases where higher-level evaluations are planned and it is important to know if actual learning is taking place. A few techniques can ensure that the process is effective:

- The self-assessment should be made anonymously so that participants feel free to express realistic and accurate assessments of what they have learned.
- The purpose of the self-assessment should be explained, along with the plans for the data. Specifically, if there are implications for project design or individual retesting, this should be discussed.
- If there has been no improvement or the self-assessment is unsatisfactory, there should be some explanation as to what that means and what the implications will be. This will help ensure that accurate and credible information is provided.

Using Reaction and Learning Data

Sometimes consulting reaction and learning data are solicited, tabulated, summarized, and then disregarded. The information must be collected and used for one or more of the purposes of evaluation. Otherwise, the exercise is a waste of the time. Too often, project evaluators use the material to feed their egos and let it quietly disappear into their files, forgetting the original purposes behind its collection. Here are a few of the more common uses of reaction and learning data.

Monitor Customer Satisfaction

Because this input is the principal measure taken from the stakeholders, it provides a good indication of the reaction to, and satisfaction with, the project. Thus, project leaders and owners will know how satisfied the customers actually are with the project. Data should be reported to clients and other key stakeholders.

Identify Strengths and Weaknesses of the Project

Feedback is helpful in identifying weaknesses as well as strengths in the project. Feedback on weaknesses can often lead to adjustments and changes. Identifying strengths can be helpful in future designs so processes can be replicated.

Develop Norms and Standards

Because reaction and learning evaluation data can be automated and are collected in nearly 100 percent of projects, it becomes relatively easy to develop norms and standards throughout the organization. Target ratings can be set for expectations; particular course results are then compared to those norms and standards.

Evaluate Consultants

Perhaps one of the most common uses of reaction and learning data is consultant evaluation. If properly constructed and collected, helpful feedback data can be provided to consultants so that adjustments can be made to increase effectiveness. Some caution needs to be taken, though, since consultant evaluations can sometimes be biased, so other evidence may be necessary to provide an overall assessment of consultant performance.

Identify Planned Improvements for a Forecast

Reaction and learning can provide a profile of planned actions and improvements to use in a forecast or impact and ROI. Also, these data can be compared with on-the-job actions as a result of the project. This provides a rich source of data in terms of what participants may be changing or implementing because of what they have learned.

Marketing Future Projects

For some organizations, reaction and learning data provide helpful marketing information. Participants' quotes and reactions provide information that may be convincing to potential participants. Learning measures help to validate the effectiveness of the project. Consulting marketing brochures often contain quotes and summaries of feedback data.

Providing Individual Feedback to Build Confidence

Learning data, when provided directly to participants, provides reinforcement for learning and enhances learning for the solutions. This reinforces the learning process and provides much-needed feedback to participants in consulting projects.

Final Thoughts

This chapter is the first of two chapters on data collection and represents two of the six measures of data reported in the ROI Methodology. Measuring reaction and learning should be included in every study and is a critical part of the success. Although there are many uses for the data, two important uses stand out. The first use is for making adjustments and changes throughout the consulting project as problems or barriers are uncovered. The second is for reporting the level of satisfaction and learning with the project and having it included as one of the six key types of data. Several methods are available to collect satisfaction and learning data, including questionnaires, surveys, interviews, focus groups, testing, and simulations. By far the questionnaire is the most common, and sometimes just a simple, one-page questionnaire will be appropriate. Whatever the method used, the important point is to collect data, react quickly, make adjustments, and summarize the data for reporting and for use in preparing the ROI impact study.

Measuring the Progress of Consulting Projects

Tracking Application and Impact

I F THE SUCCESS of a consulting project hinges on anything, it's effectively measuring the application (Level 3) and impact (Level 4). These levels of outcome data play a pivotal role in the overall success or failure of the consulting project. If the project is not implemented effectively, there will be little or no change in the business data—and thus, no business value from the consulting project.

Collecting these data well is essential, and several methods of data collection are available to capture them. The range of possibilities varies, including the use of questionnaires, interviews, focus groups, observation, action planning, performance contracting, and performance monitoring. This chapter explores how application and impact data are collected and the issues faced in applying these processes.

Why Measure Application?

The two previous measures, reaction and learning, occur during the early stages of the consulting project where there is more attention and focus directly on what must be accomplished in the consulting project. Measuring Level 3, application and implementation data, occurs at later stages and even after the project has been implemented. The focus is on measuring the success of the implementation. Sometimes, this level of evaluation measures the degree to which the project is handed off to those who are charged with its success. This is a key transition process with measures that follow the project until it has been fully implemented. Here are a few reasons to measure at this level.

The Value of the Data

As briefly discussed in Chapter 2, the value of the information increases as progress is made through the chain of impact from Level 1 to Level 5. Thus, data concerning application and implementation (Level 3) are more valuable to the client than reaction (Level 1) and learning (Level 2). While these two levels are important, measuring the extent to which the consulting project is implemented properly provides critical data for executives at this level. The success of the project includes the factors that contributed to the success as the consulting process is fully implemented.

It's the Key Focus of Many Projects

Many consulting projects focus directly on implementation. The project sponsor often speaks in these terms and is concerned about these measures of success (e.g., the system was fully implemented or the new product was successfully launched). Even a comprehensive consulting project, designed to transform an organization, will have key issues for application and implementation. The sponsor will be interested in knowing the extent to which all of the key stakeholders are adjusting to, and properly implementing, the desired new behaviors, processes, systems, and procedures. This interest in application and implementation often drives the project.

Barriers and Enablers

When a consulting project goes astray, the first question is usually, "What happened?" More importantly, when a project appears not to be adding value, the first question should be, "What can we do to change the direction of the project?" In either scenario, it is critical to have information that identifies barriers to success, problems encountered in implementation, and obstacles to the application of the process. It is at Level 3, measuring application, that these barriers are identified and examined for reduction or elimination. Sometimes, it's a matter of going around the barrier. In many cases, the key stakeholders directly involved in consulting provide important input into the recommendations for making changes or for using a different approach in the future.

When there is success, the obvious question is, "How can we repeat this success or even improve on this in the future?" The answer to this question is also found at Level 3. Identifying the factors that contribute directly to the success of the project is critical since those same items can be used to replicate the process to produce specific results in the future and to enhance results. When key stakeholders identify those issues, it not only makes the project successful but provides an important case history of what is necessary for success.

Rewards for Success

Measuring application and implementation allows the client and consulting team to reward those who are doing the best job of applying the processes and implementing the consulting project. Measures taken at this level provide clear evidence of various efforts and roles, providing an excellent basis for performance review or special recognition. Sometimes the consultants are rewarded for implementation (e.g., the project was completed on time, the system is operational, or the procedure is working properly). This often has a reinforcing value for keeping the project on track and communicating a strong message for future improvements.

Why Measure Business Impact?

A logical extension of application is the corresponding business impact. Although there are several obvious reasons for measuring impact, several issues support the rationale for collecting business impact data related to a consulting project.

Higher-Level Data

Following the assumption that higher-level data create more value for the client, the business impact measures in a five-level framework offer more valuable data. They are the data considered to be the consequence of the successful application and implementation of a consulting project. This level responds to "So what?" and "What if?" questions. The product was successfully launched, so what are the results (i.e., sales, profits, etc.)? What if the system is implemented on time (i.e., how will productivity and quality improve)? These consequences often represent the bottom-line measures that are positively influenced when a project is successful. For most executives, this is the most important data set, but only if the amount of improvement can be pinpointed to the project.

The Business Driver for Projects

For most consulting projects, the business impact data represent the initial drivers for the project. The problem of deteriorating or less-than-desired performance may have perpetuated the need for the project (e.g., a quality problem or a retention problem). The opportunity for improvement of a business measure may lead to a consulting project (e.g., improving customer satisfaction or market share). If the business needs defined by business measures are the drivers for a project, then the key measures for evaluating the project are the same business measures. The extent to which measures actually have changed is the key determinant of the success of the project.

It's the Payoff for Clients

Business impact data often reflect key payoff measures from the perspective of the client. These are the measures often desired by the client and what he or she wants to see changed or improved. They often represent hard, indisputable facts that reflect performance critical to the business and operating unit level of the organization. And these measures are the ones converted to money to calculate the ROI. Without impact data, a credible ROI calculation cannot be delivered.

Easy to Measure

One unique feature about business impact data is that they are often easy to measure. Hard and soft data measures at this level often reflect key measures that are found in plentiful numbers throughout an organization. A typical large organization will have hundreds or even thousands of business measures reflecting output, quality, cost, time, job satisfaction, and customer satisfaction. The challenge is to connect the consulting project to the appropriate business measures. This is easily accomplished at the beginning of the consulting project because of the availability and ease with which many of the data items can be located.

Data Collection Key Issues

When collecting application and impact data, several key issues should be addressed. While these are very similar to measuring reaction and learning, a few are different due to the later collection time for this type of data and the importance of the results at this level.

Types of Data

The types of data needed are directly related to the objectives of the project. At Level 3, application and implementation, data reflect what participants have accomplished in the project. The outcomes of applications are easy to observe and evaluate. Table 5-1 shows the variety of data for this level of analysis. It's all about action and activity.

Table 5-1   Examples of Coverage Areas for Application

Action	Explanation	Example
Increase	Increasing a particular activity or action.	Increase the frequency of the use of a particular skill.
Decrease	Decreasing a particular activity or action.	Decrease the number of times a particular process has to be checked.
Eliminate	Stop or remove a particular task or activity.	Eliminate the formal follow-up meeting, and replace it with a virtual meeting.
Maintain	Keep the same level of activity for a particular process.	Continue to monitor the process with the same schedule as previously used.
Create	Design, build, or implement a new procedure, process, or activity.	Create a procedure for resolving the differences between two divisions.
Use	Use a particular process, procedure, or activity.	Use the new procedure in situations when it is appropriate.
Perform	Conduct or do a particular task, process, or procedure.	Perform a post-audit review at the end of each activity.
Participate	Become involved in various activities, projects, or programs.	Each associate should submit a suggestion for reducing costs.
Enroll	Sign up for a particular process, program, or project.	Each associate should enroll in the career advancement program.
Respond	React to groups, individuals, or systems.	Each participant in the project should respond to customer inquiries within 15 minutes.
Network	Facilitate relationships with others who are involved or have been affected by. the project	Each project participant should continue networking with contacts on at least a quarterly basis.

To help focus on the measures for impact, a distinction is made in two general categories of data: hard data and soft data. Hard data are the primary measurements of improvement, presented through rational, undisputed facts that are easily gathered. They are the most desirable type of data to collect. The ultimate criteria for measuring the effectiveness of management rest on hard data items, such as productivity, profitability, cost control, and quality control.

Hard data are:

- Easy to measure and quantify
- Relatively easy to convert to monetary values
- Objectively based
- Common measures of organizational performance
- Credible with management

Hard data can be grouped into four categories—output, quality, cost, and time—and are typical performance measures in almost every organization. Table 5-2 shows examples of these four categories.

Table 5-2 Examples of Hard Data

Output	Time
Sales	Cycle time
Completion rate	Equipment downtime
Units produced	Overtime
Tons manufactured	Delivery time
Items assembled	
Money collected	Time to project completion
Items sold	Processing time
New accounts generated	Employee time
Forms processed	Time to proficiency
Loans approved	Response time
Inventory turnover	Meeting time
Patients discharged	Repair time
Applications processed	
Students graduated	Efficiency
Projects completed	Recruiting time
Output per hour	Average delay time
Productivity	Late reporting
Work backlog	Lost time days
Incentive bonus	
Shipments	

Costs	Quality
Shelter costs	Failure rates
Treatment costs	Dropout rates
Budget variances	Scrap
Unit costs	Waste
Costs by account	Rejects
Variable costs	Reject rates
Fixed costs	Error rates
Overhead costs	Rework
Operating costs	Shortages
Project cost savings	Product defects
Accident costs	Deviations from standard
Program costs	Product failures
Sales expense	Inventory adjustments
Participant costs	Accidents
	Incidents
	Compliance discrepancies
	Agency fines
	Penalties

There are times when hard, rational numbers just do not exist. When this is the case, soft data may be meaningful in evaluating consulting projects. Table 5-3 shows common types of soft data, categorized or subdivided into five areas: work climate/satisfaction, employee development/advancement, customer service, initiative/innovation, and image. There may be other ways to divide soft data into categories. Due to the many types of soft data, the possibilities are almost limitless.

Sources

For application, the sources of data mirror those identified in Chapter 4, which covers measuring reaction and satisfaction. Essentially, all key stakeholders are candidates for sources of data. Perhaps the most important source is those who are actually involved in the application and implementation. It may involve the entire team or the specific team leaders charged with the responsibility of implementation. For impact data, sources include reports, records, and data as listed in Table 5-4.

Table 5-3 Examples of Soft Data

Work Climate/Satisfaction	Customer Service
Job satisfaction	Customer complaints
Organization commitment	Customer satisfaction
Employee engagement	Customer dissatisfaction
Employee loyalty	Customer impressions
Tardiness	Customer loyalty
Grievances	Customer retention
Discrimination charges	Customer value
Employee complaints	Lost customers
Intent to leave	
Stress	**Employee Development/Advancement**
Teamwork	Promotions
Communication	Capability
Cooperation	Intellectual capital
Conflicts	Requests for transfer
	Performance appraisal ratings
Initiative/Innovation	Readiness
Creativity	Networking
Innovation	
New ideas	
Suggestions	**Image**
New products	Brand awareness
New services	Reputation
Trademarks	Leadership
Copyrights	Social responsibility
Patents in process	Environmental friendliness
Patents improvements	Social consciousness
Partnerships	Diversity
Alliances	External awards

Timing

The timing of data collection can vary significantly. Since evaluation of application and impact is a follow-up to the consulting project, the key issue is determining the best time for data collection at these two levels. The challenge is to analyze the nature and scope of the application and impact and determine the earliest time that a trend and pattern will evolve. This occurs when the application is complete and the impact has occurred. This is a judgment call.

Table 5-4   Sources of Data

Department records	Work unit reports
Human capital databases	Payroll records
Quality reports	Design documents
Manufacturing reports	Test data
Compliance reports	Marketing data
Sales records	Service records
Annual reports	Safety and health reports
Benchmarking data	Industry/trade association data
R&D status reports	Suggestion system data
Customer satisfaction data	Project management data
Cost data statements	Financial records
Scorecards	Dashboards
Productivity records	Employee engagement data

The important point is to go in as early as possible so that potential adjustments can still be made, while at the same time, waiting until there is significant time for the implementation to be observed and measured and the impact to be evaluated. In consulting projects spanning a considerable length of time in terms of complete implementation, several measures may be taken at three- to six-month intervals. This gives successive input in terms of progress and clearly shows the extent of improvement, using effective measures at well-timed intervals, and identifies the issues that are standing in the way of a successful implementation. For some projects, there will be a lag between implementation and impact. For example, a new customer loyalty project will have a delay from the time the project is completed to the time when sales and customer tenure materialize. This will require input from the most credible sources about the amount of delay so that impact data can be collected at the appropriate time.

Responsibilities

Measuring application and impact may involve the responsibility and work of others. Because this time period follows the consulting completion, an important issue may surface in terms of who is responsible for this follow-up. There is a range of possibilities, from consulting staff to the client staff, as well as the possibility of an external, independent third party. This matter should be addressed in the planning stage so that there is no misunderstanding as to the distribution of responsibilities. More importantly, those who are responsible should fully understand the nature and scope of their responsibility and what is necessary to collect the data.

Using Questionnaires to Measure Application and Impact

Questionnaires have become a mainstream data collection tool for measuring application and impact because of their flexibility, low cost, and ease of administration. The issues involved in questionnaire design, discussed in Chapter 4, apply equally to questionnaire development for measuring application and impact. This section will be limited to the specific content issues of follow-up questionnaires for application and impact.

One of the most difficult tasks is to determine specific issues that need to be addressed on a follow-up questionnaire. Although the content items on a follow-up questionnaire can be the same as questionnaires used in measuring reaction and learning, the following content items are more desirable for capturing application and impact information (Level 3 and 4 data). Figure 5-1 presents a questionnaire used in a follow-up evaluation of a consulting project on building a sales culture. The evaluation was designed to capture the ROI, with the primary method of data collection being the follow-up questionnaire. This example will be used to illustrate many of the issues involving potential content items for a follow-up questionnaire.

Progress Bank, following a carefully planned growth pattern through acquiring smaller banks, initiated a consulting project to develop a strong sales culture. The project involved four solutions. Through a competency-based learning intervention, all branch personnel were taught how to aggressively pursue new customers and cross-sell to existing customers in a variety of product lines. The software and customer database were upgraded to provide faster access and enhanced routines to assist selling. The incentive compensation system was also redesigned to enhance payments for new customers and increase sales of all branch products. Finally, a management coaching and goal-setting system was implemented to ensure that ambitious sales goals were met. All branch employees were involved in the project.

Six months after the project was implemented, an evaluation was planned. Each branch in the network had a scorecard that tracked performance through several measures such as new accounts, total deposits, and growth by specific products. All product lines were monitored. All branch employees provided input on the questionnaire shown in Figure 5-1. Most of the data from the questionnaire covered application and impact. This type of feedback helps consultants know which parts of the intervention are most effective and useful.

Sales Culture at Progress Bank Follow-Up Questionnaire

Are you currently in a sales capacity at a branch?

Yes ☐   No ☐

1. Listed below are the objectives of the sales culture project. After reflecting on this project, please indicate the degree of success in meeting the objectives. Use the following scale:

    1 = No success

    2 = Limited success

    3 = Moderate success

    4 = Generally successful

    5 = Very successful

As a result of this project, branch employees will:	1	2	3	4	5
a. Use the tools and techniques to determine customer needs and concerns.	☐	☐	☐	☐	☐
b. Match needs with specific projects and services.	☐	☐	☐	☐	☐
c. Use the tools and techniques to convince customers to buy/use Progress Bank products and services.	☐	☐	☐	☐	☐
d. Build a productive, long-term relationship with customers.	☐	☐	☐	☐	☐
e. Increase sales of each product line offered in the branch.	☐	☐	☐	☐	☐

2. Did you implement an on-the-job action plan for this project?

    Yes ☐   No ☐

    If yes, please describe the nature and outcome of the plan. If not, explain why. ___

    _____

    _____

    _____

3. Please rate the relevance to your job of each of the following components of the project using the following scale:

    1 = No relevance

    2 = Limited relevance

    3 = Moderate relevance

    4 = General relevance

    5 = Very relevant

Figure 5-1   Example of questionnaire *(continues)*.

	1	2	3	4	5
Job aids	☐	☐	☐	☐	☐
Group learning activities	☐	☐	☐	☐	☐
Incentive opportunities	☐	☐	☐	☐	☐
Networking opportunities with other branches	☐	☐	☐	☐	☐
Reading material/videos	☐	☐	☐	☐	☐
Coaching sessions	☐	☐	☐	☐	☐
Software/system changes	☐	☐	☐	☐	☐
Database enhancements	☐	☐	☐	☐	☐

4. Have you used the job aids provided during the project?

   Yes ☐   No ☐

   Please explain. _____

   _____

   _____

   _____

5. Please indicate the change in the application of knowledge and skills as a result of your participation in the sales culture project. Use the following scale:

   1 = No change

   2 = Limited change

   3 = Moderate change

   4 = Much change

   5 = Very much change

		1	2	3	4	5	No Opportunity to Use Skill
a.	Probing for customer needs	☐	☐	☐	☐	☐	☐
b.	Helping the customer solve problems	☐	☐	☐	☐	☐	☐
c.	Understanding the features and benefits of all products and services	☐	☐	☐	☐	☐	☐
d.	Comparing products and services to those of competitors	☐	☐	☐	☐	☐	☐
e.	Selecting appropriate products and services	☐	☐	☐	☐	☐	☐
f.	Using persuasive selling techniques	☐	☐	☐	☐	☐	☐
g.	Using follow-up techniques to stay in touch with the customer	☐	☐	☐	☐	☐	☐
h.	Using new software routines for data access and transactions	☐	☐	☐	☐	☐	☐

Figure 5-1 Example of questionnaire *(continued)*.

6. What has changed about your work (actions, tasks, activities) as a result of this project?

_____

_____

_____

_____

7. Indicate the extent to which you think this program has influenced each of these measures in your branch. Use the following scale:

1 = No influence
2 = Limited influence
3 = Moderate influence
4 = Much influence
5 = Very much influence

		1	2	3	4	5
a.	New accounts	☐	☐	☐	☐	☐
b.	Sales	☐	☐	☐	☐	☐
c.	Customer response time	☐	☐	☐	☐	☐
d.	Cross-sales ratio	☐	☐	☐	☐	☐
e.	Cost control	☐	☐	☐	☐	☐
f.	Employee satisfaction	☐	☐	☐	☐	☐
g.	Customer satisfaction	☐	☐	☐	☐	☐
h.	Customer complaints	☐	☐	☐	☐	☐
i.	Customer loyalty	☐	☐	☐	☐	☐

8. Please define the most improved measure above. Use a unit of value such as one sale, one new account, or one customer complaint.

_____

_____

_____

_____

9. Provide the actual change in the unit measure since the project began. This would take the pre-program baseline data and subtract it from the current level to indicate a change.

_____

_____

_____

_____

(Continues)

10. Indicate the actual unit value for the specific measure in question. If it is a measure that is desired to improve, indicate the value-add, such as one additional sale. If it is a value that needs to be minimized, such as one customer complaint, indicate the money saved when the customer complaint is avoided. Although this can be very difficult, please follow the instructions of how this value may be obtained.

_____

_____

_____

_____

11. Provide the basis for the above unit value. If it is a standard value, please indicate that it is a standard value; if it is an expert input, indicate that it is an expert input; if it is based on an estimate, indicate how the estimate was derived.

_____

_____

_____

_____

12. Provide the total impact of the change. This involves taking the unit value times the change in the value for one year. This takes into account the frequency. If it is a monthly data item, then it would be times 12. If it is a weekly value, it would be times 52.

_____

_____

_____

_____

13. List other factors that could have influenced this improvement. Be very thoughtful and specific in listing the other influences.

_____

_____

_____

_____

14. Indicate the percent of improvement directly related to this project using a scale of 0% to 100%. Zero percent is no improvement connected to the project. One hundred percent is all the improvement connected to the project.

_____

_____

_____

_____

Figure 5-1 Example of questionnaire *(continued)*.

15. What level of confidence do you place in the previous estimations
(0% = no confidence; 100% = certainty)? _____%

Please explain. _____

_____

_____

_____

16. Do you think the sales culture project represented a good investment for Progress Bank?

Yes ☐   No ☐

Please explain. _____

_____

_____

_____

17. Please rate the success of the immediate project team and the quality of the team's leadership. Use the following scale:

1 = No success
2 = Limited success
3 = Moderately successful
4 = Generally successful
5 = Very successful

Team Characteristic	1	2	3	4	5
Capability	☐	☐	☐	☐	☐
Motivation	☐	☐	☐	☐	☐
Cooperation	☐	☐	☐	☐	☐
Communication	☐	☐	☐	☐	☐

Leadership Quality	1	2	3	4	5
Leadership style	☐	☐	☐	☐	☐
Organization	☐	☐	☐	☐	☐
Communication	☐	☐	☐	☐	☐
Team support	☐	☐	☐	☐	☐
Team training	☐	☐	☐	☐	☐

(Continues)

18. What barriers, if any, have you encountered that prevented this project from being successful. Please explain, if possible.

_____

_____

_____

_____

19. What has helped this project be successful? Please explain.

_____

_____

_____

_____

20. Which of the following statements best describes the level of management support?

   ❑ There was no management support.
   ❑ There was limited management support.
   ❑ There was a moderate amount of management support.
   ❑ There was much management support.
   ❑ There was very much management support.

21. Could other program solutions have been effective in meeting the business need(s)?

   Yes ❑   No ❑

   Please explain. _____

_____

_____

_____

22. What specific suggestions do you have for improving this project?

_____

_____

_____

_____

23. Other comments about this project:

_____

_____

_____

_____

Figure 5-1   Example of questionnaire *(continued)*.

Using Interviews and Focus Groups

Interviews and focus groups can be used on a follow-up basis to collect application and impact data. However, the steps needed to design and administer these instruments are the same as the ones presented in Chapter 4 and will not be repeated here.

Using Observation

Observing participants and recording changes in behavior and specific actions taken may be appropriate to measure application. This technique is useful when it is important to know precisely how the consulting participants are using new skills, knowledge, tasks, procedures, or systems. For example, participant observation is often used in sales and sales support projects. The observer may be a member of the consulting staff, the participant's supervisor, a member of a peer group, or an external resource, such as a mystery shopper.

Guidelines for Effective Observation

Observation is often misused or misapplied to evaluation situations, forcing some to abandon the process. The effectiveness of observation can be improved with the following guidelines:

- **Observers must be fully prepared.** Observers must fully understand what information is needed and what skills are covered in the intervention. They must be prepared for the assignment and provided a chance to practice observation skills.
- **The observations should be systematic.** The observation process must be planned so that it is executed effectively, without any surprises. The individuals observed should know in advance about the observation and why they are being observed, unless the observation is planned to be invisible. In this case, the individuals are monitored unknowingly. Observations are planned when work situations are normal. Several steps are necessary to accomplish a successful observation:
  1. Determine what behavior will be observed.
  2. Prepare the forms for the observer's use.
  3. Select the observers.
  4. Prepare a schedule of observations.
  5. Prepare observers to observe properly.

6. Inform participants of the planned observation, providing explanations.
7. Conduct the observations.
8. Summarize the observation data.

- **The observers should know how to interpret and report what they see.** Observations involve judgment decisions. The observer must analyze which behaviors are being displayed and what actions the participants are taking. Observers should know how to summarize behavior and report results in a meaningful manner.

- **The observer's influence should be minimized.** Except for "mystery" or "planted" observers and electronic observations, it is impossible to completely isolate the overall effect of an observer. Participants will display the behavior they think is appropriate, performing at their best. The presence of the observer must be minimized. To the extent possible, the observer should blend into the work environment and be unnoticeable.

- **Select observers carefully.** Observers are usually independent of the participants. They are typically members of the consulting staff. The independent observer is usually more skilled at recording behavior and making interpretations of behavior and is usually unbiased in these interpretations. Using an independent observer reduces the need to prepare observers. However, the independent observer has the appearance of an outsider, and participants may resent the observer. Sometimes it is more feasible to recruit observers from inside the organization.

Observation Methods

Five methods of observation are suggested and are appropriate depending on the circumstances surrounding the type of information needed. Each method is briefly described below:

- **Behavior checklist and codes.** A behavior checklist is useful for recording the presence, absence, frequency, or duration of a participant's behavior or action as it occurs. A checklist does not provide information on the quality, intensity, or possible circumstances surrounding the behavior observed. The checklist is useful, though, since an observer can identify exactly which behaviors should or should not occur. The behaviors listed in the checklist should be minimized and listed in a logical sequence if they normally occur in a sequence. A variation of this approach involves coding behaviors or actions on a form. While this method is useful when there are many behaviors, it is more time consuming because a code is entered that identifies a specific behavior or actions instead of checking an item.

- **Delayed report method.** With a delayed report method, the observer does not use any forms or written materials during the observation. The information is either recorded after the observation is completed or at particular time intervals during an observation. The observer tries to reconstruct what has been witnessed during the observation period. The advantage of this approach is that the observer is not as noticeable, and there are no forms being completed or notes being taken during the observation. The observer becomes more a part of the situation and less of a distraction. An obvious disadvantage is that the information written may not be as accurate and reliable as the information collected at the time it occurred. A variation of this approach is the 360° feedback process in which surveys are completed on other individuals based on observations within a specific time frame.

- **Video recording.** A video camera records behavior or actions in every detail. However, this intrusion may be awkward and cumbersome, and the participants may be unnecessarily nervous or self-conscious while they are being videotaped. If the camera is concealed, the privacy of the participant may be invaded. Because of this, video recording of on-the-job behavior is not frequently used.

- **Audio monitoring.** Monitoring conversations of participants is an effective observation technique. For example, in a large communication company's telemarketing department, sales representatives were prepared to sell equipment by telephone. To determine if employees were using the skills and procedures properly, telephone conversations were monitored on a randomly selected basis. While this approach may stir some controversy, it is an effective way to determine if skills and procedures are being applied consistently and effectively. For it to work smoothly, it must be fully explained and the rules clearly communicated.

- **Computer monitoring.** For employees who work regularly with software, computer monitoring is becoming an effective way to "observe" participants as they perform job tasks. The computer monitors times, sequence of steps, use of routines, and other activities to determine if the participant is performing the work according to specific steps and guidelines of the consulting intervention. As technology continues to be a significant part of the workplace, computer monitoring holds much promise.

Using Action Plans

In some cases, follow-up assignments can develop application and impact data. In a typical follow-up assignment, the consulting participant is asked to meet a goal or complete a particular task or project by a set date. A summary of the results of the completed assignments provides further evidence of the success of the consulting project.

With this approach, participants are required to develop action plans as part of the consulting project. Action plans contain detailed steps to accomplish specific objectives related to the project. The process is one of the most effective ways to enhance support for a consulting project and build the ownership needed for the successful application and impact of the project.

The plan is typically prepared on a printed form, such as the one shown in Figure 5-2. The action plan shows what is to be done, by whom, and the date by which the objectives should be accomplished. The action-plan approach is a straightforward, easy-to-use method for determining how participants will implement the project and achieve success with consulting.

Using Action Plans Successfully

The development of the action plan requires two major tasks: determining the measure to improve and writing the action items to improve it. As shown in Figure 5-2, an action plan can be developed with a direct focus on business impact data. The plan presented in this figure requires participants to develop an objective, which is related to the consulting project. In some cases, there may be more than one objective, which requires additional action plans. Related to the objective are the improvement measure, the current levels, and target of performance. This information requires the participant to anticipate the application of the consulting project and set goals for specific performances that can be realized. For example, an objective may be to reduce equipment downtime. The measure is the average hours of downtime for the printing presses. The current performance is six hours per week with a target of two hours per week.

The action plan is completed during the early stages of the consulting project, often with the input, assistance, and facilitation of the consultant. The consultant actually approves the plan, indicating that it meets the particular requirements of being very **S**pecific, **M**easurable, **A**chievable, **R**ealistic, and **T**ime-based (SMART). The plan can actually be developed in a one- to two-hour time frame and often begins with action steps related to the implementation of the project. These action steps are actually Level 3 activities that

Action Plan

Name: _____ Consultant signature: _____ Follow-up date: _____
Objective: _____ Evaluation period: _____ to _____
Improvement measure: _____ Current performance: _____ Target performance: _____

Action Steps	Analysis
1. _____	A. What is the unit of measure? _____
2. _____	B. What is the value (cost) of one unit? $ _____
3. _____	C. How did you arrive at this value? _____
4. _____	_____
5. _____	_____
6. _____	D. What other factors could have caused the improvement? _____
7. _____	_____
	E. How much did the measure change during the evaluation period? (monthly value) _____
Intangible Benefits:	F. What percent of this change was actually caused by this program? _____ %
	G. What level of confidence do you place on the above information (100% = certainty; 0% = no confidence)? _____ %

Comments: _____

Figure 5-2 Action plan example.

detail the application of the consulting project. All of these steps build support for, and are linked to, business impact measures:

- **Define the unit of measure.** The next important issue is to define the actual unit of measure. In some cases, more than one measure may be used and will subsequently be contained in additional action plans. The unit of measure is necessary to break the process down into the simplest steps so that the ultimate value of the project can be determined. The unit can be output data, such as an additional unit manufactured or additional hotel room rented. In terms of quality, the unit can be one reject, error, or defect. Time-based units are usually measured in minutes, hours, days, or weeks, such as one minute of downtime. Units are specific to their particular type of situation, such as one turnover of key talent, one customer complaint, or one escalated call in the call center. The important point is to break them down into the simplest terms possible.
- **Require participants to provide monetary values for each improvement.** During the consulting project, participants are asked to determine, calculate, or estimate the monetary value for each improvement outlined in the plan. The unit value is determined using standard values, expert input, external databases, or estimates (the consultant will help with this). The process used to arrive at the value is described in the action plan. When the actual improvement occurs, participants will use these values to capture the annual monetary benefits of the plan. For this step to be effective, it is helpful to provide examples of common ways in which values can be assigned to the actual data.
- **Participants implement the action plan.** Participants implement the action plan during the consulting project, which often lasts for weeks or months following the intervention. Upon completion, a major portion, if not all, of the consulting project is slated for implementation. The consulting participants implement action-plan steps, and the subsequent results are achieved.
- **Participants estimate improvements.** At the end of the specified follow-up period—usually three months, six months, nine months, or one year—the participants indicate the specific improvements made, sometimes expressed as a monthly amount. This determines the actual amount of change that has been observed, measured, or recorded. It is important for the participants to understand the necessity for accuracy as data are recorded. In most cases, only the changes are recorded, as those amounts are needed to calculate the value of the project. In other

cases, before and after data may be recorded, allowing the evaluator to calculate the actual differences.

- **Ask participants to isolate the effects of the project.** Although the action plan is initiated because of the project, the improvements reported on the action plan may be influenced by other factors. Thus, the action planning process, initiated in the consulting project, should not take full credit for the improvement. For example, an action plan to reduce employee turnover in a division could take only partial credit for an improvement because of the other variables that affect the turnover rate. While there are several ways to isolate the effects of a consulting project, participant estimation is usually most appropriate in the action-planning process. Consequently, participants are asked to estimate the percentage of the improvement actually related to this particular intervention. This question can be asked on the action plan form or in a follow-up questionnaire.

- **Ask participants to provide a confidence level for estimates.** Because the process to convert data to monetary values may not be exact and the amount of the improvement actually related to the project may not be precise, participants are asked to indicate their level of confidence in those two values, collectively. On a scale of 0 to 100 percent, where 0 percent means no confidence and 100 percent means the estimates represent certainty, this value provides participants a mechanism for expressing their uneasiness with their ability to be exact with the process.

- **Collect action plans at specified time intervals.** An excellent response rate is essential, so several steps may be necessary to ensure that the action plans are completed and returned. Usually participants will see the importance of the process and will develop their plans in detail early in the consulting project. Some organizations use follow-up reminders by mail or e-mail. Others call participants to check progress. Still others offer assistance in developing the final plan as part of the consulting project. These steps may require additional resources, which must be weighed against the importance of having more data.

- **Summarize the data and calculate the ROI.** If developed properly, each action plan should have annualized monetary values associated with improvements. Also, each individual should have indicated the percentage of the improvement directly related to the project. Finally, participants should have provided a confidence percentage to reflect their uncertainty with the process and the subjective nature of some of the data that may be provided.

Advantages/Disadvantages of Action Plans

Although there are many advantages to using action plans, there are at least two concerns:

1. The process relies on direct input from the participant. As such, the information can sometimes be inaccurate and unreliable. Participants must have assistance along the way.
2. Action plans can be time consuming for the participant, and, if the participant's manager is not involved in the process, there may be a tendency for the participant not to complete the assignment.

As this section has illustrated, the action-plan approach has many inherent advantages. Action plans are simple and easy to administer; are easily understood by participants; are suitable in a wide variety of consulting projects; and are appropriate for all types of data.

Because of the tremendous flexibility and versatility of the process and the conservative adjustments that can be made in analysis, action plans have become important data collection tools for consulting project evaluation.

Using Performance Contracts

The performance contract is essentially a slight variation of the action-planning process. Based on the principle of mutual goal setting, a performance contract is a written agreement between a participant, the participant's manager, and the consultant. The participant agrees to improve performance on measures related to the consulting project. The agreement is in the form of a goal to be accomplished during or after the consulting project. The agreement spells out what is to be accomplished, at what time, and with what results.

Although the steps can vary according to the specific kind of contract and the organization, a common sequence of events follows:

1. The consulting participant becomes involved in the implementation of the consulting project.
2. The participant and the consultant mutually agree on a measure for improvement related to the consulting project (i.e., "What's in it for me?").
3. The consultant and the participant's manager agree on the amount of improvement.

4. Specific, measurable goals are set.
5. The participant is involved in the project as the contract is discussed, and plans are developed to accomplish the goals.
6. During the consulting project, the participant works on the contract against a specific deadline.
7. The participant reports the results of the effort to the manager and the consultant.
8. The manager and participant document the results and forward a copy to the consultant along with appropriate comments.

The process of selecting the area for improvement is similar to the process used in the action-planning process.

The topic selected should be stated in terms of one or more objectives. The objectives should state what is to be accomplished when the contract is complete. The objectives should be:

- Written
- Understandable by all involved
- Challenging (requiring an unusual effort to achieve)
- Achievable (something that can be accomplished)
- Largely under the control of the participant
- Measurable and dated

The details required to accomplish the contract objectives are developed following the guidelines for action plans presented earlier.

Monitoring Business Performance Data

Data are available in every organization to measure business performance. Monitoring performance data enables management to measure performance in terms of output, quality, costs, time, job engagement, and customer satisfaction. When determining the source of data in the evaluation, the first consideration should be existing databases and reports. In most organizations, performance data suitable for measuring improvement from a consulting project are available. If not, additional record-keeping systems will have to be developed for measurement and analysis. At this point, the question of economics comes to the surface. Is it economical to develop the record-keeping systems necessary to evaluate a consulting project? If the costs are greater than the expected return for the entire project, then it is pointless to develop those systems.

Existing Measures

Existing performance measures should be researched to identify those related to the proposed objectives of the project. In many situations, it is the performance of these measures that has created the need for the project. Frequently, an organization will have several performance measures related to the same item. For example, the efficiency of a production unit can be measured in several ways, some of which are outlined below:

- Number of units produced per hour
- Number of on-schedule production units
- Percentage of utilization of the equipment
- Percentage of equipment downtime
- Labor cost per unit of production
- Overtime required per unit of production
- Total unit cost

Each of these, in its own way, measures the efficiency of the production unit. All related measures should be reviewed to determine those most relevant to the consulting intervention.

Occasionally, existing performance measures are integrated with other data, and it may be difficult to keep them isolated from unrelated data. In this situation, all existing related measures should be extracted and tabulated again to be more appropriate for comparison in the evaluation. At times, conversion factors may be necessary. For example, the average number of new sales orders per month may be presented regularly in the performance measures for the sales department. In addition, the sales costs per sales representative are also presented. However, in the evaluation of a consulting project, the average cost per new sale is needed. The average number of new sales orders and the sales cost per sales representative are required to develop the data necessary for comparison.

Developing New Measures

In some cases, data are not available for the information needed to measure the effectiveness of a consulting project. The consulting staff must work with the client organization to develop record-keeping systems, if economically feasible. In one organization, a turnover problem with new professional staff prompted a consulting project to fix the problem. To help ensure success of the project, several measures were planned, including early turnover defined as the percentage of employees who left the company in the first three months of employment. Initially this measure was not available. When the intervention was implemented, the organization began collecting early turnover figures for comparison.

Several questions regarding this issue should be addressed:

- Which department will develop the measurement system?
- Who will record and monitor the data?
- Where will it be recorded?
- Will new forms or documentation be needed?

These questions will usually involve other departments or a management decision that extends beyond the scope of the consultants. Often the administration department, operations, or the information technology unit may be instrumental in helping determine whether new measures are needed and, if so, how they will be developed.

Selecting the Appropriate Method
for Each Level

This chapter and the previous chapter presented several methods to capture data. Collectively, they offer a wide range of opportunities for collecting data in a variety of situations. Eight specific issues should be considered when deciding which method is appropriate for a situation. These should be considered when selecting data collection methods for other evaluation levels as well.

Type of Data

Perhaps one of the most important issues to consider when selecting the method is the type of data to be collected. Some methods are more appropriate for Level 4, while others are best for Level 3. Table 5-5 shows the most appropriate types of data for specific methods of Level 3 and 4 data collection. Follow-up surveys, observations, interviews, and focus groups are best suited for Level 3 data, sometimes exclusively. Performance monitoring, action planning, and questionnaires can easily capture Level 4 data.

Table 5-5 Collecting Application and Impact Data

Data Collection Method	Level 3	Level 4
Follow-up surveys	✓	
Follow-up questionnaires	✓	✓
Observation on the job	✓	
Interviews with participants	✓	
Follow-up focus groups	✓	
Action planning	✓	✓
Performance contracting	✓	✓
Business performance monitoring		✓

Participants' Time for Data Input

Another important factor in selecting the data collection method is the amount of time participants must spend with data collection and evaluation systems. Time requirements should always be minimized, and the method should be positioned so that it is a value-added activity (i.e., the participants understand that this activity is something valuable so they will not resist). This requirement often means that sampling is used to keep the total participant time to a minimum. Some methods, such as performance monitoring, require no participant time, while others, such as interviews and focus groups, require a significant investment in time.

Manager Time for Data Input

The time that a participant's direct manager must allocate to data collection is another important issue in the method selection. This time requirement should always be minimized. Some methods, such as performance contracting, may require much involvement from the supervisor before and after the intervention. Other methods, such as questionnaires administered directly to participants, may not require any supervisor time.

Cost of Method

Cost is always a consideration when selecting the method. Some data collection methods are more expensive than others. For example, interviews and observations are very expensive. Surveys, questionnaires, and performance monitoring are usually inexpensive.

Disruption of Normal Work Activities

Another key issue in selecting the appropriate method—and perhaps the one that generates the most concern with managers—is the amount of disruption the data collection will create. Routine work processes should be disrupted as little as possible. Some data collection techniques, such as performance monitoring, require very little time and distraction from normal activities. Questionnaires generally do not disrupt the work environment and can often be completed in only a few minutes, or even after normal work hours. On the other extreme, some items such as observations and interviews may be too disruptive to the work unit.

Accuracy of Method

The accuracy of the technique is another factor to consider when selecting the method. Some data collection methods are more accurate than others. For example, performance monitoring is usually very accurate, whereas questionnaires can be distorted and unreliable. If actual on-the-job behavior must be captured, observation is clearly one of the most accurate methods.

Utility of an Additional Method

Because there are many different methods to collect data, it is tempting to use too many data collection methods. Multiple data collection methods add to the time and costs of the evaluation and may result in very little additional value. Utility refers to the added value of the use of an additional data collection method. As more than one method is used, this question should always be addressed. Does the value obtained from the additional data warrant the extra time and expense of the method? If the answer is no, the additional method should not be implemented.

Cultural Bias for Data Collection Method

The culture or philosophy of the organization can dictate which data collection methods are used. For example, some organizations are accustomed to using questionnaires and find the process fits in well with their culture. Some organizations will not use observation because their culture does not support the potential invasion of privacy often associated with it.

Final Thoughts

This chapter outlined techniques for measuring application and impact—a critical issue in determining the success of the project. These essential measures determine not only the success achieved, but areas where improvement is needed and areas where the success can be replicated in the future. A variety of techniques is available, ranging from observation and questionnaires to action planning and business performance monitoring. The method chosen must match the scope of the project resources available and the accuracy needed. Complicated projects require a comprehensive approach that measures all of the issues involved in application and impact. Simple projects can take a less formal approach and collect data only from a questionnaire. The next chapter focuses on another critical issue: isolating the effects of the consulting project from other influences.

Analysis

CHAPTER

Separating the Consulting Impact from Other Factors

How to Isolate the Effects of the Consulting Project

W HEN A SIGNIFICANT INCREASE in a business measure is noted after a consulting project has been conducted, the two events appear to be linked. The client asks, "How much of this improvement was caused by the consulting project?" When this potentially challenging question is posed, it is not always answered with the accuracy and credibility needed. While the change in performance may be linked to the consulting project, other nonconsulting factors usually contribute to the improvement as well. This chapter explores useful techniques for isolating the effects of consulting. These proven techniques are used in some of the most successful organizations as they attempt to measure the return on investment in consulting.

Why Isolate the Effects of Consulting Projects?

In almost every consulting project, multiple influences will drive the business measures targeted for the consulting project's success. With multiple influences present, it is critical to measure the actual effect of each of the different factors, or at least the extent that is attributed to the consulting project. Without this isolation step, the consulting project's success will be in question. The results will be overstated if it is suggested that all of the change in the business impact measure is attributed to the actual consulting project. When this issue is ignored, the impact study is considered invalid and inconclusive. This harsh reality places tremendous pressure on consultants to show the business value of consulting when compared to other factors.

Preliminary Issues

The cause-and-effect relationship between consulting and business performance can be confusing and difficult to prove but can be developed with an acceptable degree of accuracy. The challenge is to develop one or more specific techniques to isolate the effects of consulting early in the process, usually as part of an evaluation plan. Up-front attention ensures that appropriate techniques will be used with minimum costs and time commitments. Here are the most important issues when isolating the effects of a consulting project.

Early Evidence: Chain of Impact

Before presenting the isolation techniques, it is helpful to examine the chain of impact implied in the different levels of evaluation. Measurable results achieved from a consulting project should be derived from the application of the consulting recommendations over a specified period of time after the project has been completed. Application is Level 3 in the five evaluation levels. Continuing with this logic, successful application of the project should stem from participants learning new skills or acquiring new knowledge from the consulting project, which is a Level 2 evaluation. Therefore, for a business impact improvement from the project (Level 4 evaluation), this chain of impact implies that measurable application and implementation are realized (Level 3 evaluation), and new knowledge and skills are acquired (Level 2 evaluation). Without this preliminary evidence, it is difficult to isolate the effects of a consulting project. In other words, if there is no learning and application, it is virtually impossible to conclude that any performance improvements were caused by the consulting project. From a practical standpoint, this issue requires data collection at four levels for an ROI calculation. If data are collected on business impact, they should also be collected for other levels of evaluation to ensure that the consulting project helped produce the business results. While this requirement is a prerequisite to isolating the effects of a consulting intervention, it does not prove that there was a direct connection, nor does it pinpoint how much of the improvement was caused by the consulting project. It merely shows that without improvements at previous levels, it is difficult to make a connection between the ultimate outcome and the consulting project.

Identifying Other Factors: A First Step

A first step in isolating a consulting project's impact on performance is to identify the factors that may have contributed to the performance improvement. This step underscores that consulting is not the sole source of improvement and that the credit for improvement is shared with several possible sources—an approach that is likely to gain the respect of the client.

Several potential sources are available to identify major influencing variables. In many situations, the client may be able to identify factors that will influence or already have influenced the business measure. The client usually is aware of other projects, events, initiatives, or promotions that may be present to influence the output.

Participants in the consulting project are usually aware of other influences that may have caused performance improvement. After all, it is the impact of their collective efforts that is being monitored and measured. In many situations, they have witnessed previous changes in the business measures and can pinpoint reasons for the changes.

Project consultants are another source for identifying variables that impact results. Although the needs analysis will usually uncover these influencing variables, consultants usually analyze these variables while addressing the issues in the consulting project implementation.

In some situations, immediate managers of participants (e.g., work unit managers) may be able to identify variables that influence the performance improvement. This is particularly useful when participants are nonexempt employees (operatives) who may not be fully aware of the variables that can influence performance.

Finally, subject matter experts may be able to identify other influences based on their experience and knowledge of the situation. In the role of expert, they have monitored, examined, and analyzed the variables previously. The authority of these individuals often increases the data's credibility.

Taking time to focus attention on variables that may influence performance brings additional accuracy and credibility to the process. It moves beyond presenting results with no mention of other influences—a situation that often destroys the credibility of a consulting impact study. It also provides a foundation for some of the techniques described in this book by identifying the variables that must be isolated to show the effects of a consulting project.

Use of Control Groups

The most accurate approach for isolating the impact of a consulting project is the use of control groups in an experimental design process. This approach involves the use of an experimental group that experiences the consulting project and a control group that does not. The composition of both groups should be as identical as possible and, if feasible, each group should be selected randomly from a list of potentials. When this is achieved, and both groups are subjected to the same environmental influences, the difference in the performance of the two groups can be attributed to the consulting project.

As illustrated in Figure 6-1, the control group and experimental groups do not necessarily have pre-project measurements. Measurements can be taken after the project is implemented, and the difference in the performance of the two groups shows the amount of improvement that is directly related to consulting.

Sometimes the use of control groups may create an image that the consultants are producing a laboratory setting, which can cause a problem for some executives. To avoid this stigma, consultants use the term *pilot project* instead of the experimental group. A similarly matched nonparticipating group is referred to as the *comparison group*.

For example, in a consulting project for a major United States–based computer company, a pilot group was used. The consulting project involved regional and local sales managers, account managers, account executives, account representatives, and sales representatives. The business measures involved profit-margin quota attainment, total revenue attainment, profit margin, and various sales volumes. A comparison group (the control group) was carefully matched with the initial pilot group. The same number of participants for the comparison group was selected at random using the company database. This effort ensured that the comparison group and the pilot group had equivalent job roles. A distinct difference in the two groups emerged after the project was implemented.

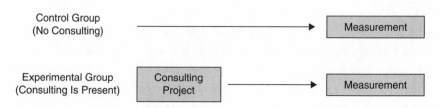

Figure 6-1 Pre-project measures.

The control arrangement does have some inherent problems that may make it difficult to apply in practice. The first major problem is the selection of the groups. From a theoretical perspective, it is virtually impossible to have identical control and experimental groups. Dozens of factors can affect business performance, some of them individual, others contextual. To address this issue on a practical basis, it is best to select four to six variables that will have the greatest influence on performance. For example, in a consulting project designed to boost direct sales in a large retail store chain, three stores were selected, and their performances were compared to three similar stores that constituted the control group. The selection of these particular groups of stores was based on four variables store executives thought would have the greatest influence on sales performance from one store to another: the household income in market area, store size, customer traffic, and previous store performance. Although there are other factors that could have influenced performance, these four variables were used to make the selection.

Another problem is contamination, which can develop when participants in the consulting group (experimental group) actually communicate with others who are in the control group. Sometimes the members of the control group model the actions of the consulting project. In either case, the experiment becomes contaminated as the influence of the consulting intervention is passed on to the control group. This can be minimized by ensuring that control groups and consulting groups are at different locations (i.e., different stores, branches, plants, cities, etc.), have different shifts, or are on different floors in the same building. When this is not possible, it may be helpful to explain to both groups that one group will be involved in the consulting project now, and the other will be involved at a later date if it works. It is not unusual to try a new system, process, or procedure in one area first and then implement it in other areas if it is successful. Also, it may be helpful to appeal to the sense of responsibility of those involved in the consulting project and ask them not to share the information with others.

Another problem occurs when the different groups function under different environmental influences. This is usually the case when groups are at different locations. Sometimes the selection of the groups can help prevent this problem from occurring. Another tactic is to use more groups than necessary and discard those with some environmental differences.

Because the use of control groups is an effective approach for isolating the impact of consulting, it should be considered as a technique when a major ROI impact study is planned. In these situations, it is important that the consulting impact is isolated with a high level of accuracy, and the primary advantage of the control group process is accuracy. Best practice data among users of the ROI Methodology show that about 30 percent of the ROI studies are using this isolation technique.

Analytical Approaches

The control group is the most credible process if it works. If it does not work, the next set of approaches is categorized as analytical approaches, because they involve various mathematical relationships and calculations. Three approaches are in this category, including trend-line analysis; forecasting, which can involve regression analysis; and calculating the effects of other factors.

Trend-Line Analysis

A useful technique for approximating the impact of consulting is trend-line analysis. With this approach, a trend line is drawn to project the future, using previous performance as a base. When the consulting project is conducted, actual performance of the business measure is compared to the trend-line projection. Any improvement of performance over what the trend line predicted can then be reasonably attributed to the consulting project. While this is not an exact process, it provides a reasonable estimation of consulting impact.

Figure 6-2 shows an example of a trend-line analysis taken from a shipping department of a large book distribution company. The percentage reflects the

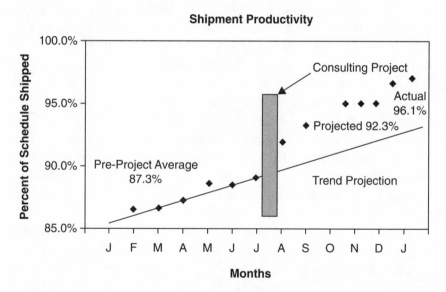

Figure 6-2   Example of trend-line analysis.

level of actual shipments compared to scheduled shipments. Data are presented before and after a consulting project was implemented in July. As shown in the figure, there was an upward trend on the data prior to conducting the intervention. Although the consulting apparently had a dramatic effect on shipment productivity, the trend line shows that some improvement would have continued anyway, based on the trend that had previously been established. It is tempting to measure the improvement by comparing the average six months' shipments prior to the project (87.3 percent) to the value six months after the project (96.1 percent), yielding a 10.1 percent difference. However, a more accurate comparison is the value after the project (96.1 per cost) compared to the trend line (92.3 percent). In this example, the difference is 3.8 percent. Using this more conservative measure increases the accuracy and credibility of the process to isolate the impact of consulting.

A primary disadvantage of the trend-line approach is that it is not always accurate. This approach assumes that the events that influenced the business measure prior to the consulting project are still in place after the project is implemented (i.e., the trends that were established prior to consulting will continue in the same relative direction). Also, it assumes that no new influences entered the situation at the time consulting was conducted. This may not always be the case. These two conditions must be met to use this solution technique.

The primary advantage of this approach is that it is simple and inexpensive. If historical data are available, a trend line can quickly be drawn and differences estimated. While not exact, it does provide a quick assessment of the consulting impact.

Forecasting Methods

A more analytical approach to trend-line analysis is the use of forecasting methods that predict a change in performance variables. This approach represents a mathematical interpretation of the trend-line analysis when other factors (variables) enter a situation at the time the consulting project is implemented. With this approach, the business measure targeted by consulting is forecast based on the influence of other variables that have changed during the implementation or evaluation period of the consulting project. The actual value of the measure is compared to the forecasted value. The difference reflects the contribution of consulting.

An example will help explain the application of this process. A large retail computer store chain routinely develops a revised sales forecast. The sales forecasting model has a reputation for being accurate and is based on several inputs such as staffing levels, advertising, economic indicators, and a competition index. The model has the flexibility to add new variables or remove variables that no longer influence the output measure. The sales forecast is usually revised each month, and the previous month's result is used in the model. However, it is possible to omit the influence of the previous month.

A consulting project was initiated to improve sales. The project involved changes in sales transaction processing systems. Many job aids were also part of the project. An important measure of the consulting project's success was the unit sales per sales associate. The average sale per associate prior to the consulting project was projected using a trend-line analysis. Six months after the project, the average daily sale per employee was $1,500. Two related questions must be answered: Is the difference in these two values attributable to the consulting program? Did other factors influence the sales level?

As illustrated in Figure 6-3, the consulting project was completed, and changes were implemented in January. After reviewing potential influencing factors with several store executives, two factors—the level of advertising and competitor pricing—appeared to have changed significantly during the period of evaluation. The trend-line projection using the previous sales-per-associate data was not appropriate because of these two factors. As expected, when advertising expenditures and competitor pricing increased, the sales per associate increased proportionately. The forecasting model was used to predict sales with the two changes. Figure 6-3 shows the forecasted value. The influence of the previous month was omitted to isolate the effect of the consulting project.

The values in Figure 6-3 need further explanation. In this figure, four lines are presented. The first line, A, represents the pre-project value that

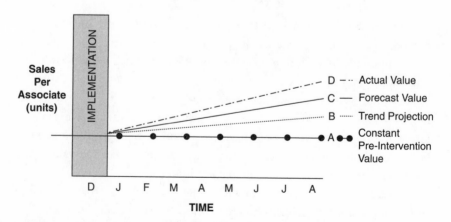

Figure 6-3 Forecasted value of sales.

would be achieved if sales remained flat, or constant. However, some influences were already there, and B represents the trend value that would have been achieved if the pre-project influences had remained constant. Line C represents the forecasted value with the two new influences (advertising and competitor pricing), and line D represents the actual value. The difference in the actual value and the forecasted value represents the monthly impact of the consulting project (D minus C). This six-month snapshot is annualized to develop the first-year impact (the monthly difference times 12). Assuming that the other factors possibly influencing sales were constant, this value represents the impact of the consulting intervention.

With the forecasting approach, a major disadvantage occurs when several variables enter the process. The complexity multiplies, and the use of sophisticated statistical packages for multiple variable analysis is necessary. Even then, a good fit of the data to the model may not be possible. Unfortunately, some organizations have not developed mathematical relationships for business measures as a function of one or more inputs, and without them, the forecasting method is difficult to use.

The primary advantage of this process is that it can accurately predict business performance measures without the consulting if appropriate data and models are available. The presentation of specific methods is beyond the scope of this book.

Calculating the Impact of Other Factors

Although not appropriate in all cases, sometimes it is possible to calculate the impact of factors (other than consulting) that influence a portion of the improvement and credit the consulting project with the remaining portion. In this approach, the consulting project takes credit for improvement that cannot be attributed to other factors.

An example will help explain the approach. In a consulting project to improve consumer loans for a large bank, a significant increase in consumer loan volume was generated after the consulting project was completed. Part of the increase in volume was attributed to consulting, and the remaining was due to the influence of other factors in place during the same time period. Two other factors were identified: an increase in sales promotion and declining interest rates, which caused an increase in consumer volume.

With regard to the first factor, as sales promotion increased, so did consumer loan volume. The impact of this factor was estimated using input from several internal experts in the marketing department. For the second factor, industry sources were used to estimate the relationship between increased consumer loan volume and lower interest rates. These two estimates together accounted for a modest percentage of increased consumer loan volume. The remaining improvement was attributed to the consulting project.

This method is appropriate when the other factors are easily identified and the appropriate mechanisms are in place to calculate their impact on the improvement. In some cases it is just as difficult to estimate the impact of other factors as it is the impact of consulting, leaving this approach less advantageous. This process can be very credible if the method used to isolate the impact of other factors is credible.

Estimates from Credible Sources

If analytical approaches will not work, then the next set of approaches is estimates of the program impact. A variety of different inputs can be used to provide estimates of how much of the improvement in a business measure is related to the consulting project. The challenge is to find the most credible sources to provide the data. The participants involved in the consulting project may be the most credible. Another possibility may be the managers of those participants, if they are active in the project, and still another is to use the senior management team, but only if they are familiar with all the factors that could affect the business performance measures. And finally, inputs from customers may be appropriate, but only if the customers can clearly see the factors.

Participant's Estimate of Impact

An easily implemented method for isolating the impact of consulting is to obtain information directly from the participants in the consulting. The effectiveness of this approach rests on the assumption that participants are capable of determining or estimating how much of a performance improvement is related to the consulting project. Because their actions have produced the improvement, participants may have an accurate input on the issue. They should know how much of the change was caused by implementing the consulting project. Although an estimate, this value will usually have considerable credibility with management because they know participants are at the center of the change or improvement. Participant estimation is obtained by asking participants the series of questions in Table 6-1 after describing the improvement. The credibility is enhanced with an error adjustment obtained through a confidence estimate. Table 6-2 illustrates this approach with an example of one participant's estimations.

Table 6-1 Questions for Participant Estimation

Please define the performance measure improved by the consulting project.

How much improvement has been realized since the consulting project began?

What other factors have contributed to this improvement in performance?

What percentage of this improvement can be attributed to the consulting project?

What is the basis for this estimation?

What confidence do you have in this estimate, expressed as a percentage (0% = no confidence; 100% = complete confidence)?

What other individuals or groups could estimate this percentage?

Table 6-2 Example of a Participant's Estimation

Factor That Influenced Improvement	% of Improvement Caused By	Confidence Expressed as a %	Adjusted % of Improvement Caused By
Consulting project	60%	80%	48%
System changes	15%	70%	10.50%
Environmental changes	5%	60%	3%
Compensation changes	20%	80%	16%
Other	__%	__%	__%
Total	100%		

Participants who do not provide information on these questions are excluded from the analysis. Also, erroneous, incomplete, and extreme information should be discarded before analysis. To be conservative, the confidence percentage can be factored into the values to provide an error adjustment. The confidence percentage is actually a reflection of the error in the estimate. An 80 percent confidence level equates to a potential error range of 20 percent, which could be plus or minus. With this approach, the level of confidence is multiplied by the estimate using the lower side of the range. In the example, the participant allocates 60 percent of the improvement to the consulting project and is 80 percent confident in the estimate. The confidence percentage is multiplied by the estimate to develop a usable consulting factor value of 48 percent. This adjusted percentage is then multiplied by the actual amount of the improvement (post-project minus pre-project value) to isolate the portion attributed to consulting. The adjusted improvement is now ready for conversion to monetary values and, ultimately, for use in the return on investment calculation.

Although it produces only an estimate, this approach does have considerable accuracy and credibility. Five adjustments are effectively applied to the participant estimation to reflect a conservative approach:

1. Participants who do not provide usable data are assumed to have experienced no improvements.
2. Extreme data and incomplete, unrealistic, and unsupported claims are omitted from the analysis, although they may be included in the intangible benefits.
3. For short-term consulting projects, it is assumed that no benefits from the consulting intervention are realized after the first year of implementation. For long-term projects, more than one year of consulting benefits is used in the analyses.
4. The improvement amount is adjusted by the amount directly related to the consulting project, expressed as a percentage.
5. The confidence level, expressed as a percentage, is multiplied by the improvement value to reduce the amount of the improvement by the potential error.

When presented to senior management, the result of an impact study is perceived to be an understatement of a project's success. The data and the process are considered to be credible and accurate. As an added enhancement to this method, the next level of management above the participants may be asked to review and approve the estimates from participants.

An example will illustrate the process for participant estimates. A restaurant chain initiated a consulting project on performance improvement. The project was designed to improve the operating performance of the restaurant chain using a variety of tools to establish measurable goals for employees, provide performance feedback, measure progress toward goals, and take action to ensure that goals are met. As part of the project, each store manager developed an action plan for improvement. Managers also learned how to convert measurable improvements to an economic value for the restaurant. Their action plans could focus on any improvement and converted the improvements to either cost savings or restaurant profits. Some of the improvement areas were inventory, food spoilage, cash shortages, employee turnover, absenteeism, and productivity.

As part of the follow-up evaluation, each action plan was thoroughly documented, showing results in quantitative terms that were converted to monetary values. The annual monetary value for each improvement for each participant was calculated from action plans. Realizing that other factors could have influenced the improvement, managers were asked to estimate the percent of the improvement that resulted directly from the consulting project (the contribution estimate). Restaurant managers are aware of factors that influence costs and profits and usually know how much of an improvement is traceable to the project. Each manager was asked to be conservative and provide a confidence estimate for the above contribution estimate (100 percent = certainty; 0 percent = no confidence). The results are shown in Table 6-3.

Estimation of the consulting impact can be calculated using the conservative approach of adjusting for the contribution of the project and adjusting for the error of the contribution estimate. For example, the $5,500 annual value for labor savings is adjusted to consider the consulting contribution ($5,500 × 60% = $3,300). Next, the value is adjusted for the confidence in this value ($3,300 × 80% = $2,640). The conservative approach yields an overall improvement of $68,386. Participant 5 did not submit a completed

Table 6-3 Estimates of Consulting Project Impact from Participants

Participant	Total Annual Improvement (Dollar Value)	Basis Measure	Contribution Estimate from Manager (Participants)	Confidence Estimate from Manager (Participants)	Conservative Value Reported
1	$5,500	Labor savings	60%	80%	$2,640
2	15,000	Employee turnover	50%	80%	6,000
3	9,300	Absenteeism	65%	80%	4,836
4	2,100	Daily shortages	90%	90%	1,701
5	0	—— Cash	——	——	——
6	29,000	Employee turnover	40%	75%	8,700
7	2,241	Inventory adjustments	70%	95%	1,490
8	3,621	Overtime	100%	80%	2,897
9	21,000	Employee turnover	75%	80%	12,600
10	1,500	Food spoilage	100%	100%	1,500
11	15,000	Labor savings	80%	85%	10,200
12	6,310	Accidents	70%	100%	4,417
13	14,500	Absenteeism	80%	70%	8,120
14	3,650	Productivity	100%	90%	3,285
Total	$128,722				$68,386

action plan and was discarded from the analysis, although the costs are still included in the ROI calculation, based on guiding principle #6.

Another interesting observation emerges from this type of analysis. When the average of the three largest improvements is compared with the average of the three smallest values, important information is revealed about the potential for return on investment. If all the participants in the consulting project had focused on high-impact improvements, a substantially higher ROI could have been achieved. This information can be helpful to the management group, whose support is often critical to the success of consulting. While an impressive ROI is refreshing, a potentially greater ROI is outstanding.

This process has some potential disadvantages. It produces only an estimate, and consequently, it may not have the accuracy desired by some consultants and clients. Also, the input data may be unreliable since some participants may be incapable of providing these types of estimates. They may not be aware of the factors that contributed to the results.

Several advantages make this technique attractive. It is a simple process, easily understood by most participants and by others who review evaluation data. It is inexpensive, takes very little time and analysis, and thus results in an efficient addition to the evaluation process. Also, these estimates originate from a credible source—the individuals who produced the improvement, the consulting participants.

The advantages of this approach seem to offset the disadvantages. Isolating the effects of a consulting project will never be precise, and this estimate may be accurate enough for most clients and management groups. The process is appropriate when the participants are managers, supervisors, team leaders, sales associates, engineers, and other professional or technical employees.

Manager's Estimate of Impact

In lieu of, or in addition to, participant estimates, the participants' managers may be asked to provide input as to the extent of the consultant's role in producing improved performance. In some settings, the participants' managers may be more familiar with the other factors influencing performance. Consequently, they may be better equipped to provide estimates of impact. The recommended questions to ask managers, after describing the improvement caused by the participants, are provided in Table 6-4.

These questions are essentially the same ones described in the participant's questionnaire. Manager estimates should be analyzed in the same manner as participant estimates. To be more conservative, actual estimates

Table 6-4 Questions for Manager's Estimate

Are you closely involved in the consulting project?

Please define the performance measure improved by the consulting project.

How much did the measure change since the consulting project began?

What other factors could have contributed to this success?

What percentage of the improvement in performance measures of the participant resulted from the intervention program?

What is the basis for this estimate?

What is your confidence in this estimate, expressed as a percentage (0% = no confidence; 100% = complete confidence)?

What other individuals or groups would know about this improvement and could estimate this percentage?

---

are adjusted by the confidence percentage. When participants' estimates have also been collected, the decision of which estimate to use becomes an issue. If there is some compelling reason to think that one estimate is more credible than the other, then it should be used. If both are credible, the most conservative approach is to use the lowest value and include an appropriate explanation. This is guiding principle #4.

In some cases, upper management may estimate the percent of improvement that should be attributed to a project. After considering additional factors that could contribute to an improvement, such as technology, procedures, and process changes, management applies a subjective factor to represent the portion of the results that should be attributed to the consulting project. While this is quite subjective, the individuals who provide or approve funding for the consulting usually accept the input. Sometimes their comfort level with the process is the most important consideration.

This approach of using management estimates has the same disadvantages as participant estimates. It is subjective and, consequently, may be viewed with skepticism by some. Also, managers may be reluctant to participate or may be incapable of providing accurate impact estimates. In some cases, they may not know about other factors that contributed to the improvement.

The advantages of this approach are similar to the advantages of participant estimation. It is simple, inexpensive, and enjoys an acceptable degree of credibility because it comes directly from the managers of individuals who are involved in the consulting project. When combined with participant estimation, the credibility is enhanced considerably. Also, when factored by the level of confidence, its value further increases.

Customer Estimates of Consulting Impact

Another helpful approach in some narrowly focused situations is to solicit input on the impact of consulting directly from customers. In these situations, customers are asked why they chose a particular product or service or to explain how their reaction to the product or service has been influenced by individuals or systems involved in the consulting project. This technique often focuses directly on what the consulting project is designed to improve. For example, after a customer service consulting project involving customer response was conducted for an electric utility, market research data showed that the percentage of customers who were dissatisfied with response time was reduced by 5 percent when compared to market survey data before the consulting project. Since response time was reduced by the consulting project and no other factor contributed to the reduction, the 5 percent reduction in dissatisfied customers was directly attributable to the consulting project.

Routine customer surveys provide an excellent opportunity to collect input directly from customers concerning their reaction to an assessment of a new or improved product, service, process, or procedure. Pre- and post-data can pinpoint the changes related to an improvement driven by a consulting project.

When collecting customer input, it is important to link it with the current data collection methods and avoid creating new surveys or feedback mechanisms if at all possible. This measurement process should not add to the data collection systems. Customer input could, perhaps, be the most powerful and convincing data if they are complete, accurate, and valid.

Expert Estimation of Consulting Impact

External or internal experts can sometimes estimate the portion of results that can be attributed to a consulting intervention. When using this technique, experts must be carefully selected based on their knowledge of the process, program, and situation. For example, an expert in quality might be able to provide estimates of how much change in a quality measure can be attributed to a consulting intervention and how much can be attributed to other factors.

An example will illustrate this process. Omega Consultants provides consulting services to the banking industry and implements sales consulting projects in a variety of settings. Utilizing control group arrangements, Omega determined that a typical project would generate a 30 percent increase in sales volume three months after implementation. Given this value, implementation should result in a 30 percent improvement in another financial institution with a similar target audience and a similar need. Although the situations may vary considerably, this is a very rough estimate that may be used in comparisons. If more than 30 percent was achieved, the additional amount could be due to factors other than the consulting. Experts, consultants, or researchers are usually available for almost any field. They bring their experience with similar situations into the analysis.

This approach does have disadvantages. It will be inaccurate unless the project and setting in which the estimate is made are quite similar to the project in question. Also, this approach may lose credibility because the estimates come from external sources and may not necessarily involve those who are close to the process.

This process has an advantage in that it is a quick source of input from a reputable expert or independent consultant. Sometimes top management will place more confidence in external experts than in its own internal staff.

Using the Techniques

With all these techniques available to isolate the impact of consulting, selecting the most appropriate techniques for a specific project can be difficult. Some techniques are simple and inexpensive, while others are more time consuming and costly. When attempting to make the selection decision, the following factors should be considered:

- Feasibility of the technique
- Accuracy of the technique
- Credibility of the technique with the target audience
- Specific cost to implement the technique
- Amount of disruption to normal work activities as the technique is implemented
- Participant, staff, and management time needed for the particular technique

Multiple techniques or multiple sources of data input should be considered since two sources are usually better than one. When multiple sources are utilized, a conservative method is recommended for combining the inputs. A conservative approach builds credibility and acceptance. The target audience should always be provided with explanations of the process and the various subjective factors involved. Multiple sources allow an organization to experiment with different strategies and build confidence with a particular technique. For example, if management is concerned about the accuracy of participants' estimates, a combination of a control group arrangement and participants' estimates could be attempted to check the accuracy of the estimation process.

It is not unusual for the ROI of a consulting project to be extremely large. Even when a portion of the improvement is allocated to other factors, the numbers are still impressive in many situations. The audience should understand that, although every effort is made to isolate the impact, it is still a figure that is not precise and may contain error. It represents the best estimate of the impact given the constraints, conditions, and resources available. Chances are it is more accurate than other types of analysis regularly used in other functions within the organization.

Final Thoughts

This chapter presents a variety of techniques for isolating the effects of consulting. The techniques represent the most effective approaches to address this issue and are used by some of the most progressive organizations. Too often, results are reported and linked with the consulting project without any attempt to isolate the portion that can be attributed to consulting. If professionals in the consulting field are committed to improving their image as well as meeting their responsibility for obtaining results, this issue must be addressed early in the process for all major projects. The next chapter focuses on converting data to money, another challenge for consultants.

How to Convert Business Measures to Monetary Values

Iᴛ's ɴoᴛ ᴀ ɴᴜᴍʙᴇʀ, does it mean as much? For most of today's leading consultants, they are learning that the answer is "no." Transforming or converting data into monetary values is an essential step in calculating the return on investment for a consulting assignment. Many consulting projects stop with a tabulation of business results. While these results are important, it is more valuable to convert the positive outcomes into monetary values and weigh them against the cost of consulting. This is the ultimate level in the five-level evaluation framework, presented in Chapter 2. This chapter explains how leading consultants are moving beyond simply tabulating business results to developing monetary values used in calculating ROI.

Consulting project results include both tangible and intangible measures. Intangible measures are the benefits directly linked to a consulting project that cannot or should not be converted to monetary values. These measures are often monitored after the consulting project has been completed. Although they are not converted to monetary values, they are still an important part of the evaluation process.

Why Convert Data to Monetary Values?

The answer to this question is not always clearly understood by some consultants. A consulting project could be labeled a success without converting to monetary values, just by using business impact data showing the amount of change directly attributed to the project. For example, an improvement in production, waste, cycle time, customer satisfaction, or employee engagement could represent a significant improvement linked directly to consulting. For some projects this may be sufficient. However, if the client desires more insight into the impact data or return on investment calculation with the actual monetary benefits compared to the costs, then this extra step of converting data to monetary values will be necessary. Sometimes the monetary value has more impact on the client than just the change in the number itself. For example, consulting project success in terms of a reduction of 10 customer complaints per month may not seem to be significant. However, if the value of a customer complaint had been determined to be $3,000, this change equates to an annual value of at least $36,000—a more impressive improvement.

The Five Key Steps to Convert Data to Money

Before describing specific techniques to convert both hard and soft data to monetary values, there are five general steps that should be completed for each data item.

1. **Focus on a unit of measure.** First, define a unit of measure. For output data, the unit of measure is one item produced, one service provided, one project completed, or one sale consummated. Time measures might include one hour of cycle time, or one minute of customer-response time. The unit is usually expressed in minutes, hours, or days. Quality is a common measure, with a unit being defined as one error, one reject, one customer complaint, or one reworked item. Soft data measures vary, with a unit of improvement representing such things as one conflict, a one-point change in the customer satisfaction index, or one point on the employee engagement survey.

2. **Determine the value of each unit.** Place a value (V) on the unit identified in the first step. For measures of production, quality, cost, and time, the process is relatively easy. Most organizations maintain records or reports that can pinpoint the cost of one unit of production, or one defect. Soft data are more difficult to convert to money. For example, the value of one customer complaint or a one-point change in employee engagement is often difficult to determine. The techniques described in this chapter provide an array of approaches for making this conversion.

When more than one value is available, the most credible or the lowest value is used in the calculation.

3. **Calculate the change in performance data.** Calculate the change in output data after the effects of the consulting project have been isolated from other influences. The change (Δ) is the performance improvement, measured as hard or soft data, that is directly attributed to consulting. The value may represent the performance improvement for an individual, a team, a group of participants, or several groups of participants.

4. **Determine an annual amount for the change.** Annualize the Δ value to develop a total change in the performance data for at least one year (ΔP). Using annual values has become a standard approach for organizations seeking to capture the benefits of many consulting projects, although the benefits may not remain constant through the entire year. First-year benefits are used even when the consulting project is considered to be short term. This approach is considered conservative. (Note: For long-term projects, multiple years would be used.)

5. **Calculate the annual value of the improvement.** Arrive at the total value of improvement by multiplying the annual performance change (ΔP) by the unit value (V) for the complete group in question. For example, if one group of participants is involved in a consulting project being evaluated, the total value will include total improvement for all participants in the group. This value for annual project benefits is then compared to the cost of consulting, usually with the ROI formula presented in Chapter 1.

An example taken from a team-building consulting project at a manufacturing plant describes the five-step process of converting data to monetary values. This project was developed and implemented after the initial needs assessment and analysis revealed that a lack of teamwork was causing an excessive number of labor grievances. Thus, the actual number of grievances resolved at Step 2 in the four-step grievance process was selected as an output measure. Table 7-1 shows the steps taken in assigning a monetary value to the data, arriving at a total consulting impact of $546,000.

Several strategies for converting data to monetary values are available. Some are appropriate for a specific type of data or data category, while others may be used with virtually any type of data. The consultant's challenge is to select the strategy that best suits the situation. These strategies are presented next, beginning with the most credible approach.

Table 7-1 An Example Illustrating the Steps for Converting Data to Monetary Values

---

Setting: Team-Building Consulting Project in a Manufacturing Plant

Step 1	**Focus on a unit of measure.**
	One grievance reaching Step 2 in the four-step grievance resolution process.
Step 2	**Determine the value of each unit.**
	Using internal experts (i.e., the labor relations staff), the cost of an average grievance was estimated to be \$6,500, when time and direct costs were considered ($V = \$6{,}500$).
Step 3	**Calculate the change in performance data, Δ.**
	Six months after the project was completed, total grievances per month reaching Step 2 declined by 10. Seven of the 10 reductions were related to the consulting project, as determined by first-level managers (isolating the effects of the consulting project).
Step 4	**Determine an annual amount for the change, ΔP.**
	Using the six-month value of seven grievances per month yields an annual improvement of 84 ($\Delta P = 84$).
Step 5	**Calculate the annual value of the improvement, ΔPV.**
	Annual value = $\Delta P \times V$
	$= 84 \times \$6{,}500$
	$= \$546{,}000$

Standard Monetary Values

Most hard data items (output, quality, costs, and time) have standard values developed, because these are often the measures that matter to the organization. They reflect problems, and their conversion to monetary values shows their impact on the operational and financial well-being of the organization.

For the last two decades, quality programs have typically focused only on the cost of quality. Organizations have been obsessed with placing a value on mistakes or the payoff from avoiding these mistakes. This assigned value—the standard cost of an item—is one of the critical outgrowths of the quality management movement.

In addition, a variety of process improvement programs—such as reengineering, reinventing the corporation, transformation, and continuous process improvement—have included a component in which the cost of a particular measure is determined.

Finally, the development of a variety of cost control, cost containment, and cost management systems—such as activity-based costing—has forced organizations, departments, and divisions to place costs on activities and, in some cases, relate those costs directly to the revenues or profits of the organization. The following discussion describes how measures of output, quality, and time can be converted to standard values.

How Much Is a Widget Worth? Converting Output Data

When a consulting project produces a change in output, the value of the increased output can usually be determined from the organization's accounting or operating records. For organizations operating on a profit basis, this value is typically the marginal profit contribution of an additional unit of production or service provided. For example, an assembly team within a major appliance manufacturer is able to boost the production of small refrigerators after an operations consulting project. The unit of improvement is the operating margin of one refrigerator. For organizations that are nonprofit or in the public sector, this value is usually reflected in the savings accumulated when an additional unit of output is realized for the same input resources. For example, in the visa section of a government office, an additional visa application is processed at no additional cost in terms of resources. Thus, an increase in output translates into a cost savings equal to the unit cost of processing a visa application.

The formulas and calculations used to measure this contribution depend on the type of organization and the status of its record keeping. Most organizations have standard values readily available for performance monitoring and setting goals. A standard value is defined as a value that has been previously developed and is accepted by the managers involved in the functional area where the consulting project takes place.

The benefit of converting output data to money using standard values is that these calculations are already available for the most important data items. Perhaps no area has as much experience with standard values as the sales and marketing area. Table 7-2 shows a sampling of the sales and marketing measures that are often calculated and reported as standard values.

What Does Quality Cost? Calculating the Standard Cost of Quality

Because many consulting projects are designed to increase quality, the consulting staff must find a value of the improvement in certain quality measures. Quality and the cost of quality are important issues in most manufacturing and service firms. In recent years it has worked its way into governments (the U.S. Department of Defense), nongovernment organizations (the United Nations),

Table 7-2   Standard Values in Sales and Marketing

Metric	Definition	Converting Issues
Sales	The sale of the product or service is recorded in a variety of different ways: by product, by time period, by customer.	This data must be converted to monetary value by applying the profit margin for a particular sales category.
Profit margin (%)	Price – cost/cost for the product, customer, time period.	Factored to convert sales to monetary value-add to the organization.
Unit margin	Unit price less the unit cost.	This shows the value of incremental sales.
Channel margin	Channel profits as a percent of channel selling price.	This would be used to show the value of sales through a particular marketing channel.
Retention rate	The ratio of customers retained to the number of customers at risk of leaving.	The value is the saving of money necessary to acquire a replacement customer.
Churn rate	The ratio of customers leaving compared to the number who are at risk of leaving.	The value is the saving of money necessary to acquire a new customer.
Customer profit	The difference between the revenues earned from and the cost associated with the customer relationship during the specified period.	The monetary value added is the profit obtained from customers. It all goes to the bottom line.
Customer value lifetime	The present value of the future cash flows attributed to the customer relationship.	Bottom line; as customer value increases, it adds directly to the profits. Also, as a new customer is added, the incremental value is the customer lifetime average.
Cannibalization rate	The percentage of the new product sales taken from existing product lines.	This is to be minimized, as it represents an adverse effect on existing product, with the value added being the loss of profits due to the sales loss.

Metric	Definition	Converting Issues
Workload	Hours required to service clients and prospects.	This includes the salaries, commissions, and benefits from the time the sales staff spends on the workloads.
Inventories	The total amount of product or brand available for sale in a particular channel.	Since inventories are valued at the cost of carrying the inventory, space, handling, and the time value of money, insufficient inventory is the cost of expediting the new inventory or lost sales because of the inventory outage.
Market share	Sales revenue as a percentage of total market sales.	Actual sales are converted to money through the profit margins. This is a measure of competitiveness.
Loyalty	The length of time the customer stays with the organization, the willingness to pay a premium, and the willingness to search.	This is calculated as the additional profit from the sale or the profit on the premium.

Adapted from *Marketing Metrics: 50+ Metrics Every Executive Should Master* by Paul W. Farris, Neil T. Bendle, Phillip E. Pfeifer, and David J. Ribstein. (Upper Saddle River, NJ: Wharton School Publishing, 2006), pp. 46–47.

and nonprofits (American Cancer Society). The beginning point in these analyses is to calculate the cost of poor quality. For some quality measures, the task is easy. For example, if quality is measured with the defect rate, the value of the improvement is the cost to repair or replace the product. The most obvious cost of poor quality is the scrap or waste generated by mistakes. Defective products, spoiled raw materials, and discarded paperwork are all the result of poor quality. Scrap and waste translate directly into a monetary value. In a production environment, for example, the cost of a defective product is the total cost incurred to the point the mistake is identified, minus the salvage value.

Employee mistakes and errors can cause expensive rework. The most costly rework occurs when a product is delivered to a customer and must be returned for correction. The cost of rework includes both labor and direct costs. In some organizations, rework costs can be as much as 35 percent of operating expenses.

In one example, a consulting project focused on customer service provided by dispatchers in an oil company. The dispatchers processed orders and scheduled deliveries of fuel to service stations. A measure of quality that was considered excessive was the number of pullouts experienced. A pullout occurs when a delivery truck cannot fill an order for fuel at a service station. The truck must then return to the terminal for an adjustment to the order. This is essentially a rework item. The average cost of a pullout was previously developed by tabulating the cost from a sampling of actual pullouts. The elements in the tabulation included driver time, the cost of using the truck for adjusting the load, the cost of terminal use, and estimated administrative expenses. This value became the accepted standard to use in the consulting project.

Organizations have made great progress in developing standard values for the cost of quality. Quality costs can be grouped into six major categories: internal failure, penalties, external failure, analysis, prevention, and customer dissatisfaction.

1. **Internal failure** represents costs associated with problems detected prior to product shipment or service delivery. Typical costs are reworking, retesting, and redesigning.
2. **Penalty costs** are the fines and charges incurred as a result of unacceptable quality.
3. **External failure** refers to problems detected after product shipment or service delivery. Typical cost items are technical support, complaint investigation, remedial upgrades, and fixes.
4. **Analysis costs** are the expenses involved in determining the condition of a particular product or service. Typical costs are testing and related activities, such as product-quality audits.
5. **Prevention costs** include actions to avoid unacceptable product or service quality. These efforts include service quality administration, inspections, process studies, and improvements.
6. **Customer dissatisfaction** is perhaps the costliest element of inadequate quality. In some cases, serious mistakes result in lost business. Customer dissatisfaction is difficult to quantify, and arriving at a monetary value may be impossible using direct methods. The judgment and expertise of sales, marketing, or quality managers are usually the best resources to draw upon in measuring the impact of dissatisfaction.

More and more quality experts are measuring customer and client dissatisfaction with the use of market surveys. However, other strategies discussed in this chapter may be more appropriate for the task.

How Much Is Time Worth? Converting Employee Time Using Compensation

Decreasing the workforce or employee time is a common objective for consulting projects. In a team environment, a project may enable the team to complete tasks in less time or with fewer people. A major consulting project could effect a reduction of several hundred employees. On an individual basis, consulting may be designed to help professional, sales, supervisory, and managerial employees save time in performing daily tasks. The value of the time saved is an important measure, and determining the monetary value is a relatively easy process.

The most obvious timesavings are from reduced labor costs for performing the same amount of work. The monetary savings are found by multiplying the hours saved by the labor cost per hour. For example, after participating in personal time-management consulting, participants estimated that they saved an average of 74 minutes per day, worth $31.25 per day or $7,500 per year. The timesavings were based on the average salary plus benefits for the typical participant. This is a benefit only if the time saved is used in other productive ways.

The average wage, with a percent added for employee benefits, will suffice for most calculations. However, employee time may be worth more. For example, additional costs in maintaining an employee (office space, furniture, telephones, utilities, computers, secretarial support, and other overhead expenses) could be included in calculating the average labor cost. Thus, the average wage rate may escalate quickly. In a large-scale employee reduction effort, calculating additional employee costs may be more appropriate for showing the value. However, for most projects, the conservative approach of using salary plus employee benefits is recommended.

Beyond reducing the labor cost per hour, timesavings can produce benefits such as improved service, avoidance of penalties for late projects, and additional profit opportunities. These values can be estimated using other methods discussed in this chapter.

A word of caution is in order when developing timesavings. Savings are realized only when the amount of time saved translates into a cost reduction or profit contribution. Even if a consulting project produces savings in manager time, a monetary value is not realized unless the manager puts the additional time to productive use. Having measures estimate the percentage of time saved that is devoted to productive work may be helpful, if it is followed up with a request for examples of how the extra time was used. If a team-based project sparks a new process that eliminates several hours of work each day, the actual savings will be based on a reduction in staff or overtime pay. Therefore, an important preliminary step in developing timesavings is determining whether the expected savings will be genuine.

Finding Standard Values

Standard values are available for all types of data. Virtually every major department will develop standard values that are monitored for that area. Typical functions in a major organization where standard values are tracked include:

- Finance and accounting
- Production
- Operations
- Engineering
- IT
- Administration
- Sales and marketing
- Customer service and support
- Procurement
- Logistics
- Compliance
- Research and development
- HR

Thanks to enterprise-wide systems software, standard values are commonly integrated and made available for access by a variety of people. In some cases, access may need to be addressed to ensure that the data can be obtained by those who require them.

When Standard Values Are Not Available

When standard values are not available, several alternative strategies for converting data to monetary value are available. Some are appropriate for a specific type of data or data category, while others may be used with virtually any type of data. The challenge is to select the strategy that best suits the situation.

How about Cost Savings? Using Historical Costs from Records

Sometimes historical records contain the value of a measure and reflect the cost (or value) of a unit of improvement. This strategy relies on identifying the appropriate records and tabulating the actual cost components for the item in question. For example, a large construction firm initiated a consulting project to improve safety. The consulting project improved several safety-related performance measures, ranging from government fines to total workers' compensation costs. By examining the company's records using one year of data, the average cost for each safety measure was obtained.

This value included the direct costs of medical payments, insurance payments and premiums, investigation services, and lost-time payments to employees, as well as payments for legal expenses, fines, and other direct services. The amount of time to investigate, resolve, and correct the issues was also factored. This time involved not only the health and safety staff but other personnel as well. In addition, the costs of lost productivity, disruption of services, morale, and dissatisfaction were estimated to obtain a full cost. The corresponding costs for each item were then developed.

Managers often use marginal cost statements and sensitivity analyses to pinpoint values associated with changes in output. If the data are not available, the consulting staff must initiate or coordinate the development of appropriate values. In one case involving a commercial bank, a consulting project in the consumer-lending department produced increased consumer loan volume. To measure the ROI for the project, it was necessary to calculate the value (profit contribution) of one additional consumer loan. Although a standard value existed (the profit on a loan), the client wanted the consultant to calculate this value independently—for comparison with the current value. This was relatively easy to calculate from the bank's records. As shown in Table 7-3, the calculation involved several components.

Table 7-3 Loan Profitability Analysis

Profit Component	Unit Value
Average loan size	$15,500
Average loan yield	9.75%
Average cost of funds (including branch costs)	5.50%
Direct costs for consumer lending	0.82%
Corporate overhead	1.61%
Net profit per loan	1.82%

The first step was to determine the yield, which was available from bank records. Next, the average spread between the cost of funds and the yield realized on the loan was calculated. For example, the bank could obtain funds from depositors at 5.5 percent on average, including the cost of operating the branches. The direct costs of making the loan—such as advertising expenditures and salaries of employees directly involved in consumer lending—were subtracted from this difference. Historically, these direct costs amounted to 0.82 percent of the loan value. To cover overhead costs for other corporate functions, an additional 1.61 percent was subtracted from the value. The remaining 1.82 percent of the average loan value represented the bank's profit margin on a loan. The good news in this situation and with this approach is that these calculations are already completed for the most important data items and are reported as standard values.

Historical cost data are usually available for most hard data. Unfortunately, this is generally not true for soft data, so other techniques explained in this chapter must be employed to convert the data to monetary values.

- **Time.** Sorting through databases, cost statements, financial records, and activity reports takes a tremendous amount of time—time that may not be available for the project. It is important to keep this part of the process in perspective. Converting data to monetary values is only one step in the ROI Methodology. Time needs to be converted.
- **Availability.** In some cases, data are not available to show all of the costs for a particular item. In addition to the direct costs associated with a measure, an equal number of indirect or invisible costs may be present that cannot be obtained easily.
- **Access.** Compounding the problems of time and availability is access. Monetary values may be needed from a system or record set that is under someone else's control. In a typical implementation, the project leader may not have full access to cost data. Cost data are more sensitive than other types of data and are often protected for a number of reasons, including competitive advantage. Therefore, access can be difficult and sometimes is even prohibited unless an absolute need to know can be demonstrated.
- **Accuracy.** Finally, the need for accuracy is this analysis should not be overlooked. A measure provided in current records may appear to be based on accurate data, but this may be an illusion. When data are calculated, estimations are involved, access to certain systems is denied, and different assumptions are made (all of which can be compounded by different definitions of systems, data, and measures). Because of

these limitations, the calculated values should be viewed as suspect unless means are available to ensure that they are accurate.

Calculating monetary value using historical data should be done with caution and only when these two conditions exist:

- The sponsor has approved the use of additional time, effort, and money to develop a monetary value from the current records and reports.
- The measure is simple and can be found by searching only a few records.

Otherwise, an alternative method is preferred.

Is There an Expert in the House?
Using Input from Internal and External Experts

When converting data items for which historical cost data are not available, it might be feasible to consider input from experts on the processes. Internal experts provide the cost (or value) of one unit of improvement. Individuals with knowledge of the situation and the respect of management are often the best prospects for expert input. They must understand the processes and be willing to provide estimates—as well as the assumptions made in arriving at the estimates. Most experts have their own methodology for developing these values. So when requesting their input, it is important to explain the full scope of what is needed, providing as many specifics as possible.

Internal experts are everywhere. They may be found in:

- The obvious department (quality)
- The place that produces and sends the report (human resources)
- The job title (customer complaint coordinator)

The key is to find them. Asking may help.

In the example described earlier of the team building intervention designed to reduce grievances, other than actual settlement costs and direct external expenses, the company had no records reflecting the total cost of grievances (i.e., there were no data for the time required to resolve a grievance). Therefore, an educated estimate was needed. The manager of labor relations, who had credibility with senior management and thorough knowledge of the grievance process, provided a cost estimate. He based it on the average settlement when a grievance was lost; the direct costs related to the grievances (arbitration, legal fees, printing, research); the estimated amount of supervisor and employee time expended; and a factor for reduced morale. This internal estimate, although not a precise figure, was appropriate for the analysis and had credibility with management.

If internal experts have a strong bias regarding the measure or are not available, external experts are sought. External experts should be selected based on their experience with the unit of measure. Fortunately, many experts are available who work directly with important measures such as employee attitudes, customer satisfaction, turnover, absenteeism, and grievances. They are often willing to provide estimates of the costs (or value) of these intangibles.

External experts—including consultants, professionals, or suppliers in a particular area—can also be found in obvious places. For example, the costs of accidents can be estimated by the worker's compensation carrier, or the costs of a grievance may be estimated by the labor attorney defending the company in grievance transactions. The process of locating an external expert is similar to the external database search, which is described later.

The credibility of the expert, whether internal or external, is a critical issue if the monetary value of a measure is to be reliable. Foremost among the factors behind an expert's credibility is the individual's experience with the process or measure at hand. Ideally, he or she would work with this measure routinely. Also, the person must be unbiased. Experts should be neutral in connection with the measure's value and should have no personal or professional interest in it.

In addition, the credentials of external experts—published works, degrees, and other honors or awards—are important in validating their expertise. Many of these people are tapped often, and their track records can and should be checked. If their estimate has been validated in more detailed studies and was found to be consistent, this can serve as a confirmation of their qualifications in providing such data.

Are There Data Available? Using Values from External Databases

For some soft data, it may be appropriate to use cost (or value) estimates based on the research of others. This technique taps external databases that contain studies and research projects focusing on the cost of data items. Fortunately, there are many databases that include cost studies of many data items related to consulting projects, and most are accessible through the Internet. Data are available on the cost of turnover, absenteeism, grievances, accidents, and even customer satisfaction. The difficulty is in finding a database with studies or research appropriate to the current intervention. Ideally, the data should come from a similar setting in the same industry, but that is not always possible. Sometimes data on all industries or organizations are sufficient, perhaps with some adjustments to suit the project at hand.

An example illustrates the use of this process. A consulting project was designed to reduce turnover of branch managers in a financial services company. To complete the evaluation and calculate the ROI, the cost of turnover was needed. To develop the turnover value internally, several costs were identified, including the expense of recruiting, employment processing, orientation, training new managers, lost productivity while training new managers, quality problems, scheduling difficulties, and customer satisfaction problems. Additional costs include the time regional managers spend working with turnover issues and, in some cases, the costs of litigation, severance, and unemployment. Obviously, these expenses are significant. Most consultants do not have time to calculate the cost of turnover, particularly if it is needed for a one-time event, such as evaluating a consulting project. In this example, turnover cost studies in the same industry for the same job group placed the value at about one and a half times the average annual salary of employees. Most turnover cost studies report the cost of turnover as a multiple of annual base salaries. In this example, management decided to be conservative and adjust the value downward to equal the average base salary of branch managers.

An example will illustrate the power of an external database. Employee turnover is very costly and difficult to capture on a precise basis, especially considering the indirect and direct costs of turnover. One excellent database for finding studies on a fully loaded cost of turnover is a database called ERIC, Educational Resources Information Center, which is available at www.eric.ed.gov or any public or university library.

Table 7-4 shows selected turnover cost data captured from dozens of impact studies arranged by job category and ranging from entry-level, non-skilled jobs to middle managers. The cost of turnover is shown as a percentage of base pay of the job group. The ranges are rounded off. The costs include exit cost of departing employees, recruiting, selection, orientation, initial training, wages and salaries while in training, lost productivity, quality problems, customer dissatisfaction, loss of expertise/knowledge, supervisor's time for turnover, and temporary replacement costs. The sources for these studies follow these general categories:

- Industry and trade magazines where the costs have been reported for a specific job within the industry.
- Practitioner publications in general management, human resources management, human resources development, and performance improvement.

Table 7-4 Turnover Costs Summary

Job Type/Category	Turnover Cost Ranges as a Percent of Annual Wage/Salary
Entry level—hourly, nonskilled (such as fast food worker)	30 to 50
Service/production workers—hourly (such as courier)	40 to 70
Skilled hourly (e.g., machinist)	75 to 100
Clerical/administrative (e.g., scheduler)	50 to 80
Professional (e.g., sales representative, nurse, accountant)	75 to 125
Technical (e.g., computer technician)	100 to 150
Engineers (e.g., chemical engineer)	200 to 300
Specialists (e.g., computer software designer)	200 to 400
Supervisors/team leaders (e.g., section supervisor)	100 to 150
Middle managers (e.g., department manager)	125 to 200

Notes:

Percentages are rounded to reflect the general range of costs from studies. Costs are fully loaded to include all of the costs of replacing an employee and bringing him or her to the level of productivity and efficiency of the former employee.

- Academic and research journals where professors, consultants, and researchers publish the results of their work on retention.
- Independent studies conducted by organizations and not reported in the literature, but often available on a Web site or through membership arrangements. These are research-based groups supported by professional and management associations.
- In addition, a few consulting firms develop and report on cost impact studies.

This list is not intended to be all-inclusive, but it illustrates the availability of current studies and the tremendous cost associated with turnover. Unfortunately, finding a study in a specific field is sometimes difficult and can tax the search skills of even the most adept Internet browser.

Is There a Connection with Other Data? Linking with Other Measures

When standard values, records, experts, and external studies are not available, a feasible approach might be developing a relationship between the measure in question and some other measure that may be easily converted to a monetary value. This involves identifying existing relationships, if possible, that show a strong correlation between one measure and another with a standard value.

For example, another useful technique is finding a correlation between a customer satisfaction measure and another measure that can easily be converted to a monetary value. Figure 7-1 shows a relationship between customer satisfaction and customer loyalty. Many organizations are able to show a strong connection between these two measures. Furthermore, there is often a strong correlation between customer loyalty—which may be defined in terms of customer retention or defection—and the actual profit per customer. By connecting these two variables, it becomes possible to estimate the actual value of customer satisfaction by linking it to other measures.

Another example, a classical relationship depicted in Figure 7-2, shows a correlation between increasing job satisfaction and employee turnover. In a consulting project designed to improve job satisfaction, a value is needed for changes in the job satisfaction index. A predetermined relationship showing the correlation between improvements in job satisfaction and reductions in

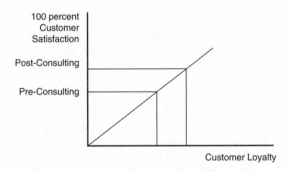

Figure 7-1   The relationship between customer satisfaction and loyalty.

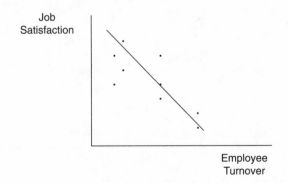

Figure 7-2   The relationship between job satisfaction and employee turnover.

turnover can link the changes directly to turnover. Using standard data or external studies, the cost of turnover can easily be developed as described earlier. Thus, a change in job satisfaction is converted to a monetary value or, at least, an approximate value. It is not always exact because of the potential for error and other factors, but the estimate is sufficient for converting the data to monetary values.

In some situations, a chain of relationships may be established to show the connection between two or more variables. In this approach, a measure that may be difficult to convert to a monetary value is linked to other measures that, in turn, are linked to measures that a value can be placed on. Ultimately these measures are traced to a monetary value often based on profits. Figure 7-3 shows the model used by Sears, one of the world's largest retail chains.[1] The model connects job attitudes (collected directly from the employees) to customer service, which is directly related to revenue growth. The rectangles in the chart represent survey information, while the ovals represent hard data. The shaded measurements are collected and distributed in the form of Sears's total-performance indicators.

As the model shows, a 5-point improvement in employee attitudes will drive a 1.3-point improvement in customer satisfaction. This, in turn, drives a 0.5 percent increase in revenue growth. Thus, if employee attitudes at a

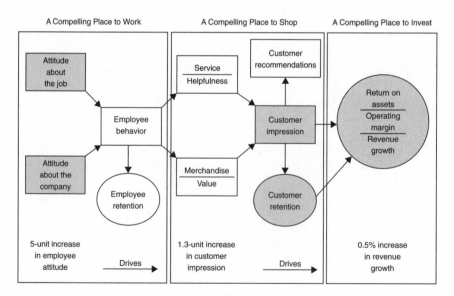

Figure 7-3   Sears model of service-profit chain.
Source: Copyright 1998. President and Fellows of Harvard College 1998. Used with permission.

local store improved by 5 points, and previous revenue growth was 5 percent, the new revenue growth would be 5.5 percent.

These links between measures, often called the service-profit chain, create a promising way to place monetary values on hard-to-quantify measures. This research practice is significant, and the opportunity for customized work is tremendous.

Who Can Estimate This Value? Using Estimates from Participants

In some cases, participants in the consulting project should estimate the value of soft data improvement. This technique is appropriate when participants are capable of providing estimates of the cost (or value) of the unit of measure improved through consulting solutions. When using this approach, participants should be provided clear instructions, along with examples of the type of information needed. The advantage of this approach is that the individuals closest to the improvement are often capable of providing the most reliable estimates of its value.

An example illustrates this process. A group of supervisors was involved in a major absenteeism reduction project. Successful application of the project should produce a reduction in absenteeism. To calculate the ROI for the project, it was necessary to determine the average value of one absence in the company. As is the case with most organizations, historical records for the cost of absenteeism were not available. Experts were not available, and external studies were sparse for this particular industry. Consequently, supervisors (consulting participants) were asked to estimate the cost of an absence. In a focus group format, each participant was asked to recall the last time an employee in his or her work group was unexpectedly absent and describe what was necessary to adjust to the absence. Because the impact of an absence varies considerably from one employee to another within the same work unit, the group listened to all explanations. After reflecting on what actions to take when an employee is absent, each supervisor was asked to provide an estimate of the average cost of an absence in the company.

Although some supervisors are reluctant to provide estimates, with prodding and encouragement they usually will. The group's values are averaged, and the result is the cost of an absence that may be used in evaluating the project. Although this is an estimate, it is probably more accurate than data from external studies, calculations using internal records, or estimates from experts. And because it comes from supervisors who wrestle with the issue daily, it will carry weight with senior management.

Can the Managers Estimate the Value?
Using Estimates from the Management Team

In some situations, participants in a consulting project may be incapable of placing a value on the improvement. Their work may be so far removed from the output of the process that they cannot reliably provide estimates. In these cases, the team leaders, supervisors, or managers of participants may be capable of providing estimates. Consequently, they may be asked to provide a value for a unit of improvement linked to the intervention.

For example, a consulting project involving customer service representatives was designed to reduce customer complaints. While the project resulted in a reduction of complaints, the value of a single customer complaint was still needed to determine the value of improvement. Although customer service representatives had knowledge of some issues surrounding customer complaints, they could not gauge the full impact, so their managers were asked to provide a value. In other situations, managers are asked to review and approve participants' estimates and confirm, adjust, or discard the values.

In some cases, senior management provides estimates of the value of data. With this approach, senior managers interested in the consulting project are asked to place a value on the improvement based on their perception of its worth. This approach is used when it is difficult to calculate the value or when other sources of estimation are unavailable or unreliable. An example illustrating this strategy is a hospital chain that was attempting to improve patient satisfaction with a consulting project. Patient satisfaction was measured by an external customer satisfaction index. To determine the value of the consulting project, the value of a unit of improvement (one point on the index) was needed. Because senior managers were interested in improving the index, they were asked to provide input on the value of a unit before the project was completed. In a routine executive meeting, each senior manager and hospital administrator was asked to describe what it means for a hospital when the index increases. After some explanation and discussion using a focus group format, each individual was asked to provide an estimate of the monetary value gained when the index moves one point. Although the senior managers were initially reluctant to provide the information, with some encouragement they did. The values were then averaged. The result was a monetary estimate of one unit of improvement, and it was used in calculating the projected and actual benefits of the project. Although this process is subjective, it does have the benefit of ownership from senior executives—the same executives who approved the consulting budget.

Should We Estimate This?
Using Consultant Staff Estimates

The final strategy for converting data to monetary values is using consultants' estimates. Using all the available information and experience, the consultants most familiar with the situation provide estimates of the value. For example, a consulting project for an international oil company was designed to reduce dispatcher absenteeism and improve other performance problems. Unable to identify a value using other strategies, the consultants estimated the cost of an absence to be $200. This value was then used in calculating the savings for the reduction in absenteeism that followed the consulting project. Although the staff may be capable of providing accurate estimates, this approach is sometimes perceived as being biased. It should therefore be used only when other approaches are unavailable or inappropriate.

When Conversion Should Not Be Pursued:
The Intangible Benefits

Consulting project results include both tangible and intangible measures. Intangible measures are the benefits directly linked to a consulting project that cannot or should not be converted to monetary values. These measures are often monitored after the consulting project has been completed. Although they are not converted to monetary values, they are still an important part of the evaluation process. The range of intangible measures is almost limitless, and Table 7-5 lists common examples of these measures. This listing is not meant to imply that these measures cannot be converted to monetary values. In one study or another, each item has been monetarily quantified. However, in typical impact studies, these variables are considered intangible benefits.

Not all measures can or should be converted to monetary values. By design, some are captured and reported as intangibles. Although they may not be perceived as being as valuable as the quantifiable measures, intangibles are critical to the overall evaluation process. In some consulting projects, teamwork, job engagement, communications, image, and customer satisfaction may be more important than monetary measures. Consequently, these measures should be monitored and reported as part of the overall evaluation. In practice, every project, regardless of its nature, scope, and content, will produce intangible measures. The challenge is to identify them effectively and report them appropriately.

Table 7-5 Typical Intangible Measures Linked with Programs

- Job satisfaction
- Organizational commitment
- Climate
- Engagement
- Employee complaints
- Recruiting image
- Brand awareness
- Stress
- Leadership effectiveness
- Resilence
- Level of caring
- Career-mindedness
- Customer satisfaction
- Customer complaints
- Customer response time
- Teamwork
- Cooperation
- Conflict
- Decisiveness
- Communication

Where Do They Come From?

Intangible measures can be taken from different sources and at different times in the process, as depicted in Figure 7-4. They can be uncovered early in the process, during the needs assessment, and planned for collection as part of the overall data collection strategy. For example, one consulting project has several hard data measures linked to the project. An intangible measure, employee satisfaction, is identified and monitored with no plans to convert it to a monetary value. Thus, from the beginning, this measure is destined to be a nonmonetary benefit reported along with the ROI results.

A second opportunity to identify intangible benefits is to discuss the issue with clients or sponsors of the consulting project. Clients can usually identify the intangible measures they expect to be influenced by the project. For example, an environmental consulting project at a large multinational company was conducted, and an ROI analysis was planned. Consultants, participants, participants' managers, and senior executives identified potential intangible measures that were perceived to be influenced by the project, including corporate social

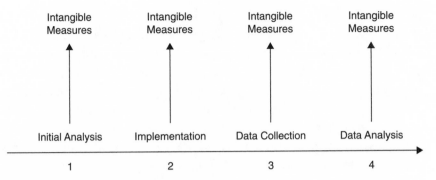

Figure 7-4 When intangibles are identified.

responsibility image, reputation, brand awareness, and eco-friendliness of the organization.

The third opportunity to identify intangible measures presents itself during data collection. Although the measure is not anticipated in the initial project design, it may surface on a questionnaire, in an interview, or during a focus group. Questions are often asked about other improvements linked to a consulting project, and participants usually provide several intangible measures for which there are no plans to assign a value. For example, in the evaluation of a new technology consulting project, participants (financial advisors) were asked what specifically had improved about their work area and relationships with customers as a result of the project. Participants provided more than a dozen intangible measures that managers attributed to the project.

The fourth opportunity to identify intangible measures is during data analysis and reporting, while attempting to convert data to monetary values. If the conversion loses credibility, the measure should be reported as an intangible benefit. For example, in a project to standardize procedures in a large nongovernment organization, timesavings were identified early in the process as a measure of the consulting success. A conversion to monetary values was attempted, but it lacked the accuracy and credibility needed. Consequently, timesavings were reported as an intangible benefit.

How Are Intangibles Analyzed?

For each intangible measure identified, there must be some evidence of its connection to the consulting project. However, in many cases no specific analysis is planned beyond tabulating responses. Early attempts to quantify intangible data sometimes result in aborting the entire process; thus, no further data analysis is conducted. In some cases, isolating the effects of the consulting project may be undertaken using one or more of the methods outlined in Chapter 6. This step is necessary when there is a need to know the specific amount of change in the intangible measure linked to the project. Intangible data often reflect improvement. However, neither the precise amount of improvement nor the amount of improvement directly related to consulting is usually identified. Since the value of this data is not included in the ROI calculation, intangible measures are not normally used to justify additional consulting or continuing an existing project. A detailed analysis is not necessary. Intangible benefits are viewed as additional evidence of the consulting success and are presented as supportive qualitative data.

Selecting the Techniques and Finalizing the Values

With so many techniques available, the challenge is selecting one or more strategies appropriate for the situation and available resources. It may be helpful to develop a table or list of values or techniques appropriate for the situation. Table 7-6 shows the common conversion process for a group of output measures in a manufacturing firm. This process could be expanded to other categories and tailored specifically to the organization.

Table 7-6 Common Measures and the Methods to Convert to Monetary Values

Output Measures	Example	Strategy	Comments
Production unit	One unit assembled	Standard value	Available in almost every manufacturing unit.
Service unit	Parts delivered on time	Standard value	Developed for most service providers when it is a typical service delivery unit.
Sales	Monetary increase in revenue	Margin (profit)	The profit from one additional dollar of sales is a standard item.
Market share	10% increase in market share in one year	Margin of increased sales	Standard for most units.
Productivity measure	10% change in productivity index	Standard value	This measure is very specific to the type of production or productivity measured. It may include per unit of time.

Selection Guidelines

The following guidelines may help determine the proper selection and finalize the values.

- **Use the technique appropriate for the type of data.** Some strategies are designed specifically for hard data, while others are more appropriate for soft data. Consequently, the type of data often dictates the strategy. Hard data, while always preferred, are not always available. Soft data are often required and, thus, must be addressed using appropriate strategies.
- **Move from most accurate to least accurate.** The strategies are presented in order of accuracy, beginning with the most accurate. Working down the list, each strategy should be considered for its feasibility in the situation. The strategy with the most accuracy is always recommended if it is feasible in the situation.
- **Consider availability and convenience.** Sometimes the availability of a particular source of data will drive the selection. In other situations, the convenience of a technique may be an important selection factor.
- **When estimates are sought, use the source with the broadest perspective on the issue.** The individual providing the estimate must be knowledgeable of the processes and the issues surrounding the value of the data.
- **Use multiple techniques when feasible.** Sometimes it is helpful to have more than one technique for obtaining values for the data. When multiple sources are feasible, they should be used to serve as comparisons or to provide additional perspectives. The data must be integrated using a convenient decision rule, such as the lowest value (guiding principle #4). A conservative approach must be taken.
- **Minimize the amount of time to use a technique.** As with other processes, it is important to keep the time invested in this phase to a minimum, so that the total effort for the ROI study does not become excessive. Some techniques can be implemented in less time than others. Too much time on this step may dampen otherwise enthusiastic attitudes about the process.

Apply the Credibility Test

The techniques presented in this chapter assume that each data item collected and linked with consulting projects can be converted to a monetary value. Although estimates can be developed using one or more strategies, the process of converting data to monetary values may lose credibility with the target audience, which may question its use in analysis. Highly subjective data, such as changes in employee attitudes or a reduction in the number of employee conflicts, are difficult to convert. The key question in making this determination is: "Could these results be presented to senior management with confidence?" If the process does not meet this credibility test, the data should not be converted to monetary values but, rather, listed as intangibles. Other data, particularly hard data items, may be used in the ROI calculation, leaving the highly subjective data expressed in intangible terms.

Review the Client's Needs

The accuracy of data and the credibility of the data conversion process are important concerns. Consultants sometimes avoid converting data because of these issues. They are more comfortable reporting that an intervention reduced absenteeism from 6 percent to 4 percent, without attempting to place a value on the improvement. They may assume that the client will place a value on the absenteeism reduction. Unfortunately, the target audience may know little about the cost of absenteeism and will usually underestimate the actual value of the improvement. Consequently, there should be some attempt to include this conversion in the ROI analysis.

Consider a Potential Management Adjustment

In organizations where soft data are used and values are derived with imprecise methods, senior management is sometimes offered the opportunity to review and approve the data. Because of the subjective nature of this process, management may factor (reduce) the data so that the final results are more credible. In one example, senior managers at Litton Industries adjusted the value for the benefits derived from implementing self-directed teams.

Consider an Adjustment for the Time Value of Money

Since an intervention investment is made in one time period and the return is realized at a later time, some organizations adjust consulting benefits to reflect the time value of money using discounted cash-flow techniques. The actual monetary benefits of the consulting project are adjusted for this time period. The amount of adjustment, however, is usually small when compared with the typical benefits of consulting projects.

Final Thoughts

In consulting interventions, money is an important value, but so are intangibles, which are crucial in reflecting the success of a consulting project. Consultants are striving to be more aggressive in defining the monetary benefits of a consulting project. Progressive consultants are no longer satisfied to simply report the business performance results from projects. Instead, they are taking additional steps to convert impact data to monetary values and weigh them against the consulting cost. In doing so, they achieve the ultimate level of evaluation: the return on investment. Additionally, consultants are concentrating on intangible measures because they add a unique dimension to the consulting report since most, if not all, projects involve intangible variables. This chapter presented several strategies used to convert business results to monetary values, offering an array of techniques to fit any situation and consulting project as well as exploring some of the most common intangible measures.

Costs and ROI

Monitoring the Costs of Consulting and Calculating ROI

W HEN THE MONETARY BENEFITS from Chapter 7 are combined with consulting costs, the ROI can be developed. This chapter outlines the specific costs that should be captured and economical ways in which they can be developed. One of the important challenges addressed in this chapter is deciding which costs should be tabulated and which should be estimated. In consulting, some costs are hidden and never counted. The conservative philosophy presented here is to account for all costs, direct and indirect. Several checklists and guidelines are also included in the chapter. The ROI calculation is presented with examples and interpretation.

The Importance of Costs and ROI

Monitoring the consulting costs is an essential step in developing the ROI calculation since it represents the denominator in the ROI formula. It is just as important to pay attention to costs as it is to benefits. In practice, however, costs are often more easily captured than benefits. Costs should be monitored in an ongoing effort to control expenditures and keep the project within budget. Monitoring cost activities not only reveals the status of expenditures, but also gives visibility to expenditures and influences the entire project team to spend wisely. And of course, monitoring costs in an ongoing fashion is much easier, more accurate, and more efficient than trying to reconstruct events to capture costs retrospectively.

As discussed in earlier parts of the book, ROI is becoming a critical measure demanded by many stakeholders, including clients and senior executives. It is the ultimate level of evaluation showing the actual payoff of the consulting project, expressed as a ratio or percentage and based on the same formula as the evaluation for other types of investment. Because of its perceived value and familiarity to senior management, it is now becoming a common requirement for consulting projects. When ROI is required or needed, ROI must be developed; otherwise it may be optional unless there is some compelling reason to take the evaluation to this level.

Developing Costs

The first step in monitoring costs is to define costs and explore critical issues about costs and their use. Several concerns about a cost-monitoring system are examined next. A good understanding of these issues can prevent problems later.

Costs Are Critical

Capturing costs is challenging because the numbers must be reliable and realistic. Although most organizations develop costs with much more ease than the monetary value of the benefits, the true cost of consulting is often an elusive figure even in some of the easiest projects. While the direct charges are usually easily developed and are part of the problem, it is more difficult to determine the indirect costs of a project. While the major costs are known up front, the hidden costs to the organization that are linked to the project are not usually detailed. To develop a realistic ROI, costs must be complete and credible. Otherwise, the painstaking difficulty and attention to the monetary benefits will be wasted because of inadequate or inaccurate costs.

Why Disclose All Costs?

Today, there is more pressure than ever before to report all consulting costs, or what is referred to as *fully loaded costs*. This takes the cost profile beyond the direct cost of consulting fees and expenses and includes the time that others are involved in the project, including their benefits and other overhead. For years, management has realized that there are many indirect costs of consulting. Now they are asking for an accounting of these costs.

Perhaps this point is best illustrated in a situation that recently developed in state government, where the state auditor examined the management controls of a large state agency. The agency prefers not to be identified. A portion of the audit focused on internal consulting costs. Costs tracked for a project usually focus on direct or "hard" costs and largely ignore the cost of time spent participating in or supporting the consulting project. The costs of participant time to prepare for and attend meetings with consultants are not tracked. For one consulting project, including the indirect costs raised the total consulting costs dramatically. The agency stated that the total two-year cost for the specific project was about $600,000. This figure included only direct, out-of-pocket costs to the consulting firm and, as such, was substantially less than the cost of the time spent by staff in preparing for and attending the various meetings, the facilities used for the project, and the coordination costs for the project. When the time involved was added to the cost of travel, meals, and lodging for participants involved in the consulting project, as well as the salaries and benefits of staff providing administrative and logistic support, the number came to $1.39 million. If the statewide average of 45.5 percent for employee benefits was also considered, the total indirect cost of staff time to prepare for, participate in, and support the project was $2 million, when facilities and coordination costs were added. Finally, when the agency's direct costs of $600,000 were added to the $2 million total indirect cost just noted, the total became more than $2.6 million.

The audit report suggested that the failure to consider all indirect or "soft" costs might expose the agency to noncompliance with the Fair Labor Standards Act (FLSA), particularly as the consulting spreads through the rank and file. Since the FLSA requires that such staff be directly compensated for overtime, it is not appropriate for the agency to ask employees to be involved in consulting activities and attend meetings on their own time. This situation may encourage false overtime reporting, skew overtime data, and/or increase the amount of uncompensated overtime.

While this case may be an extreme, it demonstrates that the cost of consulting is much more than direct expenditures, and some consultants are expected to report fully loaded costs in their projects.

Fully Loaded Costs

When using a conservative approach to calculating the ROI, it is recommended that consulting costs be fully loaded. With this approach, all costs that can be identified and linked to a particular consulting assignment are included. The philosophy is simple: for the denominator of the ROI equation, when in doubt, include it (i.e., if it is questionable whether a cost should be included, it is recommended that it be included, even if the cost guidelines for the organization do not require it). When an ROI is calculated and reported to target audiences, the process should withstand even the closest scrutiny in terms of its completeness and credibility. The only way to meet this test is to ensure that all costs are included. Of course, from a realistic viewpoint, if the controller or chief financial officer insists on not using certain costs, then it is best to leave them out.

The Danger of Reporting Costs without the Benefits

It is dangerous to communicate the costs of a consulting project without presenting benefits. Unfortunately, many organizations have fallen into this trap for years. Because costs can easily be collected, they are presented to management in ingenious ways, such as cost of the project, cost per employee involved, and cost per unit of product or service. While these may be helpful for efficiency comparisons, it may be troublesome to present them without benefits. When most executives review consulting costs, a logical question comes to mind: what benefit was received from the project? This is a typical management reaction, particularly when costs are perceived to be high.

In one organization, all of the costs associated with a major transformation-consulting project were tabulated and reported to the senior management team to let it know the total investment in the project. The total figure exceeded the perceived value of the project, and the executive group's immediate reaction was to request a summary of benefits (monetary and nonmonetary) derived from the complete transformation. The conclusion was that there were few, if any, economic benefits from the project. Consequently, future consulting projects were drastically reduced. While this may be an extreme example, it shows the danger of presenting only half of the equation. Because of this, some organizations have developed a policy of not communicating consulting cost data unless the benefits can be captured and presented along with the costs. Even if the benefits are subjective and intangible, they are included with the cost data. This helps to maintain a balance between the two issues.

Developing and Using Cost Guidelines

For some consulting groups, it may be helpful to detail the philosophy and policy on costs in guidelines for the consultants or others who monitor and report costs. Cost guidelines detail specifically which cost categories are included with consulting projects and how the data are captured, analyzed, and reported. Standards, unit cost guiding principles, and generally accepted values are included in the guidelines. Cost guidelines can range from a one-page brief to a hundred-page document in a large, complex organization. The simpler approach is better. When fully developed, cost guidelines should be reviewed and approved by the finance and accounting staff. The final document serves as the guiding force in collecting, monitoring, and reporting costs. When the ROI is calculated and reported, costs are included in a summary form or table, and the cost guidelines are referenced in a footnote or attached as an appendix.

Cost-Tracking Issues

The most important task is to define which specific costs are included in consulting project costs. This task involves decisions that will be made by consultants and usually approved by the client. If appropriate, the client's finance and accounting staff may need to approve the list.

Sources of Costs

It is sometimes helpful to first consider the sources of consulting costs. There are three major categories of sources, as illustrated in Table 8-1. The charges and expenses from the consulting firm will usually represent the latest segment of costs and are transferred directly to the client for payment. These are often placed in categories under fees and expenses. The second major cost category comprises those related expenses absorbed by the client organization—both direct and indirect. In many consulting projects, these costs are not identified but nevertheless reflect the cost of the consulting project.

Table 8-1 Sources of Costs

Source of Costs	Cost Reporting Issues
1. Consulting firm—fees and expenses	A Costs are usually accurate.
	B Variable expenses may be underestimated.
2. Client expenses—direct and indirect	A Direct expenses are usually not fully loaded.
	B Indirect expenses are rarely included in costs.
3. Other expenses, such as equipment and services	A Sometimes understated.
	B May lack accountability.

The third cost is the cost of payments made to other organizations as a result of the consulting project. These include payments directly to suppliers for equipment and services prescribed in the consulting project. The finance and accounting records should be able to track and reflect the costs from these three different sources, and the process presented in this chapter has the capability of tracking these costs as well.

Consulting Process Steps and Cost

Another way to consider consulting costs is in the characteristics of how the project unfolds. Figure 8-1 shows the specific functions of a complex consulting

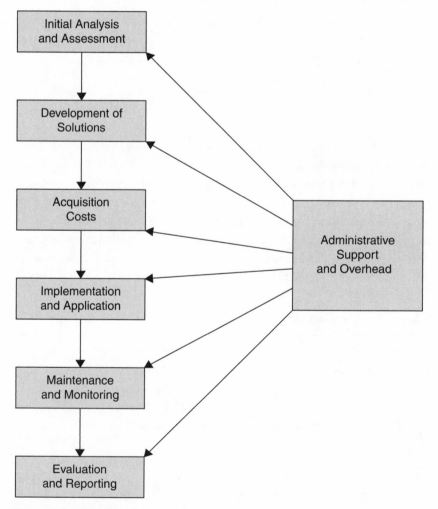

Figure 8-1   Costs based on consulting process steps.

assignment, beginning with the initial analysis and assessment and migrating to the evaluation and the reporting of the results. These are the functional process steps that were outlined earlier in the book and later in this chapter. They represent the typical flow of work. As a problem is addressed, a solution is developed or acquired and implemented in the organization. There are maintenance and monitoring processes usually put in place that will result in ongoing costs. The entire process is routinely reported to the client, and evaluation is undertaken to show the success of the project. There is also a group of costs that will support the process primarily from the client perspective, as these represent important administrative support and overhead costs. To be fair, the consulting project should be analyzed in these different categories, as will be described later in the chapter.

This may be a bit complex for consulting processes that are small in scope and involve only a few consultants—in some cases maybe only one consultant. In these situations, a more simplistic approach is taken following a simplified process flow described in Figure 8-2, which represents the consulting process reflected in fees, the direct cost of the expenses, and the client cost. These occur as the consultant allocates time and generates costs, and the client has some recurring or ongoing costs in the project. The important point is to consider costs as they occur naturally and systematically in the consulting intervention.

Prorated versus Direct Costs

Usually all costs related to a consulting project are captured and expensed to that project. However, some costs are prorated over a longer period of time. Equipment purchases, software development and acquisition, and the construction of facilities are all significant costs with a useful life that may extend beyond a specific consulting project. Consequently, a portion of these costs should be prorated to the consulting project. Using a conservative approach,

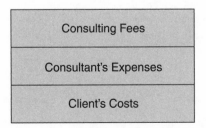

Figure 8-2 Simplified fully loaded costs.

the expected life of the consulting project is fixed. Some organizations will consider one year of operation for a simple project. Others may consider three to seven years. If there is some question about the specific time period to be used in the proration formula, the finance and accounting staff should be consulted, or appropriate guidelines should be developed and followed.

Employee Benefits Factor

Employee time is valuable, and when time is required on a consulting project, the costs must be fully loaded, representing total compensation. This means that the employee benefits factor should be included. This number is usually well known in the organization and is used in other costing formulas. It represents the cost of all employee benefits expressed as a percentage of payroll. In some organizations, this value is as high as 50 to 60 percent. In others, it may be as low as 25 to 30 percent. The average in the United States is about 38 percent.

Major Cost Categories

Table 8-2 shows the recommended cost categories for a fully loaded, conservative approach to estimating costs. In this table, there are four categories. The first is the cost that could be prorated from one consulting project to another. There are not many of these, but sometimes an item is purchased or

Table 8-2   Consulting Cost Categories

Cost Item	Prorated	Consulting Expenses	Client Proposal Costs	Client Expenses
A Initial analysis and assessment		✓		✓
B Design and development of project	✓	✓	✓	
C Acquisition costs	✓	✓	✓	
D Capital expenditures	✓			✓
E Application and implementation				
Salaries/benefits for consultant time		✓	✓	
Salaries/benefits for coordination time		✓		✓
Salaries/benefits for participant time		✓		✓
Consulting materials and supplies		✓	✓	
Travel/lodging/meals		✓	✓	✓
Use of facilities		✓		✓
F Maintenance and monitoring		✓	✓	✓
G Administrative support and overhead	✓			✓
H Evaluation and reporting		✓	✓	✓

equipment is acquired that will serve other purposes rather than just this consulting project. These would be prorated to other initiatives as well. The second column would be the direct charges to the consulting project, and these are the substantial costs, which are, by far, the largest costs for most projects. The third column is the expense absorbed by the consulting firm. These costs would be in the proposal, agreed to at the beginning of the project, and these are traditional costs of consulting. However, they may be less than the other costs. The last column is the cost to the client. For any consulting project, the client does have some involvement and some expenses. In some cases, they may be significant, and this table is an attempt to sort them out. The important part is to think of each project on its own, considering all possible costs.

Initial Analysis and Assessment

One of the most underestimated items is the cost of conducting the initial analysis and assessment. In a comprehensive project, this involves data collection, problem solving, assessment, and analysis. In some consulting projects, this cost is near zero because the project is launched without an appropriate assessment of need. However, as more consultants and clients place increased attention on needs assessment and analysis, this item will become a significant cost in the future. All costs associated with the analysis and assessment should be captured to the fullest extent possible. These costs include consulting time, direct expenses, and internal services and supplies used in the analysis.

Design and Development of the Project

One of the more significant items is the cost of designing and developing the solutions for a consulting project of the project itself. These costs include consulting time in both design and development and the purchase of supplies, technology, and other materials directly related to the project or solutions. As with needs assessment costs, design and development costs are usually fully charged to the project. However, in some situations, major expenditures may be prorated over several projects.

Acquisition Costs

In lieu of development costs, many organizations purchase hardware, software, equipment, or facilities from other sources to use directly or in a modified format. The acquisition costs for these projects include the purchase price, support materials, and licensing agreements. Many consulting projects have both acquisition costs and design and development costs.

Capital Expenditures

For expenses that represent significant investment, such as in a major remodeling of facilities, the purchase of a building, and purchases of major equipment, the expenses should be recorded as capital expenditures and allocated over a period of time. If the equipment, building, or facility is used for other projects, then the costs should be allocated over the different projects and only a portion captured for a particular assignment.

Application and Implementation Costs

Usually the largest cost segment in a consulting project is associated with implementation and delivery. Eight major categories are reviewed below:

1. **Salaries and benefits for consulting time.** This includes all of the charges for consultants assigned directly to the staff. This cost represents specific fees for the time they are involved in the project. These are direct charges only and are usually allocated directly from the consulting organization.

2. **Salaries and benefits for coordinators and organizers.** The salaries of those who implement the consulting project should be included. These are usually client staff members. If a coordinator is involved in more than one project, the time should be allocated to the specific project under review. If external facilitators are used, all expenses should be included in the project. The important issue is to capture all of the time of internal employees or external providers who work directly with the consulting project. The benefits factor should be included each time direct labor costs are involved. This factor is a widely accepted value, usually generated by the finance and accounting staff and in the 30 to 50 percent range.

3. **Participants' salaries and benefits.** The salaries plus employee benefits of consulting participants represent an expense that should be included. These client costs are significant and can be estimated using average or midpoint values for salaries in typical job classifications.

4. **Consulting materials and supplies.** Consulting materials and supplies, such as field journals, instructions, reference guides, case studies, job aids, and participant workbooks should be included in the

delivery costs, along with license fees, user fees, and royalty payments. CD-ROMs and supplies are also included in this category.

5. **Travel, lodging, and meals.** Direct travel and lodge costs for consultants, consulting participants, facilitators, coordinators, and managers are included. Entertainment and refreshments during the intervention are included as well.

6. **Use of facilities.** The direct cost for the use of facilities for the consulting project should be included. For external meetings, this is the direct charge from the conference center, hotel, or motel. If the meetings are conducted in-house, the conference room represents a cost for the organization, and the cost should be estimated and included—even if it is uncommon to include facilities costs in other reports. A commonsense approach should be taken with this issue. Charging excessively for space or charging for small intervals may be unreasonable, underscoring the need for formal guidelines.

Maintenance and Monitoring

Maintenance and monitoring involves routine expenses to maintain and operate a system process, procedure, or solution implemented as part of the consulting project. Although not always present, these represent ongoing expenses to make the new solution continue to work. These may involve staff members and additional expenses, and they may be significant for some projects.

Administrative Support and Overhead

Another charge is the cost of support and overhead, the additional costs of consulting not directly related to a particular project. The overhead category represents any consulting cost not considered in the above calculations. Typical items include the cost of administrative support, telecommunication expenses, office expenses, salaries of client managers, and other fixed costs. A rough estimate will usually suffice.

Evaluation and Reporting

Usually the total evaluation cost is included in consulting costs to compute the fully loaded cost. This category includes the cost of developing the evaluation strategy, designing instruments, collecting data, data analysis, report preparation and distribution, and communication of results. Cost categories include time, materials, purchased instruments, or surveys.

Basic ROI Issues

Before presenting the formulas for calculating the ROI, a few basic issues are described and explored. Because of the myths and mysteries about ROI, an adequate understanding of these issues is necessary to address the concerns.

Definitions

The term "return on investment" is occasionally misused, sometimes intentionally. In these situations, a very broad definition for ROI is offered to include any benefit from the consulting project. ROI is thus defined as a vague concept in which even subjective data linked to a project are included in the concept. In this book, the return on investment is more precise and is meant to represent an actual value by comparing consulting costs to monetary benefits. The two most common measures are the benefit/cost ratio and the ROI formula. Both are presented along with other approaches to calculate the return or payback.

For many years, consultants sought to calculate the actual return on investment for a consulting intervention. If the consulting intervention is considered an investment, not an expense, then it is appropriate to place consulting in the same funding process as other investments, such as the investment in equipment and facilities. Although the other investments are quite different, management often views them in the same way. Thus, it is critical to the success of the consulting intervention to develop specific values that reflect the return on the investment.

Annualized Values: A Fundamental Concept

All of the formulas presented in this chapter use annualized values so that the first-year impact of the consulting investment can be calculated. Using first-year annual values is becoming a generally accepted practice for developing the ROI in many organizations' projects (guiding principle #9). This approach is a conservative way to develop the ROI, since many short-term consulting projects have added value in the second or third year. For long-term consulting projects, first-year values are inappropriate, and longer time frames need to be used. For example, in an ROI analysis of a technology-consulting project involving software implementation at a hospital, a three-year time frame was used. However, for most short-term consulting projects that last only a few weeks, first-year values are appropriate.

ROI Measures

When selecting the approach to measure ROI, it is important to communicate to the target audience the formula used and the assumptions made in arriving at the decision to use it. This helps avoid misunderstandings and confusion surrounding how the ROI value was actually developed. Although several approaches are described in this chapter, two stand out as the preferred methods: the benefit/cost ratio and the basic ROI formula. These two approaches are described next, along with brief coverage of the other approaches.

Benefit/Cost Ratio

One of the earliest methods for evaluating a consulting project is the benefit/cost ratio. This method compares the monetary benefits of consulting intervention to the costs, using a ratio. In formula form, the ratio is:

$$BCR = \frac{\text{Consulting monetary benefits}}{\text{Consulting costs}}$$

In simple terms, the BCR compares the annual economic benefits of the consulting project to the cost of the consulting project. A BCR of 1 means that the benefits equal the costs. A BCR of 2, usually written as 2:1, indicates that for each dollar spent on consulting, two dollars are returned in benefits.

The following example will illustrate the use of the benefit/cost ratio. A consulting project designed to improve the efficiency of procurement was implemented at a nonprofit. In a follow-up evaluation, direct cost savings and timesavings were captured. The first-year payoff for the project was $439,480. The total fully loaded implementation cost was $141,500. Thus, the ratio was:

$$BCR = \frac{\$439,480}{\$141,500} = 3.1:1$$

For every dollar invested in consulting, 3.1 dollars in benefits were returned. There are no standards that constitute an acceptable benefit/cost ratio from the client perspective. A standard should be established within the organization, perhaps even for a specific type of consulting intervention. A 1:1 ratio (break-even status) is unacceptable for many consulting projects. In others, a 1.25:1 ratio is required, where the benefits are 1.25 times the cost of the consulting.

ROI Formula

Perhaps the most appropriate formula for evaluating consulting investments is net program benefits divided by cost. The ratio is usually expressed as a percentage when the fractional values are multiplied by 100. In formula form, the ROI becomes:

$$\text{ROI (\%)} = \frac{\text{Net consulting monetary benefits}}{\text{Consulting costs}} \times 100$$

Net benefits are consulting benefits minus costs. The ROI value is related to the BCR by a factor of one. For example, a BCR of 2.45 is the same as an ROI value of 145% (1.45 × 100%). This formula is essentially the same as the ROI in other types of investments. When a firm builds a new plant, the ROI is developed by dividing annual earnings by the investment. The annual earnings are comparable to net benefits (annual benefits minus the cost). The investment is comparable to fully loaded consulting project intervention costs, which represent the investment in consulting.

An ROI of 50 percent on a consulting project means that the costs are recovered and an additional 50 percent of the costs are reported as "earnings." A consulting ROI of 150 percent indicates that the costs have been recovered and an additional 1.5 times the costs are captured as "earnings." An example illustrates the ROI calculation. A quality-improvement consulting project was implemented in a small manufacturing company in Italy. The results of the project were impressive. Quality improvements alone yielded an annual value of €243,340. The total fully loaded costs for the project were €79,400. Thus, the return on investment becomes:

$$\text{ROI (\%)} = \frac{€243,340 - €79,400}{€79,400} \times 100 = 206\%$$

For each euro invested, this company received €2.06 in return after the costs of the consulting project had been recovered. Using the ROI formula essentially places consulting investments on a level playing field with other investments using the same formula and similar concepts. Key management and financial executives who regularly use ROI with other investments easily understand the ROI calculation.

While there are no generally accepted standards, some organizations establish a minimum requirement or objective for the ROI. This objective could be is based on the accepted ROI for other investments, which is determined by the cost of capital and other factors. When there is low inflation in a country, this value may be in the range of 10 to 15 percent. An ROI objective of 25 percent is set by many organizations in North America, Western Europe, and the Asia Pacific regions. This target value is usually greater than the percentage required for other types of investments. The rationale? The ROI process for consulting is still relatively new and sometimes involves subjective input, including estimations. Because of that, a higher standard is required or suggested, with 25 percent being the desired figure for most organizations. Sometimes it is helpful to let the client set the ROI objective with the caution of keeping it reasonable.

BCR/ROI Case Application

A large national domestic merchandise chain located in most major U.S. markets attempted to boost revenues by changing its point-of-sale automation system used by sales associates. The system, developed and implemented by a consulting firm, was a response to a clearly defined need to increase the quality of information obtained from the customer and to reduce customer response time by speeding up transactions. With a successful system, sales per associate would increase as each associate had more time to take care of more customers. Also, the customer marketing information would provide data to drive a new telemarketing program. The system was designed during the first four weeks of the consulting project, followed by three weeks of implementation at each of 10 pilot stores. The third part of the project addressed operations and maintenance issues.

The management team was willing to experiment with the application to see if it added enough value to overcome its investment. If not, the system could be modified to add value. Realistically, it was a good bet because there was a definite need and the system showed great promise.

ROI Analysis

Post-program data collection was accomplished using four methods. First, the average weekly sales per associate for each store were monitored (business performance monitoring of Level 4, output data). Second, a follow-up questionnaire was distributed to all sales associates three months after the implementation was completed to determine the success of the implementation (Level 3, application data). They also discussed techniques to overcome the barriers to program implementation. Third, routine customer survey data were examined to spot changes in customer satisfaction (Level 4, impact data). Finally, telemarketing records were analyzed to track the success of the telemarketing program (Level 4, sales data). The method used to isolate the effects of the consulting project was a control group arrangement. Ten store locations were identified for the control group and compared with 10 stores in the pilot group. The variables of store size, store location, customer traffic levels, previous store performance, and experience levels were used to match the two groups so that they could be as identical as possible.

The method to convert data to monetary values was a direct profit contribution of the increased output (sales). The profit obtained from additional sales was readily available and used in the calculation (standard data). Sales increases in the stores were converted, as well as the sales generated from the telemarketing program.

BCR and ROI Calculations

Although the consulting project was evaluated at all five levels, the emphasis of this study was on the Level 5 calculation. Level 1, 2, and 3 data either met or exceeded expectations. Table 8-3 shows the Level 4 data, which are the average weekly sales of both store groups after the consulting project. For convenience and at the request of management, a three-month follow-up period was used. A longer period of review was recommended. However, management wanted to make the decision to implement the project at other locations quickly if it appeared to be successful in the first three months of operation. Data for the first three weeks after implementation are shown in Table 8-3 along with the last three weeks of the evaluation period (weeks 13, 14, and 15). The data show what appears to be a significant difference in the two values of the pilot and control groups.

Table 8-3   Level 4 Data: Average Weekly Sales

	Post-Consulting Data	
Weeks after Implementation	10 Stores with New System	10 Stores without New System
1	$324,395	$321,755
2	329,447	323,101
3	332,932	322,982
13	399,785	334,871
14	407,612	336,775
15	411,374	340,439
Average for weeks 13, 14, 15	**$406,257**	**$337,362**

Table 8-4 Annualized Implementation Benefits

Average weekly sales (last three weeks) 10 stores with system	$406,257
Average weekly sales (last three weeks) 10 stores without system	337,362
Increase	68,895
Profit contribution (21% of stores' sales)	14,468
Total annual benefits ($14,468 × 52 weeks)	**$752,336**

Two steps are required to move from the Level 4 data to Level 5. In step one, Level 4 data must be converted to monetary values. In step two, the cost of the program must be tabulated. Table 8-4 shows the annualized benefits from the consulting project. The total benefit was $752,336. The profit contribution at the store level, obtained directly from the accounting department, was 21 percent. For every one dollar of additional sales attributed to the new system, only 21 cents would be considered to be the added value. At the corporate level, the number was even smaller, about 9 percent. First-year values were used to reflect the total impact of the consulting. Ideally, if the new system was effective, as indicated in the Level 3 evaluation, there should be some value for its use in years two, three, or perhaps even year five. However, for short-term consulting, only first-year values are used, requiring the investment to have an acceptable return in a one-year time period.

Table 8-5 shows the cost summary for this program. Costs are fully loaded, including data for all 10 stores. Since the consulting firm installs the system, there are no direct costs. With another contractor, the costs included prorated development costs as well as equipment and software costs. Client time included estimated salaries plus a 35 percent factor for employee benefits. Meeting facility costs were included in client expenses, although the company does not normally capture the costs when internal facilities are used, as was the case with this project. The estimated costs for maintenance and monitoring, overhead, and evaluation were also included. The total cost was rounded off to $581,000. Thus, the benefit/cost ratio became:

$$\text{BCR} = \frac{\$752,336}{\$581,000} = 1.29:1$$

And the return on investment became:

$$\text{ROI (\%)} = \frac{\$752,336 - \$581,000}{\$581,000} \times 100 = 29\%$$

Table 8-5 Cost Summary

New System in 10 Stores	
Initial analysis	$15,000
Development costs (prorated across all stores)	4,000
Software and equipment costs (prorated)	72,000
Consulting fees	220,000
Expenses for consultants	23,000
Client time (training/meetings)	101,000
Client expenses (one year)	17,000
Maintenance and monitoring (client and consultants; one year)	85,000
Overhead/support (estimated one year)	20,000
Evaluation and reporting	24,000
Total costs	**$581,000**

Thus, the consulting project had an excellent return on investment, exceeding the ROI objective of 20 percent in its initial trial run after three months of on-the-job application of the new system.

Other ROI Measures

In addition to the traditional ROI formula, described above, several other measures are occasionally used under the general heading of return on investment. These measures are designed primarily for evaluating other types of projects but sometimes work their way into consulting intervention evaluations.

Payback Period

The payback period is a common method for evaluating capital expenditures. With this approach, the annual cash proceeds (savings) produced by an investment are equated to the original cash outlay required by the investment to arrive at some multiple of cash proceeds equal to the original investment. Measurement is usually in terms of years and months. For example, if the cost savings generated from a consulting project are constant each year, the payback period is determined by dividing the total original cash investment (development costs, expenses, etc.) by the amount of the expected annual or actual savings. The savings represent the net savings after the program expenses are subtracted.

To illustrate this calculation, assume that an initial project cost is $100,000 with a three-year life. The annual net savings from the project is expected to be $40,000. Thus, the payback period becomes:

$$\text{Payback period} = \frac{\text{Total investment}}{\text{Annual savings}} = \frac{\$100,000}{\$40,000} = 2.5 \text{ years}$$

The project will "pay back" the original investment in 2.5 years. The payback period is simple to use but has the limitation of ignoring the time value of money. It has not enjoyed widespread use in evaluating consulting investments.

Discounted Cash Flow

Discounted cash flow is a method of evaluating investment opportunities in which certain values are assigned to the timing of the proceeds from the investment. The assumption, based on interest rates, is that money earned today is more valuable than money earned a year from now.

There are several ways of using the discounted cash flow concept to evaluate the consulting investment. The most common approach is the net present value of an investment. This approach compares the savings, year by year, with the outflow of cash required by the investment. The expected savings received each year is discounted by selected interest rates. The outflow of cash is also discounted by the same interest rate. If the present value of the savings should exceed the present value of the outlays after discounting at a common interest rate, the investment is usually considered acceptable by management. The discounted cash flow method has the advantage of ranking investments, but it becomes difficult to calculate.

Internal Rate of Return

The internal rate of return (IRR) method determines the interest rate required to make the present value of the cash flow equal to zero. It represents the maximum rate of interest that could be paid if all project funds were borrowed and the organization had to break even on the projects. The IRR considers the time value of money and is unaffected by the scale of the project. It can be used to rank alternatives and can be used to accept/reject decisions when a minimum rate of return is specified. A major weakness of the IRR method is that it assumes all returns are reinvested at the same internal rate of return. This can make an investment alternative with a high rate of return look even better than it really is and a project with a low rate of return look even worse. In practice, the IRR is rarely used to evaluate consulting investments.

Benefits of the ROI Process

Although the benefits of adopting the ROI evaluation may appear to be obvious, several important benefits can be derived from the implementation of ROI for consulting. Here is a brief summary of the advantages of the ROI process.

Measures the Contribution

With this methodology, consultants will know the contribution of a specific consulting project. The mystery of the success and contribution of consulting is removed. The ROI will show how the benefits, expressed in monetary values, compare to costs. It will determine if the project made a business contribution to the organization and if it was a good investment.

Develops Priorities for Consulting Projects

Sometimes there is a need to identify which projects are adding the most value. Calculating the ROI for different types of consulting projects will determine which projects contribute the most to the organization, allowing priorities to be established for high-impact projects.

Improves the Consulting Process

As with any evaluation system, an ROI study provides a variety of data to make adjustments and changes to the consulting process. Barriers and enablers to success are identified and used as a basis for changes and improvement. Because different data are collected at different levels, from different sources, the opportunity for improvement is significant. This allows for a complete analysis.

Focuses on Results

The ROI Methodology is a results-based process that focuses on outcomes from all consulting projects, even for those not targeted for an ROI calculation. The process enhances business alignment in the beginning and requires consultants and support teams to concentrate on measurable objectives (i.e., what the consulting is designed to accomplish). In short, the use of ROI drives results. Expectations are created with stakeholders. Key managers, who make the project successful, are involved in the project.

Builds Management Support for the Consulting Process

The ROI Methodology, when applied consistently and comprehensively, can convince the management group that consulting is an investment and not an expense. Managers will see consulting as making a viable contribution to their objectives, thus increasing the respect and support for the process. ROI use is an important step in building a partnership with senior management and increasing the commitment to consulting.

Alters Perceptions of Consulting

Routine ROI impact data, when communicated to a variety of target audiences, will alter perceptions about the value of consulting. Consulting participants, their leaders, and other client staff will view consulting as a legitimate function in the organization, adding value to work units, departments, and divisions. They will have a better understanding of the connection between consulting and results.

Simplifies a Complex Issue

As discussed in Chapter 2, developing the return on investment for consulting appears to be a complex issue. The approach presented in this book is to take a task that seems complex and simplify it by breaking it into small steps so it is understandable and acceptable to a variety of audiences. When each step is taken separately and issues are addressed for a particular topic, the decisions are made incrementally all the way through the process. This helps reduce the process to a simplified and manageable effort.

Final Thoughts

With the monetary benefits from Chapter 7, this chapter focuses on the costs of consulting and shows how costs and benefits come together to calculate ROI. This chapter presented the two basic approaches for calculating the return—the ROI formula and the benefit/cost ratio. Each has its own advantages and disadvantages. Costs should be fully loaded in the ROI calculation, but from a practical standpoint, some costs may be optional based on the organization's guidelines and philosophy. However, because of the scrutiny involved in ROI calculations, it is recommended that all costs be included, even if this goes beyond the requirements of the policy. The next chapter focuses on reporting results.

PART IV

Reporting and Implementation

Reporting Results

*How to Provide Feedback and
Results to the Client*

W ITH DATA IN HAND, what's next? Should the data be used to modify the project, change the process, show the contribution, justify new projects, gain additional support, or build goodwill? How should the data be presented? The worst course of action is to do nothing. Communicating results is as important as achieving results. Achieving results without communicating them is like planting seeds and failing to fertilize and cultivate the seedlings—the yield simply won't be as great. This chapter provides useful information to help present evaluation data to the various audiences using a variety of reporting methods.

Communicating Results: Key Issues

Communicating results is a critical issue in consulting. While it is important to communicate achieved results to interested stakeholders when the project is complete, it is also important to communicate throughout the consulting project. Routine communication ensures that information is flowing so adjustments can be made and so that all stakeholders are aware of the success and issues surrounding the consulting project.

Measurement and Evaluation Mean Nothing without Communication

As Mark Twain once said, "Collecting data is like collecting garbage—pretty soon we will have to do something with it." If success is measured and evaluation data are collected, they mean nothing unless the findings are communicated promptly to the appropriate audiences so they will be aware of what is occurring and can take action if necessary. Communication allows a full loop to be made from the project results to necessary actions based on those results.

Communication Is Necessary to Make Improvements

Because information is collected at different points during the process, the communication or feedback to the various groups that will take action is the only way adjustments can be made. Thus, the quality and timeliness of communication become critical issues for making necessary adjustments or improvements. Even after the project is completed, communication is necessary to ensure the target audience fully understands the results achieved and how the results could either be enhanced in future projects or in the current project, if it is still operational. Communication is the key to making these important adjustments at all phases of the project.

Communication Is Necessary to Explain Contributions

The contribution of the consulting project involves the six major types of outcome measures, a confusing issue at best. The varied target audiences will need a thorough explanation of the results. A communication strategy including techniques, media, and the overall process will determine the extent to which they understand the contribution. Communicating results, particularly with business impact and ROI, can quickly become confusing for even the most sophisticated target audiences. Communication must be planned and implemented with the goal of making sure the audiences understand the full contribution.

Communication Is a Sensitive Issue

Communication is one of those important issues that can cause major problems. Because the results of an intervention can be closely linked to the political issues in an organization, communication can upset some individuals while pleasing others. If certain individuals do not receive the information or it is delivered inconsistently from one group to another, problems can quickly surface. Not only is it an understanding issue, it is also a fairness, quality, and political correctness issue to make sure communication is properly constructed and effectively delivered to all key individuals who need the information.

A Variety of Target Audiences Need Different Information

Because there are so many potential target audiences for receiving communication on the success of a consulting project, it is important for the communication to be tailored directly to their needs. A varied audience will command varied needs. Planning and effort are necessary to make sure the audience receives all of the information it needs, in the proper format, and at the proper time. A single report for all audiences may not be appropriate. The scope, size, media, and even the actual information of different types and different levels will vary significantly from one group to another, making the target audience the key to determining the appropriate communication process.

Communication Must Be Timely and Consistent

Usually, consulting results should be communicated as soon as they are known. From a practical standpoint, it may be best to delay the communication until a convenient time, such as the publication of the next client newsletter or the next general management meeting. Questions about timing must be answered. Is the audience ready for the results in light of other things that may have happened? Is it expecting results? When is the best time for having the maximum effect on the audience? Are there circumstances that dictate a change in the timing of the communication? The timing and content of the communication should be consistent with past practices. A special communication at an unusual time during the consulting intervention may provoke suspicion. Also, if a particular group, such as top management, regularly receives communication on consulting outcomes, it should continue receiving communication—even if the results are not positive. If some results are omitted, it might leave the impression that only positive results are reported.

Communication Should Be Unbiased and Humble

It is important to separate fact from fiction and accurate statements from opinions. Various audiences may accept communication from consultants with skepticism, anticipating biased opinions. Boastful statements sometimes turn off recipients, and most of the content is lost. Observable, believable facts carry far more weight than extreme or sensational claims. Although such claims may get an audience's attention, they often detract from the importance of the results.

Collectively, these reasons make communication a critical issue, although it is often overlooked or underestimated in consulting interventions. This chapter builds on this important issue and shows a variety of techniques for accomplishing all types of communication for various target audiences.

Analyzing the Need for Communication

Because there may be many reasons for communicating results, the rationale should be tailored to the organization on the specific project, the setting, and the unique needs. The results are communicated in three broad categories: projected results, early feedback, and complete results. Here are the most common reasons:

1. **To secure approval for the consulting project and allocate resources of time and money.** The initial communication is in the proposal, where the anticipated results, projected ROI, or value proposition are reported to secure project approval. This communication may not have very much data but rather anticipates what is to come.
2. **To stimulate desire in participants to be involved in the project.** Ideally, consulting participants want to be involved in the consulting project if they have an option. Projected results will pique their interest in the project and the assignment, and they will show participants the importance of the project.
3. **To gain support for the project and its objectives.** Project support is needed from a variety of groups. Projected results and early feedback are needed to build the necessary support to make the project work successfully.
4. **To prepare participants for the consulting project.** It is necessary for those most directly involved in the project, the consulting participants, to be prepared for assignments, roles, and responsibilities that will be required of them as they bring success to the project.
5. **To secure agreement on the issues, solutions, and resources.** As the project begins, it is important for all those directly involved to have some agreement and understanding of the important elements

and requirements surrounding the project. Projected results and early feedback may help with this issue.

6. **To enhance results throughout the project and the quality of future feedback.** Early feedback is designed to show the status of the project and to influence decisions, seek support, or communicate events and expectations to the key stakeholders. In addition, it will enhance both the quality and quantity of information as stakeholders see the feedback cycle in action.

7. **To drive action for improvement in the consulting project.** Early feedback is designed as a process improvement tool to effect changes and improvements as the needs are uncovered and project stakeholders make suggestions. Complete results will be used to make improvements going forward and for similar projects in the future.

8. **To underscore the importance of measuring results.** Some individuals need to understand the importance of measurement and evaluation and see the need for having important data on different measures. Early feedback and complete results will help with this issue.

9. **To show the complete results of consulting and the approach used to measure it.** Perhaps the most important communication is the results of all six types of measures, communicated to the client and other appropriate individuals so they have a full understanding of the success or shortcomings of the project. Several individuals on the client team and support staff need to understand the techniques used in measuring results. In some cases, these techniques may be transferred internally to use with other projects. In short, these individuals need to understand the soundness and theoretical framework of the process used.

10. **To demonstrate accountability for client expenditures.** For those individuals who fund projects, there is the need for accountability. These ultimate clients must understand the approach of the consultant or the consulting firm to show value. This ensures accountability for expenditures on the project.

11. **To stimulate interest in the consulting firm's products.** From a consulting firm's perspective, some communications are designed to create interest in all of the products and services based on the results obtained by the current products or processes. From a consulting firm's perspective, it is important to build a database of successful projects to use in convincing others that the consulting process can add value.

12. **To build credibility for the consulting firm, its techniques, and the finished products**. Communicating a balanced set of data with recommendations will enhance the reputation of the consulting firm, based on the approach taken and the results achieved.

The reasons for communicating results are plentiful, and because there may be others, the list should be tailored to the project and situation.

Planning the Communication

Any successful activity must be carefully planned for it to produce the maximum results. This is certainly true when communicating the results of consulting projects. Planning is necessary to ensure that each audience receives the proper information at the right time and that appropriate actions are taken. Several issues are important in planning the communication of results.

Communication Policy Issues

Client and consulting firm policy issues will influence the content medium, duration, and timing of communication. Some policies may exist; others may need to be developed. Internally, the client may have policies for communicating results as part of an overall policy on consulting projects. The consulting firm may have a policy as part of the results-based approach to consulting. Seven different areas will need some attention as the policies are developed or followed:

1. **What will actually be communicated?** The types of information communicated throughout the consulting project must be detailed. In addition to the six types of data from the ROI process model, the overall progress of the consulting intervention may be a topic of communications as well.
2. **When will the data be communicated?** With communications, timing is critical. If adjustments in the project need to be made, the information should be communicated quickly so that swift actions can be taken.
3. **How will the information be communicated?** Preferences for specific types of communication media may exist. For example, some organizations prefer to have written documents sent out as reports, while others prefer face-to-face meetings, and still others want electronic communications used much as possible.

4. **The location for communication.** Some prefer that the communication take place close to the consulting project, others prefer client offices, and still others prefer the consulting firm's facilities. The location can be an important issue in terms of convenience and perception.

5. **Who will communicate the information?** Will the consultants, an independent person, or an individual on the client team communicate the information? The person communicating must have credibility so that the information is believable.

6. **The target audience.** Identify specific target audiences that should always receive information and others that will receive information when appropriate.

7. **The specific actions that are required or desired.** When information is presented, in some cases no action is needed; in others, changes are desired and sometimes even required.

Collectively, these seven issues will frame the policy for communication as a whole. If a policy does not exist, perhaps it should be created.

Planning the Communication for the Entire Project

When a project is approved, the communication plan is usually developed. This details how specific information is developed and communicated to various groups and the expected actions. In addition, this plan details how the overall results will be communicated, the time frames for communication, and the appropriate groups to receive information. The client and consultant need to agree on the extent of detail in the plan. Additional information on this type of planning is provided later.

Communicating the Complete Results

The third type of plan is aimed at presenting the results of an impact study. This occurs when a major consulting project is completed and the detailed and complete results are known. One of the major decisions is to determine who should receive the results and in what form. This is more specialized than the plan for the entire project because it involves the final study from the project. Table 9-1 shows the communication plan for a consulting project for stress reduction. Teams were experiencing high levels of stress. Through a variety of activities and job changes, stress began to diminish among the teams. The same process was made available to other teams who were experiencing similar symptoms.

Table 9-1 Consulting Project Communication Plan

Communication Document	Communication Targets	Distribution Method
Complete report with appendixes (75 pages)	• Client team • Consulting team • Team manager	Distribute and discuss in a special meeting
Executive summary (8 pages)	• Senior management in the business units • Senior corporate management	Distribute and discuss in routine meeting
General-interest overview and summary without the actual ROI calculation (10 pages)	• Participants	Mail with letter
General-interest article (1 page)	• All employees	Publish in company publication
Brochure highlighting project, objectives, and specific results	• Other team leaders with an interest in the project • Other clients	Include with other marketing materials

Five different communication pieces were developed for different audiences. The complete report was an ROI impact study, a 75-page report that served as the historical document for the project, distributed after a live meeting with the ultimate client. It went to the client, the consulting team, and the managers of each of the teams involved in the studies. An executive summary, a much smaller document, went to some of the higher-level executives. A general-interest overview and summary without the ROI calculation went to the participants. A general-interest article was developed for company publications, and a brochure was developed to show the success of the consulting project. That brochure was used in marketing the same process internally to other teams and served as additional marketing material for the consulting firm. This detailed plan may be part of the overall plan for the consulting assignment but may be fine-tuned during the actual consulting process.

Selecting the Audience for Communications

The potential target audiences to receive information on consulting results are varied in terms of job levels and responsibilities. Determining which groups will receive a particular communication piece deserves careful thought, as problems can arise when a particular group receives inappropriate information or when another is omitted altogether.

Understanding the Potential Audience

When approaching a particular audience, the following questions should be asked about each potential group:

- Are they interested in the project?
- Do they really want to receive the information?
- Has someone already made a commitment to provide information?
- Is the timing right for this audience?
- Are they familiar with the project?
- How do they prefer to have results communicated?
- Do they know the consultants? The consulting firm?
- Are they likely to find the results threatening?
- Which medium will be most convincing to this group?

For each target audience, three actions are needed. First, the consultants should get to know and understand the target audience. Next, the consultants should find out what information is needed and why. Each group will have its own needs relative to the information desired. Some will want detailed information while others will want brief information. Rely on the input from others to determine audience needs. Finally, the consultants should try to understand audience bias. Each will have a particular bias or opinion. Some will quickly support the results, whereas others may be against them or be neutral. The staff should be empathetic and try to understand differing views. With this understanding, communications can be tailored to each group. This is especially critical when the potential exists for the audience to react negatively to the results.

Basis for Selecting the Audience

A sound basis for proper audience selection is to analyze the reason for communication, as discussed in an earlier section. Table 9-2 shows common target audiences and the basis for selecting the audience.

Perhaps the most important audience is the client or client team. This group (or individual) initiates the project, reviews data, selects the consultant, and weighs the final assessment of the effectiveness of the project. Another important target audience is the top management group. This group is responsible for

Table 9-2   Common Target Audiences

Reason for Communication	Primary Target Audiences
To secure approval for the project	Client, top executives
To gain support for the project	Immediate managers, team leaders
To secure agreement with the issues	Participants, team leaders
To build credibility for the consulting firm	Top executives
To enhance reinforcement of the processes	Immediate managers
To drive action for improvement	Consultants
To prepare participants for the project	Team leaders
To enhance results and quality of future feedback	Participants
To show the complete results of the project	Client team
To underscore the importance of measuring results	Client, consultants
To explain techniques used to measure results	Client, support staff
To create desire for a participant to be involved	Team leaders
To stimulate interest in the consulting firm's products	Top executives
To demonstrate accountability for client expenditures	All employees
To market future consulting projects	Prospective clients

allocating resources to the consulting intervention and needs information to help justify expenditures and gauge the effectiveness of the efforts.

Selected groups of managers (or all managers) are also important target audiences. Management's support and involvement in the consulting process and the department's credibility are important to success. Effectively communicating program results to management can increase both support and credibility.

Communicating with the participants' team leaders or immediate managers is essential. In many cases, they must encourage participants to implement the project. Also, they often support and reinforce the objectives of the project. An appropriate return on investment improves the commitment to consulting and provides credibility for consultants.

Consulting participants need feedback on the overall success of the effort. Some individuals may not have been as successful as others in achieving the desired results. Communicating the results adds additional pressure to effectively implement the project and improve results for the future. For those achieving excellent results, the communication will serve as a reinforcement of the consulting. Communicating results to project participants is often overlooked, with the assumption that since the project is over, they do not need to be informed of its success.

Occasionally, results are communicated to encourage participation in the project. This is especially true for those projects where the participants are involved on a volunteer basis. The potential participants are important targets for communicating results.

The consulting team must receive information about program results. Whether for small projects where consultants receive a project update, or for larger projects where a complete team is involved, those who design, develop, facilitate, and implement the project must be given information on the project's effectiveness. Evaluation information is necessary so adjustments can be made if the program is not as effective as it could be.

The support staff should receive detailed information about the process to measure results. This group provides support services to the consulting team, usually in the department where the project is conducted.

Company employees and stockholders may be less likely targets. General-interest news stories may increase employee respect. Goodwill and positive attitudes toward the organization may also be by-products of communicating project results. Stockholders, on the other hand, are more interested in the return on their investment.

While Table 9-2 shows the most common target audiences, there can be others in a particular organization. For instance, management or employees could be subdivided into different departments, divisions, or even subsidiaries of the organization. The number of audiences can be large in a complex organization. At a minimum, four target audiences are always recommended: a senior management group, the consulting participants, the consulting participants' immediate manager or team leader, and the consulting team.

Developing the Information: The Impact Study

The type of formal evaluation report depends on the extent of detailed information presented to the various target audiences. Brief summaries of project results with appropriate charts may be sufficient for some communication efforts. In other situations, particularly with significant consulting projects requiring extensive funding, the amount of detail in the evaluation report is more crucial. A complete and comprehensive impact study report may be necessary. This report can then be used as the basis of information for specific audiences and various media. The report may contain the following sections.

Management/Executive Summary

The management summary is a brief overview of the entire report, explaining the basis for the evaluation and the significant conclusions and recommendations. It is designed for individuals who are too busy to read a detailed report. It is usually written last but appears first in the report for easy access.

Background Information

The background information provides a general description of the project. If applicable, the needs assessment that led to the project is summarized. The project is fully described, including the events that led to the consulting project. Other specific items necessary to provide a full description of the project are included. The extent of detailed information depends on the amount of information the audience needs.

Objectives

The objectives for the project are outlined so that the reader clearly understands desired accomplishments for the project. These are the objectives from which the different types or levels of data were collected.

Evaluation Strategy/Methodology

The evaluation strategy outlines all of the components that make up the total evaluation process. Several components of the results-based approach and the ROI Methodology presented in this book are discussed in this section of the report. The specific purposes of evaluation are outlined, and the evaluation design and methodology are explained. The instruments used in data collection are also described and presented as exhibits. Any unusual issues in the evaluation design are discussed. Finally, other useful information related to the design, timing, and execution of the evaluation is included.

Data Collection, Integration, and Analysis

This section explains the methods used to collect data as outlined in earlier chapters of this book. The data collected are usually presented in the report in summary form. Data integration issues and the methods used to analyze data are presented with interpretations.

Reaction and Satisfaction

This section details the data collected from key stakeholders, particularly the participants involved in the process, to measure the reaction to the consulting project and a level of satisfaction with various issues and parts of the process. Other input from the client group is also included to show the level of satisfaction.

Learning

This section shows a brief summary of the formal and informal measures of learning. It explains what participants have learned in terms of new processes, skills, tasks, procedures, and practices needed to make the consulting project successful.

Application and Implementation

This section shows the success with the application of new skills and knowledge. Implementation success is addressed, including progress and/or lack of progress.

Business Impact

This section shows the business impact measures representing the business needs that initially drove the project. This shows the extent to which business performance has changed during the implementation of the consulting project.

Project Costs

Project costs are presented in this section. A summary of the costs by category is included. For example, analysis, development, implementation, and evaluation costs are recommended categories for cost presentation. The assumptions made in developing and classifying costs are discussed in this section of the report.

Return on Investment

This section shows the ROI calculation along with the benefit/cost ratio. It compares the value to what was acceptable (objective) and provides an interpretation of the calculation.

Intangible Measures

This section shows the various intangible measures directly linked to the consulting project. Intangibles are those measures not converted to monetary values and not included in the ROI calculation.

Barriers and Enablers

The various problems and obstacles affecting the success of the project are detailed and presented as barriers to implementation. Also, those factors or influences that had a positive effect on the project are included as enablers. Together, they provide insight into what can inhibit or enhance projects in the future.

Conclusions and Recommendations

This section presents conclusions based on all of the results. If appropriate, brief explanations are presented on how each conclusion was reached. A list of recommendations or changes in the project, if appropriate, is provided with brief explanations for each recommendation. It is important that the conclusions and recommendations be consistent with one another and with the findings described in the previous section.

Collectively, these components make up the major parts of a complete evaluation report, an all-important document that reflects the complete project for those individuals who need much detail. Also, it's an excellent document for knowledge sharing and management for both the client and consultant.

Developing the Report

Table 9-3 shows the contents of a typical evaluation report for an ROI study on consulting. This specific study was conducted for a large financial institution and involved an ROI analysis on a consulting project for commercial banking. The typical report provides background information, explains the processes used, and, most importantly, presents the results.

While this report is an effective, professional way to present ROI data, several cautions need to be followed. Since this document reports the success of a consulting project involving a group of employees, complete credit for the success must go to the participants and their immediate leaders. Their performance generated the success. Another important caution is to avoid boasting about results. Although the ROI Methodology is accurate and credible, not all

Table 9-3   Format of an Impact Study Report

- General information
  - ○ Background
  - ○ Objectives of study
- Methodology for impact study
  - ○ Levels of evaluation
  - ○ ROI process
  - ○ Collecting data
  - ○ Isolating the effects of consulting
  - ○ Converting data to monetary values
- Data issues
- Results: general information
  - ○ Response profile
  - ○ Success with objectives
- Results: reaction and satisfaction
  - ○ Data sources
  - ○ Data summary
  - ○ Key issues
- Results: learning
  - ○ Data sources
  - ○ Data summary
  - ○ Key issues
- Results: application and implementation
  - ○ Data sources
  - ○ Data summary
  - ○ Key issues
- Results: business impact
  - ○ General comments
  - ○ Linkage with business measures
  - ○ Key issues
- Data issues
- Results: ROI and its meaning
- Results: intangible measures
- Barriers and enablers
  - ○ Barriers
  - ○ Enablers
- Conclusions and recommendations
  - ○ Conclusions
  - ○ Recommendations
- Exhibits

executives understand it. Huge claims of success can quickly turn off an audience and interfere with the delivery of the desired message.

A final caution concerns the structure of the report. The evaluation process should be clearly explained, along with assumptions made in the analysis. The reader should readily see how the values were developed and how the specific steps were followed to make the process more conservative, credible, and accurate. Detailed statistical analyses should be placed in the appendix.

Selecting the Communication Media

There are many options available to communicate program results. In addition to the impact study report, the most frequently used media are meetings, interim and progress reports, routine communication tools, electronic media, brochures and pamphlets, and case studies.

Meetings

Meetings are fertile opportunities for communicating program results, if used properly. All organizations have a variety of meetings, and, in each, the proper context and consulting results are an important part. A few examples illustrate the variety of meetings.

Regular meetings with the first-level management group are quite common. These meetings can be an excellent forum for discussing the results achieved in a consulting project when the project relates to the group's activities. A discussion of results can be integrated into the regular meeting format.

A few organizations have initiated a periodic meeting for all members of management, in which the CEO reviews progress and discusses plans for the coming year. A few highlights of consulting project results can be integrated into the CEO's speech, showing top executive interest, commitment, and support. Consulting results are mentioned along with operating profit, new facilities and equipment, new company acquisitions, and next year's sales forecast.

Whenever a management group convenes in significant numbers, evaluate the appropriateness of communicating consulting project results.

Interim and Progress Reports

Although usually limited to large projects, a highly visible way to communicate results is through interim and routine memos and reports. Published or disseminated through e-mail on a periodic basis, they usually have several purposes:

- To inform management about the status of the project

- To communicate the interim results achieved in the consulting project
- To activate needed changes and improvements

A more subtle reason for the report is to gain additional support and commitment from the management group and to keep the project intact. This report is produced by the consulting staff and distributed to a select group of managers in the organization. Format and scope vary considerably. Common topics are:

- A schedule of planned steps/activities should be an integral part of this report.
- A brief summary of reaction evaluations may be appropriate to report initial success.
- The results achieved from the consulting project should be presented in an easily understood format.
- A section that features a key support team member can be very useful, highlighting the member's efforts and involvement in consulting.
- It is important to communicate changes in personnel involved in planning, developing, implementing, or evaluating the project.
- A section that highlights a member of the client team can focus additional attention on results.

While the list may not be suited for every report, it represents topics that should be presented to the management group. When produced in a professional manner, the report can improve management support and commitment to the effort.

Routine Communication Tools

To reach a wide audience, consultants can use in-house publications. Whether a newsletter, magazine, newspaper, or electronic files, these types of media usually reach all employees. The information can be quite effective if communicated appropriately. The scope should be limited to general-interest articles, announcements, and interviews.

Results communicated through these types of media must be significant enough to arouse general interest. For example, a story with the headline "Safety Project Helps Produce One Million Hours without a Lost-Time Accident" will catch the attention of many people because they may have participated in the project and can appreciate the significance of the results. Reports on the accomplishments of a group of participants may not create interest unless the audience relates to the accomplishments.

For many consulting projects, results are achieved weeks or even months after the project is completed. Participants need reinforcement from many sources. If results are communicated to a general audience, including the participant's subordinates or peers, there is additional pressure to continue the project or similar ones in the future.

Stories about participants involved in a consulting project and the results they achieve create a favorable image. Employees are made aware that the company is investing time and money to improve performance and prepare for the future. This type of story provides information about projects that employees otherwise may not have known about and sometimes creates a desire to participate if given the opportunity.

General audience communication can bring recognition to project participants, particularly those who excel in some aspect of the project. When participants deliver unusual performance, public recognition can enhance their self-esteem. Many human-interest stories can come out of consulting projects. A rigorous project with difficult requirements can provide the basis for an interesting story on participants who implement the project.

In one organization, the editor of the company newsletter participated in a very demanding consulting project and wrote a stimulating article about what it was like to be a participant. The article gave the reader a tour of the entire project and its effectiveness in terms of the results achieved. It was an interesting and effective way to communicate about a challenging activity.

The benefits are many and the opportunities endless for consultants to utilize in-house publications and company-wide intranets to let others know about the success of projects.

E-mail and Electronic Media

Internal and external Web pages on the Internet, company-wide intranets, and e-mail are excellent vehicles for releasing results, promoting ideas, and informing employees and other target groups of consulting results. E-mail in particular provides a virtually instantaneous means with which to communicate and solicit response from large numbers of people.

Project Brochures and Pamphlets

A brochure might be appropriate for projects conducted on a continuing basis, where participants have produced excellent results. It should be attractive and present a complete description of the project, with a major section devoted to results obtained with previous participants, if available. Measurable results and reactions from participants, or even direct quotes from individuals, could add spice to an otherwise dull brochure.

Case Studies

Case studies represent an effective way to communicate the results of a consulting project. Consequently, it is recommended that a few projects be developed in a case format. A typical case study describes the situation, provides appropriate background information (including the events that led to the intervention), presents the techniques and strategies used to develop the study, and highlights the key issues in the project. Case studies tell an interesting story of how the evaluation was developed and the problems and concerns identified along the way.

Case studies have many useful applications in an organization. First, they can be used in group discussions, where interested individuals can react to the material, offer different perspectives, and draw conclusions about approaches or techniques. Second, the case study can serve as a self-teaching guide for individuals trying to understand how evaluations are developed and utilized in the organization. Finally, case studies provide appropriate recognition for those involved in the actual case. More importantly, they recognize the participants who achieved the results, as well as the managers who allowed the participants to be involved in the project. The case study format has become one of the most effective ways to learn about consulting evaluation.

Communicating the Information

Perhaps the greatest challenge of communication is the actual delivery of the message. This can be accomplished in a variety of ways and settings based on the actual target audience and the media selected for the message. Three particular approaches deserve additional coverage. The first approach is providing insight into how to provide feedback throughout the consulting project to make sure information flows so changes can be made. The second is presenting an impact study to a senior management team. This may be one of the most challenging tasks for the consultant. The third is communicating regularly and routinely with the executive management group. Each of these three approaches is explored in more detail.

Providing Early Feedback

One of the most important reasons for collecting reaction, satisfaction, and learning data is to provide feedback so adjustments or changes can be made throughout the consulting project. In most consulting projects, data are routinely collected and quickly communicated to a variety of groups. Table 9-4 shows a feedback action plan designed to provide information to several feedback audiences using a variety of media.

As the plan shows, data are collected during the project at four specific time intervals and communicated to at least four audiences—and sometimes six. Some of these feedback sessions result in identifying specific actions that need to be taken. This process becomes comprehensive and needs to be managed in a very proactive way. The following steps are recommended for providing feedback and managing the feedback process. Many of the steps and issues follow the recommendations of Peter Block in his successful consulting book, *Flawless Consulting.*[1]

1. **Communicate quickly**. Whether it is good news or bad news, it is important to let individuals involved in the project have the information as soon as possible. The recommended time for providing feedback is usually a matter of days and certainly no longer than a week or two after the results are known.

2. **Simplify the data**. Condense data into an understandable, concise presentation. This is not the format for detailed explanations and analysis.

3. **Examine the role of the consultants and the client in the feedback situation**. Sometimes the consultant is the judge, and sometimes the consultant is the jury, prosecutor, defendant, or witness. On the other hand, sometimes the client is the judge, jury, prosecutor, defendant, or witness. It is important to examine the respective roles in terms of reactions to the data and the actions that need to be taken.

4. **Use negative data in a constructive way**. Some of the data will show that things are not going so well, and the fault may rest with the consulting firm or the client. In either case, the story basically changes from "Let's look at the success we've made" to "Now we know which areas to change."

5. **Use positive data in a cautious way**. Positive data can be misleading, and if they are communicated too enthusiastically, they may create expectations beyond what may materialize later. Positive data should be presented in a cautious way—almost in a discounting mode.

Table 9-4 Feedback Action Plan

Data Collection Item	Timing	Feedback Audience	Media	Timing of Feedback	Action Required
1. Pre-project survey • Climate/environment • Issue identification	Beginning of the project	Client team participants	Meeting	One week	None
			Survey summary	Two weeks	None
		Team leaders	Survey summary	Two weeks	Communicate feedback
		Consultants	Meeting	One week	Adjust approach
2. Implementation survey • Reaction to plans • Issue identification	Beginning of actual implementation	Client team participants	Meeting	One week	None
			Survey summary	Two weeks	None
		Team leaders	Survey summary	Two weeks	Communicate feedback
		Consultants	Meeting	Two weeks	Adjust approach
3. Implementation reaction survey/interviews • Reaction to solution • Suggested changes	One month into implementation	Client team participants	Meeting	One week	Comments
		Support staff	Study summary	Two weeks	None
		Team leaders	Study summary	Two weeks	None
		Immediate managers	Study summary	Two weeks	Support changes
			Study summary	Three weeks	Support changes
		Consultants	Meeting	Three days	Adjust approach
4. Implementation feedback questionnaire • Reaction (satisfaction) • Barriers • Projected success	End of implementation	Client team	Meeting	One week	Comments
		Participants	Study summary	Two weeks	None
		Support staff	Study summary	Two weeks	None
		Team leaders	Study summary	Two weeks	Support changes
		Immediate managers	Study summary	Three weeks	Support changes
		Consultants	Meeting	Three days	Adjust approach

6. **Choose the language of the meeting and communication very carefully.** Use language that is descriptive, focused, specific, short, and simple. Avoid language that is too judgmental, macro, stereotypical, lengthy, or complex.

7. **Ask the client for reactions to the data.** After all, the client is the number one customer, and the client's reaction is critical since it is most important that the client is pleased with the project.

8. **Ask the client for recommendations.** The client may have some very good recommendations of what needs to be changed to keep a project on track or put it back on track if it derails.

9. **Use support and confrontation carefully.** These two issues are not mutually exclusive. There may be times when support and confrontation are needed for the same group. The client may need support and yet be confronted for a lack of improvement or sponsorship. The consulting group may be confronted on the problem areas that are developed but may need support as well.

10. **React and act on the data.** Weigh the different alternatives and possibilities to arrive at the adjustments and changes that will be necessary.

11. **Secure agreement from all key stakeholders.** This is essential to make sure everyone is willing to make adjustments and changes that seem necessary.

12. **Keep the feedback process short.** Don't let it become bogged down in long, drawn-out meetings or lengthy documents. If this occurs, stakeholders will avoid the process instead of being willing to participate in the future.

Following these 12 steps will help move the project forward and provide important feedback, often ensuring that adjustments are supported and made.

Presenting Impact Study Data to Senior Management

Perhaps one of the most challenging and stressful communications is presenting an impact study to the senior management team, which also serves as the ultimate client in a consulting project (they fund the project). The challenge is convincing this highly skeptical and critical group that outstanding results have been achieved (assuming they have), in a very reasonable time frame, addressing the salient points, and making sure the managers understand the process. Two particular issues can create challenges. First, if the results are very impressive, it may be difficult to make the managers believe the data. On the other extreme, if the data are negative, it will be a challenge to make sure managers don't overreact to the negative results and look for someone to blame. Following are guidelines that can help make sure this process is planned and executed properly:

- Plan a face-to-face meeting with senior team members for the first one or two major impact studies. If they are unfamiliar with the complete consulting ROI process, a face-to-face meeting is necessary to make sure they understand the process. The good news is that they will probably attend the meeting because they have not seen ROI data developed for this type of project. The bad news is that it takes a lot of time, usually one hour for this presentation.
- After a group has had a face-to-face meeting with a couple of presentations, an executive summary may suffice. At this point they understand the process, so a shortened version may be appropriate.
- After the target audience is familiar with the process, a brief version may be necessary, which will involve a one- to two-page summary with charts and graphs showing all six types of measures.
- When making the initial presentation, the results should not be distributed beforehand or even during the session but saved until the end of the session. This will allow enough time to present the process and react to it before the target audience sees the actual ROI number.
- Present the process step-by-step, showing how the data were collected, when they were collected, who provided the data, how the data were isolated from other influences, and how they were converted to monetary values. The various assumptions, adjustments, and conservative approaches are presented along with the total cost of the project. The costs are fully loaded so that the target audience will begin to buy into the process of developing the actual ROI.
- When the data are actually presented, the results are presented step by step, starting with Level 1, moving through Level 5, and ending with the intangibles. This allows the audience to see the reaction and satisfaction, learning, application and implementation, business impact, and ROI. After some discussion on the meaning of the ROI, the intangible measures are presented. Allocate time to each level as appropriate for the audience. This helps overcome the potentially negative reactions to a very positive or negative ROI.
- Show the consequences of additional accuracy if it is an issue. The trade-off for more accuracy and validity often means more expense. Address this issue whenever necessary, agreeing to add more data if required.
- Collect concerns, reactions, and issues for the process and make adjustments accordingly for the next presentation.

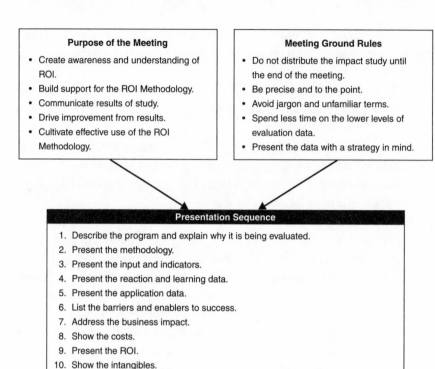

Figure 9-1 Presenting the impact study to executive sponsors.

Collectively, these steps will help prepare for and present one of the most critical meetings in the consulting ROI process. Figure 9-1 shows the details of this meeting.

Analyzing Reactions to Communication

The best indicator of how effectively the results of a consulting project have been communicated is the level of commitment and support from the management group. The allocation of requested resources and strong commitment from top management are tangible evidence of management's perception of the results. In addition to this macro-level reaction, there are a few techniques consultants can use to measure the effectiveness of their communication efforts.

Whenever results are communicated, the reaction of the target audiences can be monitored. These reactions may include nonverbal gestures, oral remarks, written comments, or indirect actions that reveal how the communication was received. Usually, when results are presented in a meeting, the presenter will have some indication of how the results were received by the group. The interest and attitudes of the audience can usually be quickly evaluated.

During the presentation, questions may be asked or, in some cases, the information is challenged. In addition, a tabulation of these challenges and questions can be useful in evaluating the type of information to include in future communications. Positive comments about the results are certainly desired and, when they are made—formally or informally—they should also be noted and tabulated.

Consulting staff meetings are an excellent arena for discussing the reaction to communicating results. Comments can come from many sources depending on the particular target audiences. Input from different members of the staff can be summarized to help judge the overall effectiveness.

When major program results are communicated, a feedback questionnaire may be used for an entire audience or a sample of the audience. The purpose of this questionnaire is to determine the extent to which the audience understood and/or believed the information presented. This is practical only when the effectiveness of the communication has a significant impact on the future actions of the consulting firm.

Another approach is to survey the management group to determine its perceptions of the results. Specific questions should be asked about results. What does the management group know about the results? How believable are the results? What additional information is desired about the project? This type of survey can help provide guidance in communicating results.

The purpose of analyzing reactions is to make adjustments in the communication process—if adjustments are necessary. Although the reactions may involve intuitive assessments, a more sophisticated analysis will provide more accurate information to make these adjustments. The net result should be a more effective communication process.

Final Thoughts

This chapter presented the final step in the results-based approach to consulting accountability. Communicating results is a crucial step in the overall evaluation process. If this step is not taken seriously, the full impact of the results will not be realized. The chapter began with general principles for communicating program results. The various target audiences were discussed, and, because of its importance, emphasis was placed on the executive group. A suggested format for a detailed evaluation report was also provided.

Much of the remainder of the chapter included a detailed presentation of the most commonly used media for communicating program results, including meetings, client publications, and electronic media. Numerous examples illustrated these concepts. The next chapter describes how to make ROI studies a routine practice.

Making It Routine

Overcoming Resistance to Measuring ROI

E VEN THE BEST-DESIGNED process, model, or technique is worthless unless it is effectively and efficiently integrated into the organization. Often, there is resistance to the use of ROI in consulting, both for the client and the consultant. Some of this resistance is based on fear and misunderstanding. Some is real, based on actual barriers and obstacles. Although the ROI Methodology presented in this book is a step-by-step, methodical, and simplistic procedure, it can fail if it is not integrated properly and fully accepted and supported by those who must make it work. This chapter focuses on the key issues needed to overcome resistance to implementing the ROI process in the client organization and the consulting firm.

The Resistance

With any new process or change, there is resistance. Resistance may be especially great when implementing a process that is perceived as complex, such as ROI. There are four key reasons why there should be a detailed plan to overcome resistance.

Resistance Is Always Present

There is always resistance to change. Sometimes there are good reasons for resistance, but often it exists for the wrong reasons. The important point is to sort out both types and try to dispel the myths. When legitimate barriers are the basis for resistance, trying to minimize or remove them altogether is the challenge.

Implementation Is Key

As with any process, effective implementation overcomes the resistance and is the key to its success. This occurs when the new technique or tool is integrated into the routine framework. Without effective implementation, even the best process will fail. A process that is never removed from the shelf will never be understood, supported, or improved. There must be clear-cut steps for designing a comprehensive implementation process that will overcome resistance.

Consistency Is Needed

As this process is implemented from one study to another, consistency is an important consideration. With consistency come accuracy and reliability. The only way to make sure consistency is achieved is to follow clearly defined processes and procedures each time the consulting ROI is tackled. Proper implementation will ensure that this occurs.

Efficiency

Cost control and efficiency will always be issues in any major undertaking, and the ROI process is no exception. Implementation must ensure that tasks are done efficiently as well as effectively. It will help ensure that the process cost is kept to a minimum, that time is utilized appropriately, and that the process remains affordable.

The Approach to Overcoming Resistance

Resistance appears in many ways—as comments, remarks, actions, or behaviors. Table 10-1 shows some comments that reflect open resistance to the ROI process. Each of these represents issues that need to be resolved or addressed in some way. A few of the comments are based on realistic barriers, while others are based on myths that must be dispelled. Sometimes, resistance to the ROI reflects underlying concerns. The consultants involved may have fear of losing control of their processes, and others may feel that they are vulnerable to

Table 10-1 Typical Consultant Objections to the Use of ROI

Open Resistance

1. It costs too much.
2. It takes too much time.
3. Who is asking for this?
4. It is not part of my responsibility.
5. I did not have input on this.
6. I do not understand this.
7. What happens when the results are negative?
8. How can we be consistent with this?
9. The ROI process is too subjective.
10. Our clients will not support this.
11. ROI is too narrowly focused.
12. This is not practical.

actions that may be taken if the process is not successful. Still others may be concerned about any process that brings change or requires additional learning efforts.

Resistance can appear in both major audiences addressed in this book. It can appear in consulting firms, as many consultants may resist ROI and openly make comments similar to those listed in Table 10-1. Heavy persuasion and evidence of tangible benefits may be needed to convince those in a consulting firm that this is a process that must be done, should be done, and is in their best interest to undertake. Clients will also experience resistance. Although most clients would like to see the results of the consulting project, they may have concerns about the information they are asked to provide and if their performance is being judged along with the evaluation of the entire project. In reality, they may express the same fears listed in Table 10-1.

The challenge is to implement the process in both organizations methodically and consistently so that it becomes normal business behavior and a routine and standard process built into consulting interventions. The implementation necessary to overcome resistance covers a variety of areas. Figure 10-1 shows actions outlined in this chapter that are presented as building blocks to overcoming resistance. They are all necessary to build the proper base or framework to dispel myths and remove or minimize actual barriers. The remainder of this chapter presents specific strategies

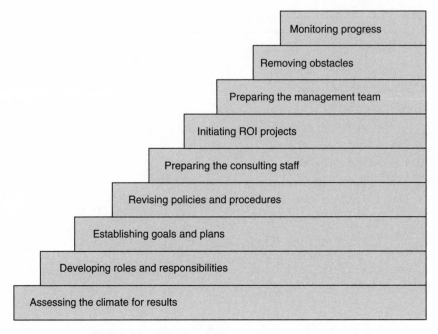

Monitoring progress

Removing obstacles

Preparing the management team

Initiating ROI projects

Preparing the consulting staff

Revising policies and procedures

Establishing goals and plans

Developing roles and responsibilities

Assessing the climate for results

Figure 10-1 Building blocks to overcome resistance.

and techniques around each of the 10 building blocks identified in Figure 10-1. They apply equally to the consulting firm and the client organization, and no attempt is made to separate the two in this presentation. In some situations, a particular strategy would work best in a consulting firm, while others may work best in client organizations. In reality, all 10 may be appropriate for both groups in certain cases.

Assessing the Climate

As a first step toward implementation, some organizations assess the current climate for achieving results. One useful tool, presented in the Appendix, reflects a results-based assessment for clients. This instrument—or some version of it—can serve as an initial assessment of how the consultants and managers perceive consulting and its results. For clients, this instrument is an excellent tool for determining current perspectives and making improvements. In some organizations, annual assessments are completed to measure progress as the consulting process is implemented. Others administer the instrument with the management group to determine the extent to which managers perceive consulting as effective. For external consultants, the instrument provides an excellent understanding of the current status with clients. Consultants should take them the instrument based on how they think their clients respond. With this awareness, the organization can plan for significant changes, pinpointing particular issues that need support as the ROI process is implemented.

Developing Roles and Responsibilities

Defining and detailing specific roles and responsibilities for different groups and individuals addresses many of the resistance factors and helps pave a smooth path for implementation. Four key issues are important.

Identifying a Champion

As an early step in the process, one or more individuals should be designated as the internal leader or champion for the process. As in most change efforts, someone must take responsibility for ensuring that the process is implemented successfully. This leader serves as a champion for ROI and is usually the one who understands the process best and sees vast potential for its contribution. More importantly, this leader is willing to teach others and will work to sustain sponsorship.

The ROI leader is a member of the consulting staff who usually has this responsibility full-time in larger consulting firms or part-time in smaller organizations. Client organizations may also have an ROI leader who pursues the ROI process from the client's perspective. The typical job title for a full-time ROI leader is manager of measurement and evaluation. Some organizations assign this responsibility to a team and empower it to lead the ROI effort.

Developing the ROI Leader

In preparation for this assignment, individuals usually obtain special training that builds specific skills and knowledge for the ROI process. The role of the implementation leader is quite broad and serves a variety of specialized duties. In some organizations, the implementation leader can take on as many as 14 roles, as shown in Table 10-2.

Leading the ROI effort is a difficult and challenging assignment that requires special skill-building. Fortunately, there are programs available that teach these skills. For example, one such program is designed to certify individuals who are assuming a leadership role in the implementation of the ROI

Table 10-2   Roles of the ROI Leader

Technical expert	Cheerleader
Consultant	Communicator
Problem solver	Process monitor
Initiator	Planner
Designer	Analyst
Developer	Interpreter
Coordinator	Teacher

process (www.roiinstitute.net). This certification is created around 10 specific skill sets linked to successful consulting ROI implementations. These are:

1. Planning for ROI calculations
2. Collecting evaluation data
3. Isolating the effects of consulting
4. Converting data to monetary values
5. Monitoring consulting costs
6. Analyzing data, including calculating the ROI
7. Presenting evaluation data
8. Implementing the ROI process
9. Providing internal consulting on ROI
10. Teaching others the ROI process

This process is quite comprehensive but may be necessary to build the appropriate skills for tackling this challenging assignment.

Establishing a Task Force

Making the process work well may require the use of a task force. A task force is usually a group of individuals from different parts of the consulting process who are willing to develop the ROI process and implement it in the organization. The selection of the task force may involve volunteers, or participation may be mandatory depending on specific job responsibilities. The task force should represent the necessary cross section for accomplishing stated goals.

Task forces have the additional advantage of bringing more people into the process and developing more ownership and support for ROI. The task force must be large enough to cover the key areas but not so large that it becomes cumbersome and difficult to function. Six to twelve members is a good size. For the client organization, the same approach may be necessary, utilizing a task force for evaluating consulting projects.

Assigning Responsibilities

Determining specific responsibilities is a critical issue because confusion can arise when individuals are unclear about their specific assignments in the ROI process. Responsibilities apply to two areas. The first is the measurement and evaluation responsibility of the entire consulting team. It is important for everyone involved in consulting to have some responsibility for measurement and evaluation. These responsibilities include providing input on the design of instruments, planning specific evaluations, analyzing data, and interpreting the results. Typical responsibilities include:

- Ensuring that the needs assessment includes specific business impact measures
- Developing specific application objectives (Level 3) and business impact objectives (Level 4) for each project
- Focusing the content of the project on performance improvement, ensuring that the project relates to the desired objectives
- Keeping participants focused on application and impact objectives
- Communicating rationale and reasons for evaluation
- Assisting in follow-up data collection to capture application and business impact data
- Providing technical assistance for data collection, data analysis, and reporting
- Designing instruments and plans for data collection and analysis

While it may be inappropriate to have each member of the staff involved in all of these activities, each individual should have at least one or more responsibilities as part of his or her routine job duties. This assignment of responsibility keeps the ROI process from being disjointed and separated from major consulting activities. More importantly, it brings accountability to those directly involved in interventions.

Another issue involves the technical support function. Depending on the size of the consulting firm or client organization, it may be helpful to establish a group of technical experts who provide assistance with the ROI process. When this group is established, it must be clear that the experts are not there to relieve others of evaluation responsibilities but to supplement technical expertise. Some firms have found this approach to be effective. For example, one of the top five consulting firms has a measurement and evaluation staff of 32 individuals who provide technical support for evaluating consulting projects. This is an extreme situation. When this type of support is developed, responsibilities revolve around six key areas:

1. Designing data collection instruments
2. Providing assistance for developing an evaluation strategy
3. Analyzing data, including specialized statistical analyses
4. Interpreting results and making specific recommendations
5. Developing an evaluation report or case study to communicate overall results
6. Providing technical support in all phases of the ROI process

The assignment of responsibilities for evaluation is also an issue that needs attention throughout the evaluation process. Although the consultants must have specific responsibilities during an evaluation, it is not unusual to require others in support functions to have responsibility for data collection. These responsibilities are defined when a particular evaluation strategy plan is developed and approved.

Establishing Goals and Plans

Establishing goals, targets, and objectives is critical to the implementation. This includes detailed planning documents for the overall process as well as individual ROI projects. Several key issues relate to goals and plans.

Setting Evaluation Targets

Establishing specific targets for evaluation levels is an important way to make progress with measurement and evaluation. Targets enable the staff to focus on improvements needed at specific evaluation levels. In this process, the percentage of projects planned for evaluation at each level is developed. The first step is to assess the present situation. The number of all consulting projects, including repeated projects of a similar nature, is tabulated along with the corresponding level(s) of evaluation presently conducted for each project. Next, the percentage of projects using reaction questionnaires is calculated. This is probably 100 percent now. The process is repeated for each level of the evaluation.

After detailing the current situation, the next step is to determine a realistic target within a specific time frame. Many organizations set annual targets. This process should involve the input of the entire consulting staff to ensure that

Table 10-3 Evaluation Targets in a Large Consulting Firm

Level	Target*
Level 1, Reaction	100%
Level 2, Learning	80%
Level 3, Application and Implementation	40%
Level 4, Business Impact	25%
Level 5, ROI	10%

*Percent of consulting projects evaluated at this level.

targets are realistic and that the staff is committed to the process. If consultants do not develop ownership of this process, targets will not be met. The improvement targets must be achievable, while at the same time challenging and motivating. Table 10-3 shows the targets for five levels established in a large consulting firm. In some organizations, half of the business impact evaluations are taken to Level 5, while in others, every one is taken to this level. Most organizations plan for the gradual improvement of increasing evaluation activity at Levels 3, 4, and 5, with a profile such as the one outlined in Table 10-3 being achieved in two years.

Target-setting is a critical implementation issue. It should be completed early in the process with the full support of the consulting staff. Also, if practical and feasible, the targets should have the approval of key managers—particularly the senior management team.

Developing a Project Plan for Implementation

An important part of implementation is to establish timetables for the complete implementation process. This document becomes a master plan for the completion of the different elements presented in this chapter, beginning with assigning responsibilities and concluding with meeting the targets previously described. From a practical standpoint, this schedule is a project plan for transitioning from the present situation to the desired future situation. The items on the schedule include, but are not limited to, developing specific ROI projects, building staff skills, developing policy, teaching managers the process, analyzing ROI data, and communicating results. The more detailed the document, the more useful it becomes. The project plan is a living, long-range document that should be reviewed frequently and adjusted as necessary. More importantly, it should always be familiar to those who are working on the ROI process. Figure 10-2 shows an ROI implementation project plan for a medium-sized firm.

	J	F	M	A	M	J	J	A	S	O	N	D	J	F	M	A	M	J	J	A	S	O	N
Team formed	■																						
Responsibilities defined	■	■																					
Policy developed		■	■	■																			
Targets set	■	■																					
ROI Project A					■	■	■	■	■														
ROI Project B						■	■	■	■	■	■	■	■										
ROI Project C									■	■	■	■	■	■	■								
ROI Project D										■	■	■	■	■	■	■	■	■	■	■			
Consultants trained								■	■	■	■	■	■										
Managers trained																	■	■	■	■			
Support tools					■											■	■						
Evaluation guidelines		■	■	■	■	■																	

Figure 10-2 ROI implementation plan of a medium-sized consulting firm.

Revising/Developing Policies and Guidelines

Another key part of planning is revising (or developing) the organization's policy concerning measurement and evaluation for consulting. The policy statement contains information developed specifically for the measurement and evaluation process. It is frequently developed with the input of the consulting staff and key managers or clients. Sometimes policy issues are addressed during internal workshops designed to build skills for measurement and evaluation. The policy statement addresses critical issues that will influence the effectiveness of the measurement and evaluation process. Typical issues include adopting the five-level framework presented in this book, requiring Level 3 and 4 objectives for some or all projects, and defining responsibilities for measurement and evaluation.

Policy statements are very important because they provide guidance and direction for the consultants and others who work closely with the ROI process. These individuals keep the process clearly focused and enable the group to establish goals for evaluation. Policy statements also provide an opportunity to communicate basic requirements and fundamental issues regarding performance and accountability. More than anything else, they serve as learning tools to teach others, especially when they are developed in a collaborative and collective way. If policy statements are developed in isolation and do not enjoy ownership from the staff and management, they will not be effective or useful.

Guidelines for measurement and evaluation are important for showing how to utilize the tools and techniques, guide the design process, provide consistency in the ROI process, ensure that appropriate methods are used, and place the proper emphasis on each of the areas. The guidelines are more technical than policy statements and often contain detailed procedures showing how the process is actually undertaken and developed. They often include specific forms, instruments, and tools necessary to facilitate the process.

Preparing the Consulting Staff

Consultants often resist ROI. They often see evaluation as an unnecessary intrusion into their responsibilities, absorbing precious time and stifling their freedom to be creative. The cartoon character Pogo perhaps characterized it best when he said, "We have met the enemy, and he is us." This section outlines some important issues that must be addressed when preparing consultants for the implementation of ROI.

Involving Consultants

On each key issue or major decision, the staff should be involved in the process. As policy statements are prepared and evaluation guidelines developed, consultant input is absolutely essential. It is difficult for consultants to resist something they helped design and develop. Using meetings, brainstorming sessions, and task forces, consultants should be involved in every phase of developing the framework and supporting documents for ROI.

Using ROI as a Learning Tool

One reason the consultants may resist the ROI process is that the effectiveness of the project will be fully exposed, putting the consultants' reputations on the line. They may have a fear of failure. To overcome this, the ROI process should be clearly positioned as a tool for learning and not a tool for evaluating consultant performance—at least during its early years of implementation. Consultants will not be interested in developing a process that can be used against them.

Evaluators can learn as much from failures as successes. If a consulting project is not working, it is best to find out quickly to understand the issues firsthand, not from others. If a consulting project is ineffective and not producing the desired results, it will eventually be known to clients and/or the management group, if they are not aware of it already. A lack of results will cause managers to become less supportive of consulting. If the weaknesses in the project are identified and adjustments are made quickly, not only will a more effective project be developed, but the credibility and respect for consulting will be enhanced.

Teaching Consultants

Most consultants have inadequate skills in measurement and evaluation and thus will need to develop some expertise in the process. Measurement and evaluation is not always a formal part of the preparation in becoming a consultant. Consequently, each consultant must be provided training on the ROI process to learn its systematic, logical steps. In addition, consultants must know how to develop an evaluation strategy and specific plan, collect and analyze data from the evaluation, and interpret results from data analysis. Sometimes a one- to two-day workshop is needed to build adequate skills and knowledge to understand the process, appreciate what the process can do for the consulting firm and client organization, see the necessity for it, and participate in a successful implementation.

Initiating ROI Projects

The first tangible evidence of the ROI process may be the initiation of the first projects where an ROI calculation is planned. This section outlines some of the key issues involved in identifying the projects and keeping them on track.

Selecting Initial Projects

Selecting a project for ROI analysis is an important and critical issue. Only specific types of projects should be selected for this comprehensive, detailed analysis. Typical criteria for identifying consulting projects for analysis are to select projects that:

- Are expected to have a long life cycle
- Are linked to major operational problems/opportunities
- Are important to overall strategic objectives
- Involve large groups of employees
- Are very expensive
- Are time-consuming
- Have high visibility
- Have management's interest in evaluation

Using these or similar criteria, the consultant must select the appropriate projects to consider for ROI evaluation. Ideally, management should concur with or approve the criteria.

The next major step is determining how many projects to undertake initially and in which particular areas. A small number of initial projects are recommended, perhaps two or three. The selected projects may represent functional areas of the business such as operations, sales, finance, engineering, and information systems. Another approach is to select projects representing functional areas of consulting, such as productivity improvement, reengineering, quality enhancement, technology implementation, and major change projects. It is important to select a manageable number so the process will be implemented.

Developing the Planning Documents

Perhaps the two most useful ROI documents are the data collection plan and the ROI analysis plan discussed in earlier chapters. These plans show which data will be collected, at what time, by whom, and how specific analyses will be conducted, including isolating the effects of consulting and converting data to monetary values. Each consultant should know how to develop, understand, and use these plans.

Reporting Progress

As the projects are developed and the ROI implementation is under way, status meetings should be conducted to report progress and discuss critical issues with appropriate team members. For example, if an intervention for operations is selected as one of the ROI projects, the key staff involved in the intervention should meet regularly to discuss the status of the project. This keeps the project team focused on the critical issues, generates the best ideas for tackling particular problems and barriers, and builds a knowledge base for better implementation evaluations in future interventions. Sometimes an external consultant, perhaps an expert in the ROI process, facilitates this group. In other cases, the internal ROI leader may facilitate the group.

In essence, these meetings serve three major purposes: reporting progress, learning, and planning. The meeting usually begins with a status report on each ROI project, describing what has been accomplished since the previous meeting. Next, the specific barriers and problems encountered are discussed. During the discussions, new issues are interjected in terms of possible tactics, techniques, or tools. Also, the entire group discusses how to remove barriers to success and focuses on suggestions and recommendations for next steps, including developing specific plans. Finally, the next steps are determined.

Preparing the Management Team

Perhaps no group is more important to the ROI process than the management team that must allocate resources for consulting and support the projects. In addition, the management team often provides input and assistance for the ROI process. Specific actions for training and developing the management team should be carefully planned and executed.

A critical issue that must be addressed before a consulting intervention is the relationship between the consultants and key managers. A productive partnership is needed, which requires each party to understand the concerns, problems, and opportunities of the other. Developing this type of relationship is a long-term process that must be deliberately planned and initiated by key consultants. Sometimes the decision to commit resources and support for consulting is based on the effectiveness of this relationship.

The Overall Importance of Consulting

Client managers need to be convinced that consulting is a mainstream function that is growing in importance and influence in modern organizations. They need to understand the results-based approach of today's progressive consulting firms. Managers should perceive consulting interventions as a critical process in the organization and be able to describe how the process contributes to strategic and operational objectives. Data from the organization should be presented to show the full scope of consulting in the organization. Tangible evidence of top management's commitment to the process should be presented in the form of memos, directives, or policies signed by the CEO or other appropriate top executives. Also, external data should be shared to illustrate the growth of consulting budgets and the increasing importance of consulting.

The Impact of Consulting

Too often, managers are unsure about the success of consulting. Managers need to be able to identify the steps to measuring the impact that consulting has on important output variables. Reports and studies should be presented, showing the impact of the consulting project using measures such as productivity, quality, cost, response time, and customer satisfaction. Internal evaluation reports, if available, should be presented to managers, revealing convincing evidence that consulting is making a significant difference in the organization. If internal reports are not available, success stories or case studies from other organizations can be utilized. Managers need to be convinced that consulting is a successful, results-based tool—not only to help with change, but to meet critical organizational goals and objectives as well.

Responsibility for Consulting

Defining who is responsible for what areas of the consulting project is important to the success of the project. Managers should know their specific responsibilities, see how they can influence consulting, and understand the degree of responsibility they must assume in the future. Multiple responsibilities for consulting are advocated, including specific responsibilities for managers, participants, participant supervisors, and consultants. In some organizations, job descriptions are revised to reflect consulting responsibilities. In other organizations, major job-related goals are established to highlight management's responsibility for consulting.

Active Involvement

One of the most important ways to enhance managers' support for consulting is to actively involve them in the process, having them commit to one or more ways to become actively involved in the future. Figure 10-3 shows several forms of manager involvement identified in one company. The information in the figure is presented to managers with a request for them to commit to at least one area of involvement. After these areas are fully explained and discussed, each manager is asked to select one or more ways in which he or she will be involved in consulting in the future. A commitment to sign up for at least one involvement role is required. If used properly, these commitments are a rich source of input and assistance from the management group. There will be many offers for involvement, and a quick follow-up on all offers is recommended.

The following are areas for present and future involvement in the consulting. Please check your areas of planned involvement.		
	In Your Area	Outside Your Area
■ Provide input on a consulting needs analysis	❑	❑
■ Serve on a consulting advisory committee	❑	❑
■ Provide input on a project design	❑	❑
■ Serve as a subject-matter expert	❑	❑
■ Serve on a task force to develop a project	❑	❑
■ Provide reinforcement to your employees as they participate in a consulting project	❑	❑
■ Coordinate a consulting project	❑	❑
■ Assist in an evaluation or follow-up	❑	❑

Figure 10-3 Form for present and future planned involvement.

Removing Obstacles

As the consulting ROI process is implemented, there will be obstacles to its progress. Many of the fears discussed in this chapter may be valid, while others may be based on unrealistic fears or misunderstandings. As part of the implementation, attempts should be made to dispel the myths and remove or minimize the barriers or obstacles. The myths should be discussed and debated in the organization so that they can be dispelled, at least in the eyes of the consultants or other support staff.

Monitoring Progress

A final part of the implementation process is monitoring the overall progress made and communicating that progress. Although it is an often-overlooked part of the process, an effective communication plan can help keep the implementation on target and let others know what the consulting ROI process is accomplishing for the consulting firm and the client organization.

The initial schedule for implementation of the ROI process provides a variety of key events or milestones. Routine progress reports should be developed to communicate the status and progress of these events or milestones. Reports are usually developed at six-month intervals but may be more frequent for short-term projects. Two target audiences, the consultants and consulting managers, are critical for progress reporting. The entire consulting team should be kept informed of the progress, and senior managers need to know the extent to which ROI is being implemented and how it is working in the organization.

Final Thoughts

In summary, the implementation of the ROI Methodology is a very critical issue. If not approached in a systematic, logical, and planned way, the ROI use will not become an integral part of consulting and, consequently, the accountability of consulting projects will suffer. This final chapter presented the different elements that must be considered and issues that must be addressed to ensure that implementation is smooth and uneventful. This is the most effective way to overcome resistance to ROI. The result provides a complete integration of ROI as a mainstream activity in the consulting process.

Do Your Consulting Projects Focus on Results?

A Self-Assessment Survey for Clients

Instructions. For each of the following statements, please circle the response that best matches the consulting activities and philosophy in your organization. If none of the answers describes the situation, select the one that best fits. Please be candid with your responses.

Select the most correct response.

1. The direction and goals of consulting at your organization:
   a. Shift with trends, fads, and industry issues.
   b. Are determined by managers of departments and adjusted as needed.
   c. Are based on a mission and a strategic plan for consulting.
2. The primary mode of operation of consultants is:
   a. To respond to requests by managers and other employees to deliver solutions.
   b. To help management react to crisis situations and reach solutions.
   c. To implement solutions in collaboration with management to prevent problems and crisis situations.
3. Consulting solutions usually focus on:
   a. Changing perceptions and opinions.
   b. Enhancing skills and job performance.
   c. Driving business measures and enhancing job performance.

4. Most consulting solutions are initiated:
   a. When a solution appears to be successful in another organization.
   b. By request of management.
   c. After analysis has indicated that the solution is needed.
5. To determine solutions:
   a. Management is asked to choose a solution from a list of existing packaged solutions.
   b. Employees and unit managers are asked about needs.
   c. Needs are systematically derived from a thorough analysis of performance problems and issues.
6. When determining the consulting solutions needed for target audiences:
   a. Nonspecific solutions for large audiences are offered.
   b. Specific needs of specific individuals and groups are addressed.
   c. Very focused projects are implemented only to those people who need it.
7. The responsibility for results from consulting:
   a. Rests primarily with the consultants.
   b. Is shared between consultants and clients, who jointly ensure that results are obtained.
   c. Rests with consultants, participants, managers, and clients all working together to ensure accountability.
8. Systematic, objective evaluation designed to ensure that consulting adds value:
   a. Is never accomplished. Evaluations are conducted during the project, and they focus on how much the participants are satisfied with the project.
   b. Is occasionally accomplished. Participants are asked if the consulting project was effective on the job.
   c. Is frequently and systematically pursued. Business performance is evaluated after the project is completed.
9. Consulting projects are staffed:
   a. Primarily with internal consultants.
   b. With one, preapproved major consulting firm.
   c. In the most economical and practical way to meet deadlines and cost objectives, using internal staff and a variety of consulting firms.
10. The objectives for consulting solutions are:
    a. Nonspecific and based on subjective input.
    b. Based on learning, application, and implementation.

c. Based on business impact, application, implementation, and satisfaction.

11. Costs for consulting are accumulated:
    a. On a total aggregate basis only.
    b. On a project-by-project basis.
    c. By specific process components such as initial analysis and implementation, in addition to a specific project.

12. Management involvement in consulting is:
    a. Very low with only occasional input.
    b. Moderate, usually by request, or on an as-needed basis.
    c. Deliberately planned for all major consulting projects, to ensure a partnership arrangement.

13. To ensure that consulting projects are translated into performance on the job, we:
    a. Encourage participants to apply what they have learned and report results.
    b. Ask managers to support and reinforce consulting project results.
    c. Utilize a variety of transfer strategies appropriate for each situation.

14. The consultant's interaction with management is:
    a. Rare. Consultants almost never discuss issues with them.
    b. Occasional, during activities such as needs analysis or project coordination.
    c. Regular, to build relationships as well as to develop and deliver solutions.

15. The investment in consulting projects is measured primarily by:
    a. Subjective opinions and relationships.
    b. Observations by management and reactions from consulting participants.
    c. ROI through improved productivity, costs, quality, or customer service.

16. New consulting projects, with no formal method of evaluation, are implemented at my organization:
    a. Regularly.
    b. Seldom.
    c. Never.

17. The results of consulting projects are communicated:
    a. When requested, to those who have a need to know.
    b. Occasionally, to members of management only.
    c. Routinely, to a variety of selected target audiences.

18. Management responsibilities for consulting:
    a. Are minor, with no specific responsibilities.
    b. Consist of informal responsibilities for selected consulting projects.
    c. Are very specific. Managers have some responsibilities for projects in their business units.

19. During a business decline at my organization, consulting will:
    a. Be the first to have its budget reduced.
    b. Be retained at the same budget level.
    c. Go untouched in reductions and possibly increased.

20. Budgeting for consulting is based on:
    a. Last year's budget.
    b. Whatever the consultant can "sell."
    c. A zero-based system based on the need for each project.

21. The principal group that must justify consulting expenditures is:
    a. The consultants.
    b. The consultants and managers of the unit where the project is initiated.
    c. Senior management over the area where the consulting project is implemented.

22. Over the last two years, the consulting budget as a percent of operating expenses has:
    a. Decreased.
    b. Remained stable.
    c. Increased.

23. Senior management's involvement in consulting projects:
    a. Is limited to introductions, announcements, and offering challenges.
    b. Includes reviewing status, opening/closing meetings, discussions of status, presentation on the outlook of the organization, etc.
    c. Includes participation in the project, monitoring progress, requiring key managers to be involved, etc.

24. When an employee is directly involved in a consulting project, he or she is required to:
    a. Follow instructions.
    b. Ask questions about the project and use the project's materials and learning.
    c. Implement the project successfully, encourage others to implement it, and report success.

25. Most managers in your organization view the consulting function as:
    a. A questionable activity that wastes too much time of employees.

      b. A necessary function that probably cannot be eliminated.

      c. An important resource that can be used to improve the organization.

Score the assessment instrument as follows. Allow:

1 point for each (a) response.

3 points for each (b) response.

5 points for each (c) response.

The total will be between 30 and 100 points.

    The interpretation of scoring is provided below. The explanation is based on the input from dozens of organizations.

Score Range	Analysis of Score
101–125	**Outstanding environment** for achieving results with consulting. Great management support. A truly successful example of results-based consulting.
76–100	**Above average** in achieving results with consulting. Good management support. A solid and methodical approach to results-based consulting projects.
51–75	**Needs improvement** to achieve desired results with consulting. Management support is ineffective. Consulting projects do not usually focus on results.
25–50	**Serious problems** with the success and status of consulting. Management support is nonexistent. Consulting projects are not producing results.

NOTES

Chapter 1

1. James O'Shea and Charles Madigan, *Dangerous Company: The Consulting Powerhouses and the Businesses They Save and Ruin*, New York: Times Business/Random House, 1997.
2. Phil Rosenzweig, *The Halo Effect: How Managers Let Themselves Be Deceived*, New York: Pocket Books, 2008.
3. Robert H. Schaffer, *High-Impact Consulting: How Clients and Consultants Can Leverage Rapid Results into Long-Term Gains*, San Francisco: Jossey-Bass Publishers, 1997.
4. Jack Welch and Suzy Welch, *Winning: The Answers*, New York: Harper-Collins, 2006.
5. Elaine Biech, *The Business of Consulting: The Basics and Beyond*, San Francisco: Jossey-Bass/Pfeiffer, 1999.
6. Scott Adams, *The Dilbert Principle: A Cubicle's-Eye View of Bosses, Meetings, Management Fads & Other Workplace Afflictions*, New York: HarperCollins Business, 1996.
7. Submitted by Dusty Miller, taken off of the Internet.
8. Gordon Perchthold and Jenny Sutton, *Extract Value from Consultants: How to Hire, Control, and Fire Them*, Austin: Greenleaf Book Group Press, 2010.

Chapter 2

1. Alan Weiss and Omar Khan, *The Global Consultant: How to Make Seven Figures Across Borders*, Hoboken, NJ: John Wiley and Sons (Asia) Pte. Ltd., 2009.
2. Jack J. Phillips and Patricia Pulliam Phillips, *The Consultant's Guide to Results-Driven Business Proposals: How to Write Proposals to Forecast Impact and ROI*, New York: McGraw-Hill, 2009.
3. Jack J. Phillips and Patricia Pulliam Phillips, *Show Me the Money: How to Determine ROI in People, Projects, and Programs*, San Francisco: Berrett-Koehler Publishers, 2007.

Chapter 7

1. Dave Ulrich, ed., *Delivering Results*, Boston: Harvard Business School Press, 1998.

Chapter 9

1. Peter Block, *Flawless Consulting: A Guide to Getting Your Expertise Used*, 2nd ed., San Francisco: Pfeiffer, 2000.

Index

Accountability:
clients' interest in, 15–17
consequences of lack of, 11–13
demonstrating to clients, 26–27
lack of, 6–8, 11–13
reasons for focus on, 27–31
Acquisition costs, 187–188
Action plans:
advantages and disadvantages
of, 124
to measure application and impact,
120–124
Activities for measuring learning, 97
Adams, Scott, 8–9
Administrative support costs, 189
Advantages brought by consultants, 9
Analysis:
costs of, 158, 187
independence from data collection, 21
of intangible measures, 173–174
of need for communication, 206–208
of reactions to communication of
results, 226–227
in report of results, 215
ROI analysis plan and, 73–75
(*See also* Initial analysis and planning)
Annualized values, 190
Anonymity for questionnaires and
surveys, 91
Application and implementation level,
32–33
costs of, 188–189
Application in report of results, 215
Application objectives, 56–57, 59, 62

Assessment:
of climate for overcoming resistance,
232–233
initial, costs of, 187
Audience:
for reporting results, selecting, 210–213
target (*see* Target audiences)
Audio monitoring for observation, 119

Background information in report of
results, 214
Bain & Company, 6–7
Balanced approach, concern for
accountability resulting from, 29
Barriers:
identifying, 102
in report of results, 216
BCR (*see* Benefit/cost ratio [BCR])
BearingPoint, 28
Behavior checklists and codes for
observation, 118–119
Benchmarking reaction data, 80–81
Benefit/cost ratio (BCR):
calculating, 38–39, 191, 194–195
case application of, 193–196
Bias:
avoiding in reporting results, 205–206
cultural, data collection method
and, 129
Biech, Elaine, 8
Block, Peter, 222, 224
Brochures for reporting results, 220–221
Budget growth, concern for
accountability resulting from, 28–29

Business games for measuring
learning, 96
Business impact:
in report of results, 215
(*See also* Implementation level)
Business impact level, 33
Business needs, 65–68
The Business of Consulting (Biech), 8
Business performance data, monitoring,
125–127

Cannibalization rate, converting to
standard monetary values, 156
Capital expenditures, 188–189
Career problems without
accountability, 13
Case studies for reporting results, 221
Cash flow, discounted, 197
Certified ROI Professionals, 42
Champion, identifying, 233
Channel margin, converting to standard
monetary values, 156
Checklists, 85
Churn rate, converting to standard
monetary values, 156
Clients:
as data source, 82
engagement of, 26
gaining confidence of, 43
needs of, converting data to monetary
values and, 176
providing feedback to (*see* Reporting
results)
self-assessment survey for,
247–251
"show me the money" requests of,
24–25
view of measures, 3–5
(*See also* Customer *entries*)
Communication:
of expectations to stakeholders, 20
(*See also* Reporting results)

Communication media for reporting
results, 218
Competitive advantage as reason for
measuring ROI, 25–26
Computer monitoring for
observation, 119
Confidence, individual feedback to
build, 99
Consistency:
for overcoming resistance, 230
of reporting results, 205
Consultants:
evaluation of, 98
involving in process, 240
overcoming resistance in, 239–240
teaching, 240
view of measures, 24–26
Consulting:
impact of, 243
overall importance of, 243
participants in, as data source, 82
responsibility for, 243–244
Consulting process, steps in, costs and,
184–185
Consulting projects:
additional, justifying, 44–45
design and development of,
costs of, 187
improving process of, 44
showing contribution of, 43
Consulting team as data source,
82–83
Contributions, need to explain, 204
Control groups for isolating effects of
consulting effort, 136–138
Converting data to monetary values,
37–38, 151–177
alternatives to standard values for,
160–171
client needs and, 176
credibility and, 175–176
estimates from participants for, 169

historical costs from records for,
161–163
input from internal and external
experts for, 163–164
linking with other measures and,
166–169
management adjustments and, 176
reasons for, 151–152
selection of measures for, 175
standard monetary values and, 154–160
steps in, 152–154
time value of money and, 176
units of measure for, 152
values from external databases for,
164–166
Costs, 179–189
acquisition, 187–188
of administrative support, 189
of analysis, 158, 187
of application and implementation,
188–189
capital expenditures and, 188–189
capturing, 38
complete disclosure of, 180–181
of consulting, 10–11, 38
consulting process steps and, 184–185
critical nature of, 180
danger of reporting without
benefits, 182
employee benefits factor and, 186
of evaluation and reporting, 189
fully loaded, 181–182
guidelines for, 182–183
historical, measuring improvement
using, 161–163
importance of, 179–180
inclusion of, as criterion for
successful ROI process, 17
of initial analysis and assessment, 187
of maintenance and monitoring, 189
major categories of, 186–188
overhead, 189

of project design and
development, 187
prorated versus direct, 185–186
of quality, 158–159
ratio of benefits to (*see* Benefit/cost
ratio [BCR])
in report of results, 215
sources of, 183–184
(*See also* Converting data to monetary
values)
Credibility as criterion for successful
ROI process, 16
Cultural bias, data collection method
and, 129
Customer dissatisfaction, cost of,
158–159
Customer profits (*see* Profits)
Customer satisfaction, 26
importance of, 80
monitoring, 98
Customer value lifetime, converting to
standard monetary values, 156
Customers:
estimates of effects of consulting
effort of, 148
estimates of impact from, 148
internal, as data source, 83
(*See also* Clients)

Data:
converting to monetary values, 37–38
integration in report of results, 215
requiring a variety of, 20–21
Data collection, 35–36
independence from analysis, 21
for learning and implementation
(*see* Data collection for learning
and implementation)
plan for, 70–73
for reaction and learning (*see* Data
collection for reaction and learning)
in report of results, 214–215

Data collection for learning and
implementation, 101–130
action plans and, 120–124
interviews and focus groups for, 117
monitoring business performance
data and, 125–127
observation for, 117–119
performance contracts and, 124–125
questionnaires for, 110–116
reasons for, 101–104
responsibilities and, 109–110
selecting method for, 127–129
sources of data for, 107–108
timing of, 108–109
types of data for, 105–107
Data collection for reaction and
learning, 79–82
accuracy of method used for, 129
cost of method used for, 128
cultural bias and, 129
disruption of normal activities by, 129
focus groups for, 93–94
informal methods for, 96–97
interviews for, 91–93
number of methods used for, 129
questionnaires and surveys for, 85–91
reasons for, 79–81
simulation for, 95–96
sources of data and, 82–83
tests for, 95
time for data input and, 128
timing of, 83–85
type of data and, 127–128
using data and, 97–99
Databases, external, measuring
improvement using data from,
164–166
Delayed report method for
observation, 119
The Dilbert Principle (Adams), 8–9
Direct costs, prorated costs versus,
185–186

Discounted cash flow, 197

Economic pressures, concern for
accountability resulting from,
27–28
Economic process as criterion for
successful ROI process, 16
Educational Resources Information
Center (ERIC), 165
Efficiency for overcoming
resistance, 230
Electronic media for reporting
results, 220
Elements of ROI Methodology,
30–31
Employee benefits, costs of, 186
Employee time, converting to standard
monetary values, 159–160
Enablers:
identifying, 103
in report of results, 216
ERIC (Educational Resources
Information Center), 165
Estimates of effects of consulting effort,
142–149
of customers, 148
of experts, 148–149
of managers, 146–147
of participants, 142–146
Evaluation:
of consultants, 98
costs of, 189
focus group applications for,
93–94
planning for, 70
setting targets for, 236–237
strategy for, in report of results, 214
Evaluation levels, 31–33
Executive managers (*see* Management)
Exercises for measuring learning, 97
Expectations, communicating to
stakeholders, 20

Experts:
    estimates of effects of consulting
        effort of, 148–149
    estimates of impact from, 148–149
    input from, measuring improvement
        using, 163–164
External databases, measuring
    improvement using data from,
    164–166
External failure, 158

Fads, concern for accountability
    resulting from, 30
Failure of consulting projects, concern
    for accountability resulting from, 27
Fair Labor Standards Act (FLSA), 181
Feedback:
    early, providing, 222–224
    individual to build confidence, 99
    (*See also* Reporting results)
Flawless Consulting (Block), 222, 224
Flexibility as criterion for successful
    ROI process, 16–17
Focus groups:
    evaluation applications of, 93–94
    guidelines for, 94
    to measure application and impact, 117
    to measure reaction and learning,
    93–94
Focus on results, ensuring, 17–21
    asking for a guarantee and, 18–19
    asking for results from other projects
        and, 17–18
    communicating expectations to
        stakeholders and, 20
    early focus on results and, 19
    independence of data collection and
        analysis and, 21
    monitoring long-term effects of
        projects and, 21
    multiple-level objectives for, 19–20
    requiring a variety of data and, 20–21

requiring an impact study and, 20
    ROI forecasting and, 19
Follow-up reminders, for
    questionnaires and surveys, 90
Forecasting:
    identifying planned improvements for
        forecasts and, 98–99
    methods for isolating effects of
        consulting effort and, 139–141
Forecasting ROI prior to implementing
    project, 19
Fully loaded costs, 181–182
Funds, waste of, without accountability,
    11–12

Games for measuring learning, 96
Goals, establishing, overcoming
    resistance and, 236–237
Guarantees, asking for, 18–19
Guidelines, revising/developing, 239

Harmful advice, without
    accountability, 13
High-Impact Consulting (Schaffer), 7
Historical costs, measuring
    improvement using, 161–163
Humility for reporting results,
    205–206

Impact objectives, 57–58, 59, 61, 62
Impact study:
    presenting data to senior
        management, 224–226
    for reporting results, selecting,
    213–221
    requiring, 20
Implementation level:
    data collection for (*see* Data collection
        for learning and implementation)
    in report of results, 215
Improvements, need for communication
    to make, 204

Incentives for questionnaires and
surveys, 89
Inclusiveness as criterion for successful
ROI process, 16
Informal measures of learning, 96–97
Initial analysis and planning, 51–75
importance of specific objectives
and, 59
levels of project objectives and, 52–59
linking evaluation with needs and,
59–75
overall project goal and, 51–52
Intangible benefits, identifying, 40
Intangible measures, 171–174
analysis of, 173–174
in report of results, 216
sources of, 172–173
Interim reports, 218–219
Internal customers as data source, 83
Internal failure, 158
Internal rate of return (IRR), 197–198
Interviews:
guidelines for, 92–93
to measure application and impact, 117
to measure reaction and learning,
91–93
types of, 92
Inventories, converting to standard
monetary values, 157
IRR (internal rate of return), 197–198
Isolating effects of consulting effort,
133–150
calculating impact of other factors
and, 141–142
chain of impact and, 134–135
control groups for, 136–138
estimates for, 142–149
forecasting methods for, 139–141
identifying contributing factors
and, 135
reasons for, 133–134
trend-line analysis for, 138–139

Isolation of effects of consulting, 36–37

Knowledge management, importance
of, 81

Learning level, 32, 33
data collection for (*see* Data collection
for learning and implementation;
Data collection for reaction and
learning)
in report of results, 215
topics for, 83
Learning needs, 70
Learning objectives, 54–55, 59, 62–63
Linking measures to convert to
standard monetary values, 166–169
Litton Industries, 176
Long-term effects of projects,
monitoring, 21
Loyalty, converting to standard
monetary values, 157

Maintenance costs, 189
Management:
active involvement of, 244
adjustment of data by, 176
concern for accountability resulting
from, 30
as data source, 82
estimates of effects of consulting
effort of, 146–147
estimates of impact from, 146–147
gaining respect of, 43–44
preparing for ROI process, 242–243
presenting impact study data to,
224–226
Management/executive summary in
report of results, 214
Market share, converting to standard
monetary values, 157
Marketing of future projects, 99
Measurement, planning for, 70

Meetings for reporting results, 218
Methodology in report of results, 214
Miller, Dusty, 9
Monetary values, converting data to
    (*see* Converting data to monetary
    values)
Monitoring costs, 189
Morale, lack of accountability and, 12
Multiple-choice questions, 85

Norms, developing, 98

Objectives:
    application, 56–57, 59, 62
    impact, 57–58, 59, 61, 62
    learning, 54–55, 59, 62–63
    levels of, 52–59
    linkage with needs, 59–75
    multiple-level, specifying, 19–20
    overall, 51–52
    reaction, 53–54, 59, 63
    in report of results, 214
    ROI, 58–59
    specific, importance of, 59
Observation:
    guidelines for, 117–118
    to measure application and impact,
    117–119
    methods for, 118–119
Open-ended questions, 85
Output data, converting to monetary
    values, 155
Overcoming resistance, 229–230
    approach to, 230–232
    assessing climate and, 222–223
    consistency and, 230
    consultants and, 240
    developing a project plan for, 237–238
    developing roles and responsibilities
    for, 233–236
    efficiency and, 230
    implementation for, 230

initiating ROI projects and, 241–244
    monitoring progress and, 245
    policies and guidelines for, 239
    preparing consulting staff for,
    239–240
    removing obstacles and, 245
    ROI as learning tool and, 240
    setting evaluation targets for,
    236–237
Overhead costs, 189

Pamphlets for reporting results, 220–221
Paradigm shifts, lack of accountability
    and, 13–15
Participants:
    estimates of effects of consulting
    effort of, 142–146
    estimates of impact from, 142–146
Payback period, 196–197
Payoff needs, 63–65
Penalty costs, 158
Performance contracts to measure
    application and impact, 124–125
Performance needs, 68–69
Planning, 35
    for data collection, 70–73
    for measurement and evaluation, 70
    overcoming resistance and, 237–238
    of reporting results, 208–210
    for ROI analysis, 73–75
    (*See also* Action plans; Initial analysis
    and planning)
Policies, revising/developing, 239
Preference needs, 70
Prevention costs, 158
Problems facing consultants, 5–11
Profit margin, converting to standard
    monetary values, 156
Profits:
    converting to standard monetary
    values, 156
    demonstrating to client, 26

Progress, monitoring, 245
Progress Bank, 110
Progress reporting, 218–219, 242
Prorated costs, direct costs versus,
    185–186

Quality, calculating standard cost of,
    155–159
Questionnaires:
    design of, 86–87
    improving response rate for, 88
    to measure application and impact,
        110–116
    to measure reaction and learning,
        85–91
    questions and statements for, 85–86
    simplicity for, 88–91

Range of response questions, 85
Ranking scales, 85
Rate of return, internal, 197–198
Reaction level, 32
    data collection for (see Data collection
        for reaction and learning)
    in report of results, 215
    topics for, 83
Reaction objectives, 53–54, 59, 63
Reactions to communication of results,
    analyzing, 226–227
Reporting progress, 218–219, 242
Reporting results, 40–41, 203–228
    analyzing need for communication
        and, 206–208
    analyzing reactions to
        communication and, 226–227
    brochures for, 220–221
    case studies for, 221
    communication policy issues and,
        208–209
    costs of, 189
    delivery of message and, 221–226
    developing the report and, 216–218

electronic media for, 220
impact study for, 213–221
interim and progress reports for,
    218–219
meetings for, 218
need for, 204
pamphlets for, 220–221
planning, 208–210
routine communication tools for,
    219–220
selecting audience for, 210–213
sensitivity of issue and, 204–205
tailoring to target audiences, 205
timeliness and consistency of, 205
unbiased and humble nature for,
    205–206
Resistance to ROI measurement,
    229–245
    overcoming (see Overcoming
        resistance)
Response rate for questionnaires and
    surveys, improving, 88
Responsibilities:
    assigning for overcoming resistance,
        235–236
    for consulting, 243–244
    data collection for learning and
        implementation and, 109–110
Results:
    developing results-focused approach
        and, 44
    ensuring a focus on (see Focus on
        results, ensuring)
    reasons for measuring, 3–5
    reporting (see Reporting results)
Results-based consulting, 14–15
Retention rate, converting to standard
    monetary values, 156
Return on investment (see ROI entries)
Return on investment level, 33
Revenues, increased, demonstrating to
    client, 26

Rewards for success, 103
ROI (return on investment), 190–200
  analysis of, 193–194
  annualized value concept and, 190
  BCR/ROI application and, 193–196
  calculating, 39, 195–196
  definition of, 190
  formula for, 192–193
  importance of, 179–180
  as learning tool, 240
  measures of, 191–193, 196–198
  objectives of, 58–59
  in report of results, 215
ROI analysis plan, 73–75
ROI Certification process, 42
ROI leader, developing, 233–234
ROI process:
  active involvement in, 244
  applications of, 42–43
  benefits of, 43–45, 198–199
  case study of, 45–50
  developing planning documents for,
    241–242
  essential criteria for, 16–17
  focus on results and (*see* Focus on
    results, ensuring)
  impact of consulting and, 243
  implementation of, 41–42
  operating standards for, 41
  overall importance of consulting
    and, 243
  preparing management team for,
    242–243
  progress reporting and, 242
  responsibility for consulting and,
    243–244
  selecting initial projects for, 231
ROI process model, 33–41
  calculating ROI in, 38–39
  capturing cost of consulting in, 38
  converting data to monetary values
    in, 37–38

  data collection in, 35–36
  identifying intangible benefits in, 40
  isolating consulting effects in, 36–37
  planning in, 35
  reporting results in, 40–41
Role-playing for measuring learning, 96

Sales, converting to standard monetary
  values, 156
SAP, 19
Satisfaction:
  in report of results, 215
  (*See also* Customer satisfaction)
Schaffer, Robert, 7
Self-assessment for measuring
  learning, 97
Self-assessment survey for clients,
  247–251
Sensitivity of communicating results,
  204–205
Simplicity as criterion for successful
  ROI process, 16
Simulation for measuring learning,
  95–96
Skill practice for measuring
  learning, 96
Staff demoralization of, without
  accountability, 12
Standard monetary values, 154–160
  alternatives to, 160–171
  converting employee time and,
    159–160
  converting output data to, 155
  finding, 160
  quality improvement and, 155–159
Standards, developing, 98
Strengths of project, identifying, 98
Surveys:
  improving response rate for, 88
  to measure reaction and learning,
    85–91
  simplicity for, 88–91

Target audiences, differing information
   needs of, 205
Tarnished image of consultants, 8–10
Task force, establishing, 234–235
Task simulation for measuring learning,
   95–96
Tests for measuring learning, 95
Theoretical foundation as criterion for
   successful ROI process, 16
Time:
   converting to standard monetary
      values, 159–160
   waste of, without accountability, 12
Timing:
   of data collection, 83–85
   of data collection for learning and
      implementation, 108–109
   of reporting results, 205

Track record as criterion for successful
   ROI process, 17
Trend-line analysis for isolating
   effects of consulting effort,
   138–139

Unit margin, converting to standard
   monetary values, 156

Video recording for observation, 119

Wasted funds without accountability,
   11–12
Wasted time without accountability, 12
Weaknesses of project, identifying, 98
Welch, Jack, 8
Workload, converting to standard
   monetary values, 157

About the Authors

Jack Phillips, Ph.D., provides consulting services for Fortune 500 companies and organizations in 54 countries. The author and editor of more than 50 books, he has received awards from several organizations, including *Meeting News* magazine, the Society for Human Resource Management, and the American Society for Training & Development.

Patricia Pulliam Phillips, Ph.D., president and CEO of the ROI Institute, Inc., consults with organizations around the globe. She is the author or coauthor of numerous articles and books, including *Show Me the Money, The Value of Learning*, and *The Consultant's Guide to Results-Driven Business Proposals*.

The authors live in Birmingham, Alabama.